Exiled Voices *Portals of Discovery*

With love,

Susan

The artist Donny Johnson has served twenty-five years in solitary confinement. His studio is a windowless cell in California's Pelican Bay State Prison, his pigments ground M&Ms and Folgers instant coffee, his brushes fashioned from his own hair wrapped in foil and plastic. Forty-eight years old now, he was sentenced in 1980 to fifteen years to life for second-degree murder. In 1989 he received consecutive sentences of nine years to life for almost fatally slashing one guard and assaulting another. Many of Donny Johnson's paintings have been sold, with the proceeds going to a charity aiding the children of prisoners. This 7"x 10" painting is titled *Scotopia II*, Out of Darkness.

Exiled Voices

Portals of Discovery

Stories, poems, and drama by imprisoned writers

Edited by Susan Nagelsen

Introduction by Robert Johnson

Photographs by Lou Jones

NEW
ENGLAND
COLLEGE
PRESS

Published in the United States by New England College Press Henniker, New Hampshire.

Library of Congress publication control number: 2007923144
ISBN- 13: 978-0-9790130-1-0
ISBN- 10: 0-9790130-1-1

Funded, in part, by the NH Bar Foundation, beneficiary of the Charles W. Dean Trust Fund of the NH Charitable Foundation.

NEW HAMPSHIRE
BAR FOUNDATION
Strengthening Justice Since 1977

First U.S. edition

Distributed by University Press of New England
Lebanon, New Hampshire
www.upne.com

For Jane

Experience teaches us that sword and fire, exile and persecution are more likely to exacerbate our ills than cure them.

JACQUES-AUGUSTE DE THOU

Contents

Hard Time

A Meditation on Prisons and Imprisonment

ROBERT JOHNSON

Americans live in a time of harsh punishment, a hard time, a time in which prisons seem natural, unremarkable. Prison sentences are handed down routinely in our courts, seemingly without a second thought. As a society, we seem smugly confident that harsh punishment, even cruel punishment, is the right thing to do when people— mostly damaged people—damage other people. We have built a veritable empire of prisons crowned with a colony of death houses. America is the world leader when it comes to prisons and a world-class contender in state-sanctioned executions, dubious distinctions for a country committed to the ideal of individual freedom.

In America today, more people are sentenced to more time in more prisons under more isolated conditions than at any time in recent memory. Prisons, sometimes opened and operated at the expense of schools, roads, social services, and even hospitals, dot the American landscape. Most of them are overcrowded and underfunded. Idle time has become a way of life behind bars. The sheer number of prisons and prisoners is remarkable, creating what amounts to a parallel penal universe, a world surrounded by fortress walls or barbed-wire barriers that hold offenders at bay, away from the world, locked in a grim suspended animation.

The numbers speak for themselves. On any given day in America, some 2.3 million men and women are confined in a state or federal prison or in a local jail. This amounts to a daily incarceration rate of roughly 750 prisoners for every 100,000 members of the general population. Incarceration rates in other Western countries range from 50 to 150 per 100,000, considerably below the American standard. Another 5 million Americans are under some form of correctional supervision, primarily probation (just over 4 million) and parole (roughly 800,000). These surveillance enterprises offer little or no help to offenders struggling to stay in the community (probationers who fail are often sent to prison) or to make the transition from prison to the free world (parolees who fail are often sent back to prison). In California, our biggest prison system and usually a bellwether for the nation, fully three out of every four parolees are returned to prison within eighteen months. Most commit technical violations of parole conditions, like missing a curfew or a meeting with a parole officer, rather than new crimes. Remarkably, there are more returning parolees in California prisons than criminals sentenced by the courts. Offenders are thought of as an unwanted group, but it would seem that our prisons want them, and sometimes seem reluctant to let them go for long.

America is the undisputed capital of capital punishment in the Western world. The death penalty, long dead to our neighbors in Europe, is alive and well in America. (There is at present a fairly robust debate about the humaneness of execution by lethal injection, but the issues in dispute are largely technical, not legal or moral.) Some 3,400 condemned prisoners are housed on death rows in the thirty-eight states that have capital punishment. Over the past three decades, starting in 1977 with the much-publicized execution of Gary Gilmore, 1,099 prisoners have been put to death in America, many by electrocution, most by lethal injection. A remarkable 123 of these prisoners— roughly 10 percent—"volunteered" for execution: prisoners who drop their appeals to expedite their executions are called volunteers, as if they diligently work their way into the death house.

These prisoners drop their appeals because they see the options before them as equally unappealing. As a practical matter, the options open to a condemned prisoner come down to death in one of two forms: death by execution or death by incarceration, which is to say, death as the culmination of a life sentence in prison. The so-called volunteers show by their actions that they prefer death in the execution chamber to a death that is the culmination of a life in prison, a life they see as empty and pointless. They know or sense that a death in prison, alone, in a cell or a prison hospital, is a prisoner's worst nightmare. As John Corley makes painfully clear in his essay, "Life in Four Parts," prison deaths are hard and lonely and horrible to behold: "They died from the recklessness and deprivation of their pasts, the drugs and booze, the poverty leading to undiagnosed health conditions. They died because years of continuous incarceration sucked the very life from them, slowly, a day at a time, a torment worse than any inquisitorial persecution. They died in dark rooms behind locked doors calling for their mamas." In light of these hard realities, known to prisoners if not to the public, one can perhaps better understand the death row prisoner who tells us that a life sentence in our prisons is a fate worse than death.

America stands alone in the world when it comes to our "other death penalty"—natural or true life sentences, sometimes called life without parole. To this beleaguered group we must add people serving terms that exceed the human lifespan; offenders get sentences of one hundred or two hundred or more years with some regularity, though no statistics are kept on the matter. All told, roughly 40,000 prisoners live under what amounts to a sentence of death by incarceration. The prison is their cemetery, the cell their tomb. If we thought of these sentences as death sentences, we might be less inclined to mete them out to juveniles and indeed to any offender convicted of a crime less egregious than premeditated murder. But we do send juveniles to prison for life without the possibility of parole—over 2,225 at last count, including some children as young as thirteen. Remarkably, some six out of ten of these child prisoners were first offenders, and many appear to have played secondary roles in violent crimes orchestrated by adults. Drug offenders, too, are regularly sentenced to life terms, though lethal violence is rarely used in these crimes.

It is the common wisdom in some circles that Americans are enamored of prisons because America is besieged by crime, particularly violent crime. The thinking is that we have no choice but to lock up serious criminals for long stretches, if not permanently, in order to incapacitate dangerous criminals and thereby reduce crime rates. Hard justice, we admit, but justice nonetheless. As appealing as this explanation may be, our crime rates do *not* explain why we have such a high rate of incarceration. While America leads the world in prison sentences by a vast margin, our crime rates are *not* extreme by international standards. When we compare our crime rates to those found in other countries in the West, we find that we are pretty much in the middle of the group when it comes to property crimes, and we are near (but not at) the top of the list when it comes to violent crimes. It is true that our violent criminals are more lethal than their counterparts in other Western countries, but violent criminals, including those who use guns, make up only a quarter of our prison population and thus cannot explain our high incarceration rate. More to the point, imprisoning offenders has little effect on crime rates. Crime rates in America have ebbed and flowed over the past few decades, while incarceration rates have simply risen year after year. The same general crime trends are found in states that use prisons freely (like California) and states that use prisons more sparingly (like Massachusetts). Prisons are not forced on us by crime; we have *chosen* prisons as our preferred way of dealing with crime.

The prisons we choose to build and fill, moreover, are increasingly isolated from the larger society and restrictive in their internal operations. More and more, prison time has become a species of dead time spent in empty activities carried out in isolation from the larger world. Meanwhile, the pace of life and productivity in the outside world have quickened dramatically. Free citizens live in what has been called an information age. Information is generated and spread like wildfire by phone and fax, computer and Internet, disseminating ideas and linking people. The technology of the information age, we are told, transcends time and space to make the world something very much akin to a global village built on the rapid exchange of information. Prisons and their prisoners are increasingly out of touch with this new world. If the free world today is one big global village, the prisons of the world are backwaters off the beaten path, places of cultural banishment. A new level of disconnection between prison and society has emerged, perhaps making prisons obsolescent as social institutions. Prisons are places most of us can readily ignore and even forget about entirely, a theme explored in this collection with disturbing insight in *Peakzone,* a play by John "Divine G" Whitfield, in which prisoners are simply forgotten by the authorities—even the correctional authorities—in the wake of a terrorist attack.

Prisons may have little redeeming value as social institutions these days, but they remain viable as economic enterprises. Building prisons stimulates industry, creates jobs, and expands local tax bases. Whether these are wise ways to expend and expand resources, and whether the collateral social and other costs outweigh any economic benefits, are open to debate. (We also can ponder the benefit society might reap if the billions of dollars spent on prisons were invested in social justice and other remedial projects, reducing the need for punishment.) The bottom line, however, is that a "prison-industrial complex" has emerged in America. Its constituency includes a vast array of organizations and individuals whose livelihoods depend on a growing prison industry—from the construction companies that build prisons, to correctional officers and others who staff them, to medical, phone, and food-service providers, not to mention impoverished rural communities desperate for a stable industry on which to hinge their precarious futures in today's fiercely competitive global economy. Trading on the misery of offenders has in fact given rise to a host of private prisons, prisons explicitly run for profit and offered as investments to the general public. (At last count, private prisons were serving thirty-three states and the federal government, housing in the neighborhood of 110,000 prisoners who were in effect outsourced to these institutions.) Private prisons aim to take the losing proposition that is crime and find, in its punishment, a kind of redemption in profit. One of the main ways these prisons turn a profit is by keeping costs down, which as a practical matter often means that fewer staff at lower salaries with little or no benefits provide unreliable and often abusive supervision to large bodies of inmates, who are explicitly warehoused for the duration of their sentences.

The routines that give form to daily existence in our isolated and isolating prisons, both public and private, are marked by a kind of casual brutality, perhaps reflecting a mixture of the contempt we feel for criminals we must punish and the indifference we feel for commodities we must store. Prisoners find themselves shunted about on buses while shackled to one another, sometimes for long hours, without access to food or toilets. They are strip-searched regularly, sometimes daily, even after noncontact visits. In a noncontact visit, prisoners speak with their loved ones through a solid (usually Plexiglas) partition; because they have no physical contact, there is no way to smuggle anything into or out of the prison. (Smuggling occurs in prison, but not by way of noncontact visits.) Strip-searching prisoners before and after such visits, a common practice, is invasive, degrading, and unnecessary and amounts to harassment, whether it is intended as such or not. Housing conditions often are invasive and degrading as well. Cells designed for one—essentially cages with toilets—are often packed with two, three, or even more prisoners. In some prisons, convicts are stacked like cordwood in minimally supervised barracks, euphemistically called dormitories in the corrections field.

Even where decent accommodations are available, the existential reality in prison is one of time that hangs heavy, time that is a punishment in itself. As poet Gary Hicks puts it, "Life in life is short, / Life in prison isn't." The key fact is captivity. Mr. Hicks continues:

"Hell has no flames, / Only windows that won't open, / doors sealed shut . . . / Year after year." A prison can be air-conditioned (some are), but the prisoners don't breathe free. A prison may offer a range of educational and recreational activities to fill time, but as we learn in Laos Chuman's moving "Diary of a Lifetime in Blue," rape may haunt the cell blocks, making one's time in prison a torment. A prison may offer a single cell, even a cell with a view. But that cell will have distinctive features, like special coat hooks, "hinged as prophylactics / against despair," in the words of Erin George, from which she "can't hang my bathrobe / or myself"—because despair and suicide are regular features of prison life.

The prison world is isolated and in varying degrees regimented, but it is not inert. Events unfold in prison with a special urgency, as if powered by the enormous frustration that comes in the wake of repression. Human hopes and aspirations are bottled up, sometimes warped by the pressure of life in captivity, and find expression in a culture or way of life that can be cold and cruel, even torturous. Violent things can happen, particularly in prisons for men, and yet be seen as normal and unremarkable. Recalcitrant prisoners may be pepper-gassed in their cells. The terrifying experience of this "intervention," as it is called in the field, is vividly described in Charles Huckelbury's "Riding the Tiger." Alternatively, a disruptive inmate may be "extracted" from his cell, pulled like a bad tooth by a "cell extraction team," a special operations team not unlike a police SWAT team. Extraction team officers line up outside the prisoner's cell dressed in a species of martial regalia, complete with helmets and (for the lead officer) an electrical shield, and then proceed on cue to charge into his cell, pin him down, carry him out to a holding area, strip him naked, and finally secure him limb by limb to a specially made bed or chair, where he may lie or sit for hours. Many of the more difficult inmates in our prisons are profoundly mentally ill, which is a story in itself. One can only wonder how these troubled people view the periodic assaults launched against them by their keepers.

Then there is the nightmare scenario of rape. In men's prisons, the main danger is inmate-on-inmate rape. (Women have more to fear from their keepers.) Statistics suggest that rapes are rare, affecting 1or 2 percent of prisoners, and it must be said that many prison systems are making a concerted effort to address this problem. But it is almost certainly the case that the vast majority of rapes are unreported because of shame and trauma, as explored in depressing detail in Chuman's "Diary": "Sobbing and lying on the floor, bleeding from my rectum, I felt filthy beyond words. I hated myself for my weakness." Rape is mortifying in itself. Moreover, as word gets out among other prisoners, pressures mount. In prison, a rape victim is fair game. The prisoner, now traumatized and demoralized, is less able to offer resistance. In extreme cases, prison gangs may orchestrate rapes and then "pimp out" their victims to other prisoners for profit, practicing what amounts to sexual slavery.

No one in authority advocates rape as a feature of prison punishment, but making prisons uncomfortable—making hard time harder still—is a cherished goal of many American politicians. This includes federal politicians, who passed the revealingly named No Frills Prison Act, which limits federal construction dollars to prison systems that cut back on a wide range of amenities and discontinue "good time," a practice that rewarded prisoners for good behavior by shortening their sentences. The federal courts have taken no explicit stand on this matter, in part because prisoners' access to the courts has been sharply limited. Prisoners who get to federal court find that the judges regularly defer to the presumed wisdom of prison officials. This leaves prisoners at the tender mercies of their keepers, who often oppose arbitrary prison conditions (in a sense the officials live there, too) but must yield to pressure from politicians and vocal members of the general public bent on making prisons more punitive and less responsive to the human needs of prisoners.

It is a truism that prisoners are first and foremost human beings, but we in the free world readily lose sight of this simple fact. Terms like "criminal" and "convict" or "murderer" and "rapist" have a way of monopolizing our attention, as if a person should be defined by his worst acts, her lowest point in life. Prisons house a disproportionate number of minority offenders, so racial and ethnic stereotypes also feed our prejudiced perceptions of prisoners. The original writings in this book offer vivid testimony to the simple and often endearing humanity of the men and women we saddle with a host of derogatory labels, people we imprison without a second thought but who are affected, often profoundly, sometimes irreparably, by the prison experience. Today's prisoners are yesterday's children. As children, they had hopes and aspirations. As adults, they retain memories, some bitter, some sweet, of their formative years. Philip Horner, in "Contraband," writes of hiding memories of love in his heart, a safe place for this contraband emotion because "the screws will never look in there."

Betrayal and loss figure prominently in the lives of prisoners. We learn from the writings in this collection that abuse may be dramatic or restrained; violations of trust may be routine and minor or occasional and profound. Sexual molestation, an often profound trauma, is explored in Erin George's poem "First Time," with a deceptive subtlety, perhaps paralleling the child's seduction. The rapist, a trusted adult, takes the young girl to a secluded place in the house (his workshop) and rapes her while she, presumably in shock, attends to small details ("The band of hiked-up nightgown . . . / The cave of cobwebs and suspended fly corpses / under your workbench"). Afterward, he cleans her up ("washing out my favorite panties, / the ones with My Pretty Pony on them") and ends the encounter expecting life to go on as if nothing happened ("promising repercussions and ice cream"). Every aspect of the event is seared into her mind; every detail lives on in the child's life until she becomes a prisoner—or rather, moves from the prison of her life to the prison we have built for her.

Yet remarkably, as we learn over and over again in this volume, these men and women do not ask for our sympathy. They do not parade themselves before us as innocent victims of a malevolent fate. They see their own flaws and hope one day to rectify them. They try to make sense of their hard lives and hope to make peace with the people who failed them. Many hope to make peace, too, with the people they have gone on to fail. For the heartbreaking legacy of abuse is that abused people all too often go on to abuse others, to fail others, even harming the loved ones who come to depend on them. All too many abused persons carry within themselves defects of character that are revealed in the predilections and limitations and addictions that mark and mar their adult lives and move them inexorably into the orbit of our justice system. Roughly 75 percent of prisoners have substance abuse problems; less than 15 percent receive treatment for their addictions. Our prison system once stressed rehabilitation and took as its call to arms the obligation to help offenders help themselves. No more. Rehabilitation has long given way to punishment. Offenders come into our police stations and courts and prisons with needs, but it is not their needs that we tend to but their culpability, their deficits and failings, what might be called their shame-worthiness.

And from that shame our prisoners are forged, one step at a

time. The prisoner we see on death row or in solitary confinement, in the prison yard or in the prison morgue, was not born to this fate. He or she is the product of a hard life compounded by policy choices that put human degradation above human decency, pain above healing. The prisoner production process, as it were, starts at arrest and in detention centers and courts, where people—mostly poor people and especially poor people of color—are processed like objects and treated with contempt. Presumed guilty from the moment they are arrested, they are threatened and cajoled, told they are human garbage, corralled in bullpens (a telling appellation), eventually offered plea bargains that come at a steep price but seem attractive, even irresistible, because going to trial means serving jail time while their case is pending and, if convicted, facing the stiffest punishment countenanced by the law. That's how sentencing works in the real world of the courts. The message is simple and clear: If you make us work to convict you, we make you pay. If you cooperate, we go easy.

Easy. It's a relative term. Those who cooperate may avoid prison for a time or perhaps receive a reduced jail or prison term, but they acquire an indelible record, one that follows them for life. The next time around—and there is likely to be a next time, since options are few for those with a record and ex-offenders are a handy pool of suspects for the police to mine—you start at a disadvantage. The deal is less sweet, your choices more limited. You go down again, this time for a longer prison term; the cycle continues, and the rest is history, your history. Before long you are a bona fide convict, a seasoned offender, a veteran of confinement. You are a class apart, consigned to a world apart. You are disreputable. People don't trust you, won't hire you, don't want you in their neighborhoods or even in their sight. You are a pariah, fit only for life with others of your despicable ilk. Prison becomes a fixture in your world, maybe the centerpiece of your world. Where else can you go? You still live and breathe and think and feel, you are still vulnerable and lonely, but nobody notices. You may be a poet, but who listens to your words? Your stories may be subtle and insightful, but who will read them?

Prisoners live in a dog-eat-dog world, the modern equivalent of a jungle. Among other things, that reality is made painfully clear in this fine book. It should come as no surprise that prisoners at times act like savages, lost in the moment, captive to raw emotion. The first law of this jungle is simple but sometimes deadly: Do unto others *before* they do unto you. Yet most prisoners tell us, in word and in deed, that they secretly yearn for order, security, and simple decency. Like the authors in this book, most prisoners are up on their toes, alert but wary, hungry for deep sleep—the kind of sleep you can find only when you are secure, when your world is ordered, when you know you are safe. The rest of us, captives of convention, are bruised daily by the firm walls of civility and in our hearts yearn for the liberation of our senses, for the sating of appetites, for moments red and redolent of life lived raw. Bored and restless, we yearn to live on the edge, to flirt with danger—at least in the safe confines of our minds. What prisoners live, however uneasily, citizens dream; what citizens live, however reluctantly, prisoners dream. Prisons thus take root at the intersection of civilization and chaos. We are advised to cross that intersection with care.

The writers in this collection have made that crossing, at great cost to themselves, and now their readers can follow. The price of admission is careful, caring attention to a wonderful collection of creative work. The reward is sweet release from the shackles of ignorance and a liberating view of crime and punishment, prisons and prisoners.

Exiled Voices *Portals of Discovery*

Yvette Louisell

Yvette Louisell began her college career at the age of sixteen at Iowa State University, in Ames, and it ended a year later, in 1987, with the murder of a partially disabled man for whom she was modeling in the nude. She was convicted for first-degree murder; she is now in her twentieth year of incarceration. Yvette spends her days at Iowa Correctional Institution for Women in Mitchellville. She is one of 2,228 people in the United States sentenced as a juvenile to life without parole. The United States is one of three countries in the world that impose this inexhaustible sentence on juveniles. There is a movement under way to urge the U.S. government to stop this cruel and unusual practice, and the Supreme Court decision in *Roper v. Simmons,* banning the use of the death penalty for juveniles, has given people fighting for this cause hope, for they contend that the logic used in the decision holds true in the sentence of life without parole as well.[1]

Yvette is long-legged and petite; her hair is long, almost to her waist, and it falls in curls. There is absolutely nothing shy about her; her straightforward, in-your-face attitude comes with laughter. Yvette and I spoke on the phone before my visit; she told me, "If they let you bring in money for the vending machines, I'll talk like a fool for chocolate." So one of the first things she said when she sat down was "Oh, damn—no chocolate?"

Our visit began with a laugh. As we sat together, Yvette's face filled with emotion; it was in her eyes, which glistened with tears of joy, and in her voice, which rose and fell with pleasure and excitement. I have spent years talking with prisoners who have done long stretches of time behind bars, but I had never spoken to someone imprisoned so young. I asked her, "How difficult was it being so young when you first came to prison?"

"I looked very young, and I was pretty naive, despite the fact that I committed a serious crime. I didn't get what was going on here at all. They put this woman in my room that was in here for child molestation. This CO came to my room and saw her and said, 'Who put her in here with you?' I told her I didn't know." Yvette told me that the CO walked away, but she came back a couple of minutes later and told the other woman to "pack up," and she moved her out of the cell.

Yvette spent the first five years she was in Iowa Correctional Institution for Women in a locked unit. She was with the same fifteen women all the time; it was done to help keep her safe. "These older women took me under their wing and kept me from being exposed to the things you might have heard about."

One woman, a lifer who lived in another unit, heard about Yvette's case on the news, and she managed to get a pass to come see her just before a church service. The service was held in the little kitchen in the unit, and when Yvette got there, "the woman came over and said, 'Honey, things are not always going to be like this. You are not always going to be here; you're going to get out one day.'" Yvette went on to say, "I guess I took it to heart and that maybe things weren't always going to be this way. So I thought maybe I should do something with myself so that when the time came I would be ready."

Because she had literally grown up in prison, I was curious about what Yvette had found most difficult about doing time. "The hardest part about being in prison is not your daily existence, because you do basically the same things. You get up; you go to work; you socialize. It is the limitations that are placed on you from an emotional standpoint, and also from the standpoint of never being able to realize your potential. There are so many small limitations being placed on you, like never having a quiet place to think, that add up to so much more than just being locked up."

In prison, chaos is constant. It is never dark; it is never quiet. Finding a place where you can think, where you can read in peace, is often a daunting task. Yvette explained, "The only time it is actually quiet or dark here is if we have a storm and the electricity goes out, and it is only quiet or dark if everyone is asleep, because if they are awake they flip out. I never have a moment to really think. I am always trying to find a place that is quieter than someplace else."

A place to think: it doesn't seem like much to ask, but with overcrowding in America's prisons it is a rare commodity. Yvette laughed and said, "One night I had an inspiration and I sat up in the middle of the night. I was trying to write in the dark. My roommate leaned over the bunk and said, 'What are you doing? Turn on the light.' I'm thinking, Ugh, I'm trying to think."

The recollection led Yvette and me to move on to a discussion of writing. "By the time I put something down on paper, it has gestated sometimes for years," she said. "When it comes out, it is born whole. It doesn't really change much after that." I nodded and then asked her how she came to write "Size." "I was in a program called Writing on the Inside, and we were given an assignment. We were to write a story from childhood that impacted our lives, and "Size" is just what came out. It is amazing how vivid all that was. It was the worst year of my life. I was smaller than everyone else. I was two years younger than everyone."

Life for Yvette at home during those years was crazy. Yvette told me that her father was abusive, and she shut down emotionally as a result. Her father moved her around continually, from school to school, from house to house, in an attempt to keep her silent; she remained silent until her third year of incarceration. "My first three years here, people thought I was stuck-up because I never said a thing. I was just closed down." Fortunately, all that changed. Writing and classes have allowed Yvette to find her voice. She will complete her bachelor's degree next year, and she is taking a class called Living Beyond Trauma that she said has helped moderate the pain of years of incest and neglect and emotional abuse.

"The Century" gives the reader another look into the life of a child who feels out of place. So much of this piece is about unreasonable expectations placed on a young child. "My parents were the Me Generation. They were going to explore their identity, and then they had kids. Well, children don't really fit in very well with self-exploration."

Yvette learned at an early age that she was alone. She said her mother was mentally ill, and her father had all the power. She did have her grandmother, who stood by Yvette throughout everything; she was always there, trying to make it better. "For a lot of my life, my grandma was the only thing that saved me." Yvette's writing is an exploration of a time in her life when everything she knew was turned upside down and inside out, and those events set in motion all that was to be.

"How have you fared throughout these years?" I asked.

"I like the COs. Sometimes they are the only avenue to the outside world, and they are people just like me." Her problems have been with the administration. "My boss told me that I have a bit of a reputation, and I said, 'Well, how hard should the truth be?'" Yvette has been known to call to the outside world when she is in need of help. "When I first got here, the clothing was inadequate. I worked maintenance and we shoveled snow. We didn't have steel-tipped boots or insulated jumpsuits, and we didn't have good thermals. The food got really, really bad. I was hungry." But as Yvette discovered, if you make enough noise to the right people, eventually something gets done.

There was a time when things in the prison were very bad. Everyone from inmates to staff was very unhappy; something needed to be done. Yvette's face took on a look of pride when she said, "Actually a whole bunch of female legislators went to the governor and complained that they didn't like the way the warden was treating the inmates, the staff, the visitors, and she was fired. Then things got much better."

The use of volunteers has made all the difference to the women in Iowa Correctional Institution for Women. The prison has opened things up to let a lot more volunteers come in. "We have classes in scrapbooking or quilting, small business, or anything you can imagine. They tie some kind of community-service component to it. You might get to make a wall hanging for your family, but you make one that goes to charity as well," and to Yvette that makes sense. It is important to give back and to feel the value in being a part of the community.

Yvette took part in a program called Match Two, which pairs up a volunteer with a prisoner. As a result, Margaret and Yvette have been visiting together for the past nineteen years; in fact, they have the longest relationship from Match Two in the entire prison system in Iowa. A group of women have adopted Yvette as their daughter, and they make sure she has what she needs. "That helps balance me a lot," she said. "I am lucky. If I hadn't had people who have been there for me the whole time I have been locked up, I don't know what I would have done." Knowing that people care, that there are people out there concerned about what is happening inside America's prisons, is something that makes Yvette's world brighter. "I am part of a spiritual program that meets twice a year, and that has been one of the most important factors in my well-being in here. Sometimes that is all you have to look forward to—people coming in from the outside, and just knowing that they care." —SUSAN NAGELSEN

Size

YVETTE LOUISELL

I'm in seventh grade, but I'm not a normal seventh grader. I'm smaller than all the other seventh graders, and I'm only eleven. All the other kids in my class at St. Joseph's are twelve, and a lot of them will turn thirteen before the end of school. I'm going to be eleven until summer. I still wear kids' sizes and have to get my green plaid skirt specially tailored so it doesn't fall off me. I'm really still the size for the jumper the younger kids wear, plus my hair is shorter even than some of the boys'.

I know I'm not going to be popular because I don't know any of the kids in my class. I went to St. Augustine's last year, until the tuition went up. I made the last cheerleading spot at St. A's because I smiled more than the other girls, but my dad made me switch schools anyway.

I try out for cheerleading at St. Joe's and make it, but they let everyone on the squad who wants to be on it. Beth Blankowicz, who is really tall with shiny dark brown hair all the way down her back, tells me I shouldn't be on cheerleading because I'm supposed to be only in sixth grade. Katie Neal calls me pygmy because I'm short, black, and have a big nose. She's fat, mean, and has a turned-up nose like a pig, but she's still more popular than I am. This isn't a school where the other kids like it when you're smart.

It's true that I'm supposed to be only in sixth grade, and I even know a few of the kids in that class, but I was told when they skipped me from fourth to sixth that I wasn't to play with the kids from my old class. I'm to adjust to my new grade. To make sure I adjusted right, my dad switched me that year from Kalamazoo Academy, where I went for fourth grade, to St. Augustine's. Now I'm switched again, to St. Joe's.

Nothing exciting happens during my first few weeks of school. Then one day I get home from school and my dad gives me an envelope and a piece of paper with directions. I'm to ride my bike to some lady's house to politely give her the envelope. My dad has to pick up one of my uncles at the airport. My dad acts really keyed up about seeing Uncle Kevin, so I figure there's drugs involved. When I went to live with Grandma Mary during third grade, my dad put a package in my suitcase. It was shaped like a big slice of my grandma's pound cake, but it was white. When Uncle Kevin got my baggage at the big wheel at LAX airport, he could barely wait until we got to the car to open my suitcase. He put some of the powder on my gums, and they felt numb for a long time, like at the dentist's office. Really, I knew what was going on, but it didn't seem all that exciting to me to feel like I was gonna get a tooth pulled out. I even heard Uncle Wayne talk about putting it on his dick, and all I could think is why would you want to feel like you were gonna have your privates pulled out.

I get to the lady's house. It's pretty small, dark greenish gray, and all on one floor. She comes to the door looking kind of dressed up, with her thick, wavy brown hair all the way to her behind. She looks at me real funny, like she's not very happy that I'm there. I tell her the message, figuring that she and my dad were supposed to go on a date. I want to warn her that her hair won't last long around my dad. His big thing is finding women with long hair and making them cut it all off. As soon as he got full custody of me, it was whack, whack, whack.

The lady's name is Pamela-not-Pam, and two weeks later we go to live in her mossy little house. All my stuff is still at our house, though. Every day I take the school bus home, shower, put all my stuff for the next day in my backpack, and ride my bike to Pamela's house. It's like getting ready for a slumber party every day, except the party never happens. I beg my dad to let me stay at home where I have the whole top floor to myself, but he says it's against the law to leave an eleven-year-old at home alone. He does take my bike back to our house every morning, at least, but I can't really study or sleep because I can hear them through the wall all night long. The wall seems too thin to be real, like the Japanese screen I see at the library's sister-city exhibit.

Finally I make friends with Jennifer Jackson and get to spend the night at her house. I'm so excited because she tells me she has twin beds. I haven't had anything but a mattress since my dad bought our house. He left my waterbed at Uncle Kevin's house, where we lived before. Uncle Kevin whispered, "Sorry. Your dad owes me money for some coke." My dad told me that the floor at our new house wasn't strong enough to hold the waterbed's weight.

Jennifer's room is all pale pink. She's got ruffles on her bedspread and on the canopies on the tops of the twin beds. She's got a bunch of dolls and stuffed animals, too. I think she's got at least twenty Cabbage Patch dolls. I could stay here forever.

Jennifer's brother, John, talks to me some after their parents tell him to keep an eye on us while they go out. He goes to Hackett, the Catholic high school. He seems nice because he lets us play his J. Geils album on his stereo. Jennifer is surprised that he's even letting her go in his room, but he tells me that he never likes Jennifer's friends, but he likes me because I'm not a brat. He says we can come back later, which we think is cool. Jennifer says we'll bring snacks so he'll let us stay and listen to his stereo longer.

We get in our pajamas, and I help Jennifer make a tray with nuts, chips, pretzels, and the little airplane liquors her dad keeps. We think we're really cool when we bring all of it to John, but he just wants to listen to the stereo. He turns out the lights so we can see the little red lights on his stereo that move to the music. I ask him how that works, and he laughs at me, but it's kind of a smiling laugh, like he's happy that I thought to ask that.

After a little while, John tells Jennifer that she's crowding him, and he makes her lie on the floor. I feel kind of bad because he lets me stay on the bed, but it's a nice waterbed, bigger than the one I used to have at my old house. He asks me a couple of questions, like do I like "Stairway to Heaven" and am I gonna go to Hackett when I get in ninth grade, because he's in tenth and will still be there. Then he whispers in my ear that he really likes me because I'm not like Jennifer's other friends. I feel kind of warm inside and just think about that for a minute. Jennifer is still on the floor. She asks can she put one of her albums on, but John ignores her.

John moves closer, and I feel his hand in my pants. It doesn't really feel bad or like much of anything, but I'm kind of scared to move. I lie there and don't say anything for a minute or two. He moves up against me, and I can hear him breathing loud. He pulls my pants down and starts rubbing me harder. I still don't say anything for a while, but finally I whisper, "Ouch! That hurts." He stops and pulls my pants back up, but he's still really close to me. His breath makes my neck feel wet. He keeps touching my face and saying he's sorry. I don't really feel anything at all.

Jennifer and I go downstairs to the rec room, and I see where there's a hose and a sink in the laundry room. I don't know why, but I go in that little room and wash my privates. Jennifer can tell that something is wrong, so I tell her what happened after she pinkie-swears not to tell anyone, not even her mom.

On Monday, I feel better about being at St. Joe's. I'm still smaller than everybody, but at least I have one good friend. Jennifer and I go to recess, and Beth actually comes up to us to talk. I stand up straighter and smile.

"So I hear you got fingered this weekend." She laughs.

I look at Jennifer; she shrugs and looks away. Two other girls start walking our way, and I run for the door to the dining hall.

Pamela moves in over first-quarter break, so I won't have to ride back and forth anymore. Her hair is to her shoulders now. My dad sends her to my parent-teacher conference even though she's only twenty-four and isn't a parent yet. When she gets back she's all red in the face and yells at me because Sister Margaret wanted to know if an older relative was molesting me. Pamela is pissed and there's no telling her anything anyway, so I don't even bother. I'm just glad the year is one fourth over, because my dad always switches my school anyway. I'm sure I'll be in a new school with all new kids next year.

We get back from break and Jennifer walks up to me on the playground and gives me a picture of John and an envelope that hasn't been opened. I read the back of the photo that John signed: "To my girl Yvette: I really like you a lot." About ten kids are watching, so I rip up the photo and envelope and throw all the pieces over the fence. I'm crying, but I'm mad, too. I kind of want to read the letter, but Jennifer had to give it to me in front of everyone. The sun is so bright white that I can't really see, but I can hear people snickering and calling me slut.

I run into the bathroom and look in the mirror. Little black spots spin around my face. I close my eyes and think about John. He has to really like me because he sent that letter and picture. I want to read the letter so I'll know what he said, but I can't go get it in front of everyone. John really likes me, and I'll never see him again because of Jennifer.

I open my eyes and look in the mirror. The spots are gone and I'm not crying anymore, but I'm not really smiling either. I see my too-short, wavy hair. I see my big nose. I see the way my white blouse with the Peter Pan collar hangs off me to one side. I take a step back and look at all of me, and I know that I'm always gonna be the smallest one in the class and that nobody will ever, ever again like me the way John did.

The Century

YVETTE LOUISELL

For most people, the sight of an old country highway conjures up memories of family vacations in early summer, all the kids piled into an old Buick. Or maybe a motorcycle ride to sightsee when the leaves turn in autumn. For me, though, the sight of an open road will always bring back memories of long bicycle rides with my dad.

It all started when I was nine, in midwinter, just before the calendar turned to 1980. My dad was part owner of a ski and bicycle shop in Schoolcraft, Michigan, one of the small rural communities that surrounded our college town of Kalamazoo. Dad had been a lifelong skier, both downhill and cross-country, and bought into the Village Cyclery both for investment purposes and for the fringe benefit of cheaper equipment. This winter, though, there was little skiing to be found in southwestern Michigan. The only snow we saw was fine powder, a huge disappointment after the '78 blizzard and another good snow year in '79.

Chandler Garrison, the primary owner of the Village Cyclery, was a tall man who owned five wiener dogs, which caused me to like him instantly. He encouraged my dad to try indoor bicycle training to compensate for the lack of good skiing conditions.

Dad, being the type never to do anything halfway, brought home a set of rollers and began training for spring competition. Each night after school, he would set his bike on top of the rollers and ride for more than an hour.

My job was to be in charge of the music: the Clash's *London Calling*, a double album. I would sit in the living room watching my dad, listening to the whir of his bike. While I memorized all the words to the Clash's political protest songs, I made sure there was as little interruption as possible between sides. The music never changed because my dad couldn't find a more constantly hard-driving album. So *London Calling* was a six-day-a-week ritual until spring. By then I knew every word to every song, plus the significance behind them all. The "Four Horsemen" were Mao's Gang of Four. I thought "Rock the Casbah" was a call to the Algerians to overthrow French colonial rule, and the coke in "Kola Kola" was not Coca-Cola.

Once the roads dried with the spring winds, my leisurely appreciation of bike riding ended. I came home from school one day and saw a bicycle like nothing I'd ever seen before. It was yellow and twice as long as a regular bike. It had a large front end and a smaller back end with pedals lower down to fit a child's legs.

Dad was excited. "It's a tandem, a bicycle built for two. I had it custom-made so that we could ride together. You can ride with me and the extra weight will help me train."

I was excited, too, when Dad presented me with a bike shirt, bike shorts with chamois, and a new Campagnolo bike cap. Although my dad wore cleats, I would wear tennis shoes and use toe straps. The bike was pretty, and I was proud when we rode around town and people honked and waved. This was fun!

After a few Saturdays of rides to the bike shop in Schoolcraft and back, my dad enthusiastically announced that we would be going on a longer ride called a "century" the following week. We'd be going with a bicycle club, and I'd get a patch when we completed the ride.

"What's a century, Dad?"

"Oh, it's a type of bike ride sponsored by a bicycle club. There'll be lots of other people on the ride, and we'll probably stop for ice cream halfway."

That was all I needed to hear. Friday night I went to bed early. Saturday morning I ate all six of my silver-dollar pancakes, half of which normally ended up as a syrupy mush in one corner of my plate. I took my Rottweiler, Atman, over to Uncle Kevin's house to play with his Great Dane cousin, Moses, while I was gone. Then we headed out along our usual route, past the Real Riders' clubhouse. Even though the Riders rode "real" bikes, as they would say, they supported our bicycling efforts by cheering, standing up, and holding up their morning beers in salute. They'd still be on the porch to cheer and salute us when we made it home, but they wouldn't be able to stand up.

We rode through the city and into Portage, where we met the other members of the bike club. They were all adults, so I went into my normal routine of watching the road and singing to myself. We crossed into the country, and my dad relaxed and got into a good rhythm. I could hear the music with every turn of the pedal.

> The ice age is coming, the sun's zooming in
> Meltdown expected . . .
> but I have no fear
> 'Cause London is drowning, and I live by the river.

I got into the rhythm of pedaling, too, pushing as hard as I could in beat with my dad. The empty road called us forward with the swirly haze that disintegrated into solid road as soon as we got close to whatever spot I'd been watching. No matter how carefully I watched, I could never see the heat off the blacktop up close. It was magic. I went back to singing.

> I get good advice from the advertising world
> Treat me nice says the party girl
> Koke adds life where there isn't any
> So freeze, man, freeze.

It was obvious that my dad was more serious than the rest of these people, because I couldn't see anyone behind us anymore.

"How are you doing?"

"Okay."

"We're going to stop pretty soon and get some ice cream. Okay?"

I saw the sign before we reached the town: a huge bear towering over everything else in sight, one half of the town's name situated on each of its outstretched hands. "Paw Paw," and then "Ice Cream Shoppe" written just above the bear's head. Usually we'd stop at a small country store and get salted nut rolls, Gatorade, and Trident gum, or maybe a banana, so this was a big treat.

"You can get whatever you want, but make sure you eat it all."

I was notorious for ordering adult-sized portions and then eating only three bites.

"Hi. I'd like a banana split with caramel and chocolate, but no strawberry sauce."

"Where are you two coming from?"

"Kalamazoo."

"Kalamazoo? That's a pretty long ride for such a little girl. You gonna ride the whole fifty miles back, too?"

I looked at my dad while he glared at the waitress. I added the numbers as she took Dad's order and went back to the counter.

"Dad, you didn't tell me we were riding a hundred miles."

"Well, we're halfway there already. You did great. We'll eat our ice cream, rest a little, and we'll be ready to ride home. Atman will be missing you."

We left the shop and got back onto our bike. I couldn't believe that my dad had tricked me into riding a hundred miles with him. A few miles outside of Paw Paw, my legs started feeling wobbly. I was still pedaling as hard as I could, trying to be tough, but I was suddenly weak. The road stretched out before us, the waves of heat looking taller and closer, until they reached all the way up to my legs. The rest of the songs left my head. All I could sing to myself was the Clash's getting-out-of-prison lament.

> Did you stand by me
> No, not at all
> Did you stand by me
> No way.

My legs ached.

"Hey. Are you pedaling back there?"

> Now I got a job
> But it don't pay
> I need new clothes
> I need somewhere to stay.

"Okay, just pedal hard every other time." We played that game with running. Dad would let me run a hundred steps, then walk a hundred steps. I could do it.

"Okay, just pedal hard every third time."

I reached for my water bottle every two minutes until we finally made it back to Portage. The bike club supporters were sitting in lawn chairs in front of their van. "Congratulations! You're the youngest rider out today. Here's your patch. You can sew it onto your jersey."

I smiled and looked at my dad. "Dad?"

"Yeah?"

"Next time I'm gonna pedal hard every time all the way back."

"You did great."

It's been almost twenty years since I've ridden a bicycle, and even longer since my last long-distance ride with my dad. Yet even today, as I look out the window of my prison cell and see the blacktop of an old country highway, I remember. The road fades into the distance, but the music remains strong.

> Did you stand by me
> No, not at all
> Did you stand by me
> No way.

Philip Horner

In prison parlance, Phil Horner is a citizen, someone who will never really believe that he is where he is, that he is in prison. Oh, he has lived it; it is real. But as I talked with him, I felt that he was still in shock, even though he has spent the last seven years living and breathing prison air. Phil is a Georgetown-trained M.D. with a wife and five children. Prior to his incarceration, he lived a busy life devoted to his family and practice, just as he had been taught by his parents, a seminary-trained father and educator mother who valued learning and books and family.

Then, at the height of his career, at the age of forty-four, he found himself caught up in a "jackpot," as they say behind the walls. In what seemed to Phil like a split second, with no time to think or prepare, he was sitting in the holding tank of the county jail. It was a sexual crime. "I became involved with a fifteen-year-old adopted daughter of family friends. She was needy, I was needy, and I took advantage of it." He is serving three consecutive three-and-a-half- to seven-year sentences, and today he has a parole hearing that will send him into the last of his sentences.

"The process of being incarcerated tore apart the things of my life upon which I had been relying to give it meaning," Phil said. He found himself sitting in a holding tank with a raised concrete slab for a bed and a hole in the floor for a toilet. "I was locked up twenty-three hours a day in a single cell in the beginning. I was alone with my thoughts. It was at that point that I started writing. I reminisced."

Phil recalled the first piece he wrote, a memory of walking with his three-year-old daughter in a sun-dappled pine grove, a memory that was filled with the innocence of a summer day and a child's voice. Even seven years after writing that piece, as Phil remembers, the pain of those lonely days in the holding cell in the county jail is etched in the lines of his face.

"The hardest thing about incarceration was being taken away from my family," he explained. In "Lullaby for My Three-Year-Old Son," Phil laments that even though he is far from his family and son, "such earthly griefs cannot erase / the brightness of these memories." "I was trying to come to terms with grief," he said. As he sat alone in the cell, pencil and paper were the only tools available to help ease the pain. Phil used memories to fill the void; he wrote stories of things he and his family had done over the years. He wrote of his children, of times they had shared. He wrote poetry. Phil's loss and grief are evident in "I Do Not Know the Way," but especially in the refrain of the last stanza: "I cling to love's existence from afar." You can also feel his pain in "Contraband," where a memory is used as "a weapon to defend against despair."

"Writing was something I could do instead of destroying myself," Phil said. "It was something I could do instead of wallowing in the self-recrimination that happens and becoming lost completely." He spoke to me of suicide and how for the first and only time in his life it was a serious consideration. "Writing was a way I could make a connection, when that connection had been almost completely severed." Phil mentioned Elisabeth Kübler-Ross's theories of death and dying, proffering the possibility that writing was a way for him to work toward acceptance of where he was, of his loss, his pain, and his shame.

The themes that emerged in Phil's early poems were heavily religious, and he needed that to survive. "I have spent most of the seven years here angry at God in some way, but that is a form of being sustained." I asked him to define his anger at God. He said, "For the first time in my life I had to come face to face with suffering, and so I had a childish understanding of the way the world operates, and now, here, I come in contact with a world filled with absurdity and suffering." Phil said that what he has experienced in prison "is probably a more real understanding of what life is like for most people."

What has that done for his writing? "It has helped me see that human life is suffering. Until I experienced suffering myself, it was hard for me to understand that."

There is cruelty in prison, but there is survival as well. "We all get wounded in one way or another, and unless we figure out how to deal with that, we'll die, what is of value in us will die," Phil said. "'Stumpy' is a metaphor for this entire experience." In "Stumpy," Phil shows the reader what happens to the wounded in prison: they become "clumsy piles / of feathers in the yard." But there is incredible resilience in Stumpy, for even though he is maimed and wounded, "Stumpy flaps uninjured wings / and you should see him fly."

"In some ways writing is the scream," Phil confided. "Prison robs you of your ability to express your emotions. There is no appropriate place to do that." For Phil, writing is the only appropriate place where that can happen. He related a story about going to see a mental health counselor when he was first in prison. He would walk into her office, and she would say, "How are you?" He would cry for the half-hour session, then dry his tears and go out to face the rest of his week. It was his release. Writing is the same for him; it is not necessarily peace for Phil, but it is release, a respite from the confining walls and the bleakness of prison.

If we are going to do anything to change the culture of revenge that prison has become, Phil believes, someone has got to write about prison "in a way that communicates to America that we are on a course that is unsustainable. There is a culture of fear around prison. We have a system that sees revenge as the goal of corrections, whereas most Western democracies see the goal as rehabilitation." He continued, "When you base public policy on an irrationality, there is no end to it. How much punishment is enough. When does it end?"

Our conversation was interrupted by his parole hearing, and Phil came back with news that he had been paroled into his third sentence. There was relief on his face.

"Were you worried?" I asked.

He nodded: "When I walked into the hearing room and saw that no one was there to object, it was a relief. When you realize that you have done something that has caused hurt to people, there is at least a little comfort in knowing that they have put it behind them."

Phil is concerned about how he will do on the outside after all this is over. He has lost his right to practice medicine, and he wonders what kind of work he will do. He thinks about the time he has missed with his children. "There is so much that I can't get back. I missed that birthday. It is gone. I don't have the memory of that event—we have lived parallel lives." His family has moved on. They live in a different house, in a different state. His children were ages three to fourteen when he left for prison; they are now seven years older. He doesn't know their friends or their schools; he has been an outsider in their lives.

Phil is lucky, though; he has family support. But it will still be a difficult road back for him. "Nothing will be able to undo the damage from this experience. I hope I can't go back to being the person that I was. I don't want to walk away and say, Whew, that is over. What do you do with the pain that can't be repaired?" In "Memory's Nacre," Phil shows us that the heart can do amazing things, "but, oh, the changing is agonizingly slow."   —SUSAN NAGELSEN

Poems

PHILIP HORNER

Stumpy

Poor Stumpy has no legs;
dismembered by the inmates
        of the Secure Housing Pod,
who pass the time by luring
hapless pigeons into snares
that amputate their feet.
        Most don't survive.
The wounded birds are clumsy piles
of feathers in the yard.
They beat against all helpers
        in their fear.
Unable to distinguish friend from foe,
        they die alone.
But Stumpy, maimed not once
but twice, survived
to wander footless
        on the concrete tier.
And when the sun, arising,
sparkles in the razor wire
and flocks of pigeons trace
concentric circles in the sky,
then Stumpy flaps uninjured wings
        and you should see him fly.

Thinking Outside the Box

Danny's in the hole—
lugged for a map that seemed to show
a world beyond the walls.
Wardens and prelates disapprove
of contraband cosmologies.
They want exclusive access to the keys.

There are a heretic few who dare
to dream a Day of Jubilee,
when minds and prisoners go free,
and blind men look through telescopes to see
a world where chains are just a memory.

Watching from the window of his cell,
Danny sees the wandering stars
and charts a universe unbarred.

I Do Not Know the Way

I do not know the way to where you are.
The road is dark. My eyes are dim with tears;
The aching emptiness of doubts and fears
All realized. There is no guiding star.
I do not know the way to where you are.

My arms reach out to hold you in the night.
The phantom of your face fast fades away,
As, with the dawning of another day,
Sleep's transient visions vanish with the light.
My arms reach out to hold you in the night.

I cling to love's existence from afar.
Though time should mar the memory of your face,
And daylight dim the dream of your embrace,
And though I lose the way to where you are,
I cling to love's existence from afar.

Reptile House

I am an animal
an animal kept in a cell
an animal nobody thinks
is cute.

I live here in the reptile house
with others of my kind.
It smells of rotting food
and stagnant urine.

Most people look the other way
when passing by my cage.
But sometimes children point at me
and laugh.

I could wish I were a panda.
But what good would that do?
Instead, I lie here on this concrete slab,
so cool and still,

watching you with hooded eyes.

Memory's Nacre

The heart,
like an oyster,
can transform each grain of sorrow
into a lustrous pearl.

But, oh,
the changing is
agonizingly slow.

Contraband

At night, I hone the memory of your love
into a blade,
a weapon to defend against despair.

By day, I hide it deep within a crevice
in my heart.
I know the screws will never look in there.

Grandpa's Dreams

When I was five years old,
my grandpa built a boat
the way his grandpa did.
He used no plans.
He shaped her lap-straked planks
with factory-roughened hands,
his landlocked shop suffused
with mackerel and motor oil,
his dreams of the sea.

She never rode the waves.
I last saw him adrift
in a box of wood and brass,
hands folded in dreamless sleep.
The room was a sea of strangers
and the scent of cologne and roses.
I watched as he was lowered
into the deep.

Our boat lay overturned
in a corner of the yard.
Her tarpaulin slowly weathered
from dun to gray;
the hulk of Grandpa's dreams
in a backwater of weeds and sumac.
One day some strangers came
and hauled her away.

Retribution

There was a time,
    the old man said,
when punishment for crimes like ours
      was swift
      and very often
      painful.

But now,
    in this enlightened age,
    sophisticated justice shuns
      such public spectacles
      of bloody vengeance.

It's now considered more humane
    to wound the soul, deliberately,
    through lonely years of waiting while
      life's tender joys,
      the blush and beauty,
      wilt and fall,

like petals from a fading rose,
    to leave at last the bitter pod,
    compressed and dry,
    a scarlet husk,
        alone amid
        an unremitting winter
        of remorse.

Hard Saying

> You have heard it said, "Eye for eye and tooth for tooth."
> But I tell you, do not resist an evil person.
>
> —Matthew 5:38

I honestly cannot begin
to love the sinner
      and hate the sin.

In theory, that's what I would do
if sinners weren't
      so tangible.

Although I pardon sins like mine,
your sins are just
      too out of line.

And when I'm hurt by your offenses,
I think there should be
      consequences.

"Eye for eye and tooth for tooth."
It has a certain
      ring of truth.

Let God forgive you way up there.
Down here, I want
      the electric chair.

Lullaby for My Three-Year-Old Son

Transience with tousled hair
sleeping, mortal, in my arms;
neither fleeting childhood's dream
nor my anguished, guilty prayer
can stop our dissolution.
In nights of grief, tears of regret,
can filmy, faithless eyes discern,
past the junkyard's twisted forms,
the clinging rust, the fever sweat,
a hint of resurrection?

From the clumsy, childish hand
slips the coin of innocence.
Ere the waking soul can sense
how great the loss, or understand,
it disappears beneath the flood
of days and weeks, of months and years.
Concentric circles spreading out
reverberate in formless doubt,
the lapping of desires and fears,
the pounding heart, the freshening blood.

Here, for this moment, sweetly sleep,
rosy cheek against my breast.
Dream no dreams of Eden lost.
Other, older eyes will weep
those ruined possibilities.
Though time and insult drive us far
from this silent, sacred place,
and other arms with you embrace,
age and care your youth will mar,
such earthly griefs cannot erase
the brightness of these memories.

Erin George

There is no portrait of the writer here because officials in the Department of Corrections for the Commonwealth of Virginia refused or ignored requests to photograph her.

I arrived at Fluvanna Correctional Center for Women armed with a pad of paper, a pencil, and my photo ID—all the administration would allow. There would be no recording of my interview and no photographs. I tried for months to gain permission to have Erin George photographed: I wrote letters, I pleaded; my editor even appealed to the governor, but each request was denied or ignored. No photographs. It didn't surprise me that it took months to arrange my visit, months to get someone to return my call. I have learned that nothing in the Department of Corrections moves quickly. I always go to prisons prepared to wait.

The officer in the reception area had no record of my scheduled visit, so the phone calls began, and I was asked to sit and wait. I had no sooner sat down than a woman in civilian clothes came into the building. She spoke to the officer, and then she walked past me, stopped, turned, looked at me, and said, "Are you from New Hampshire?"

"Yes." I laughed. "Can you tell by what I am wearing?"

She laughed too and said, "Erin George works for me, and I knew you were coming. She is just wonderful. She has been waiting for you."

We shook hands, and with that she turned to the officer and told him that the visit was approved and he should let me in, and she even volunteered to take me if necessary. The officer told her that he would escort me. He finished up a couple of things and then told me to follow him. We walked through the door and headed for the main part of the prison, where the interview would take place, and we talked about what it was like to work in a women's prison.

"I used to work in a men's prison," he said, "but it was a tough joint and very stressful, and after a couple of years I decided that I didn't want to do that, so I put in for a transfer. Working with women is very different. Men are more physical, and women are far more open with their problems."

We continued walking until we reached a medical unit, and he showed me into a tiny room that held a small desk and two chairs.

He told me to have a seat and said that Ms. George would be along shortly.

"As soon as the count clears she will be here," he said, and then he turned and walked down the hall.

It took forty-five minutes for the staff to count all the prisoners and make sure that no one had left without permission. I sat in that small white room thinking about Erin George. Her poetry is filled with grace. It is poignant and sad, funny and ironic, and I was curious to meet this woman, who at age thirty-nine was five years into a very long sentence. I heard an officer's radio squawk, and then I heard, "We have a good count; we have a good count. Begin the ten-minute movement." I knew it wouldn't be long now.

I looked up when I heard voices in the hall, and Erin George came into view. I watched her walk toward me with a hesitant gait, her right hand held awkwardly, but she was smiling.

"Erin, it is great to finally meet you after all this time," I said, with my hand extended.

"I am so glad you were able to finally get in to see me."

We made small talk for a while. I asked her how she was, and she told me that she suffers from lupus and was having a flareup. She knew she needed steroids but hated the idea of having to go through the side effects of taking those drugs. She was dressed in maroon scrubs. Her hair was short but soft around her face. It was streaked with gray but looked as if it had been frosted by a high-end salon. Erin's skin was pale, but even though I knew it was the result of not spending much time outside, I could tell that she wasn't the type to brown easily; the freckles that joined forces on her arms, creating a tan, were a dead giveaway. Her smile was genuine and warm, but it didn't reach all the way to her eyes until I asked her how she was faring in prison. Erin told me that she made the decision to do her time the only way she knew how: "I am going to be what I am—a dorky white woman." In that moment Erin's sense of humor broke through, and I knew how she would survive what she was facing.

We didn't have a lot of time, so I asked Erin to tell me about the events that had brought her to Fluvanna and her sentence. Her eyes brimmed with tears like an overfilling cup; she swallowed audibly and said, "I was sentenced to six hundred and three years for the first-degree murder of my husband, James."

She told me her story. She and her children and her husband had gone to bed on the night of his murder as they always did; the only thing different was that their dog had run away a few days before. She believes that James must have left the house in the middle of the night because he heard something and, hoping it was the family dog, he went to check. But it is just a theory. In the wee hours of the morning, a neighbor found James shot to death on the front lawn of the Georges' home. Erin and the children were asleep in bed when the police came to the door to tell her that James was dead.

What followed was a nightmare. The police found DNA evidence on James's hand, and Erin offered to submit a sample for comparison. Erin said that on the day she was to submit her DNA, the police called her lawyer and told her not to come in; they told her lawyer it wasn't necessary.

The police never found the gun that was used to kill James George, but because the Georges had once owned a gun that was among one of the top twenty most popular guns owned in America, and because the gun used in the murder was among one of the top twenty most popular guns owned in America, the police concluded that the two guns might be one and the same. The extra three years of Erin's sentence were for the gun that was never found.

The police also concluded that because the Georges had taken out a life insurance policy a few days before James was murdered—a policy that had not yet gone into effect—money was the motive for Erin to kill her husband. In 2001, Erin George was arrested for the premeditated murder of her husband.

Erin has three children, Jack, Francesca, and Gio, and she was pregnant with the couple's fourth child when the knock on the door came to tell her that the world as she knew it had been irrevocably changed. She was a "soccer mom" who was happy in her life. Erin said, "I was a rule-follower. James used to laugh at me because I was the one who would stop at the red light at two o'clock in the morning when there was no one else on the road. He would say to me, 'Honey, you can go,' but I wouldn't do that, because the rule said not to."

In a few months she lost everything. She lost her husband, she miscarried, and she eventually lost her children and her freedom. In society's eyes, because she was arrested, tried, and convicted, she also lost her right to grieve the death of the man she loved, the father of her children, and the death of her unborn child.

Erin has exhausted her appeals. Her parents, children, and in-laws have stood by her, steadfastly believing in her innocence. Erin told me that the happiest days of her life right now are the days she gets to see her children, who live in England with James's parents. She sees them only once a year, so their time together is treasured. She said, "We have a program here called MILK, Mothers Inside Loving Kids, and it is wonderful. We get to spend the entire day with our children. We have food and play games and read and spend time together. It is what I live for each year."

Her children were here for a visit in August. Jack, the oldest, is now thirteen. This year he said to his mom, "I wish you had let me testify in court. I could have told them that you were in bed the whole time. I know you never left."

"What about the Innocence Project?" I asked. "They have been helpful to a lot of people."

"I wrote to them over a year ago, but I haven't heard anything," Erin replied.

"It takes time for them to respond because they get so inundated. You can't give up hope," I offered.

"I can't live in here with hope. I have to live in here as though this is going to be my life. If I don't . . . Well, if I don't, I am not sure what will happen to me." The cup threatened to overflow, tears hovering on the lower lashes, glistening against her skin. It was time to move on to other things.

"I love your poetry," I told her. "Your poems take the reader through such a range of emotions, from laughter to the horror of the loss of a child's innocence. How did you first begin to write?"

"I never wrote a thing until I came to prison. I grew up in a word family. I read a lot, and we always did things as a family that involved words. We played Scrabble or did crossword puzzles. We just loved words." Erin attended Longwood College for several years but did not receive her degree. She told me, "I would love to continue taking courses, but courses are only available through correspondence, and it is so expensive that it is cost-prohibitive."

Erin told me a story about being held in the county jail after she was convicted. She was known in the unit as the person to go to if someone didn't know a word. "Everyone would come to me if they wanted to know how to spell something or wanted to know what a word meant. One day I was sitting on the toilet in my cell, and a girl came down and asked me how to spell a word. They were playing Scrabble and she wanted to use it on the board. She didn't even blink an eye or notice that I was on the toilet. I knew I was in a very different place."

When Erin came to Fluvanna, she became involved in the Voice Project—the Charlotte Writer's Project. The connection was profound. Erin said, "I fell like Icarus into the sea. It filled a need I didn't know I had." Her poetry is lyrical; her love of words is unmistakable in each line. In "Vacancies," it is evident in "I suffer from a superfluity/of lap." Her humor speaks to us in "Frustration." Erin George shows us her world in "With Due Respect to Randall Jarrell" when she laments, "I also fell into the State. / Not its belly, but its bowels."

Erin is grateful that she comes from a family that views the world rationally rather than emotionally. She said, "I had to take myself out of the equation. I couldn't approach what I have to do here emotionally, or I wouldn't survive." This has made life in Fluvanna livable. Erin has found that her emotions are closer to the surface in prison than they were in the free world. She told me, "I have had more true laughter in here than I did out there. Laughter in here is so rare that it is genuine and much more strongly felt."

"How will you face the time you have in front of you?" I asked.

Erin's reply left no doubt that she knows who she is and how she will manage. She said, "I have to set achievable goals for myself." Then she said, with a look of determination in her eyes, "I have five hundred ninety-eight years to go. I am going to learn to speak Spanish."   —SUSAN NAGELSEN

Poems

Erin George

Frustration

In my cell
affixed chest high
are four gunmetal steel hooks
hinged as prophylactics
against despair

can't hang my bathrobe
or myself

Vacancies

I suffer from a superfluity
of lap

not needed
as a makeshift cradle
now

nor used
as a comforter
for weeping child.

Yes, I suffer,
but perhaps
my malady

is more accurately
diagnosed
as an excess of absence

First Time

I don't remember your hands.

Rough, gentle, I can't say which.
I can't remember any pain,
and my memory is soundless.
Here is what I do remember:

The lunar surface of the garage floor,
cold and gray as a morgue,
pitted against my salty cheek.

My fingers twisting, greasy
in the square of oil-spattered green shag
crudely hacked from your old bedroom carpeting.

The band of hiked-up nightgown,
knotted as thick as an umbilical cord,
pressing against my stomach.

The cave of cobwebs and suspended fly corpses
under your workbench,
my only focus.

You, afterward, washing out my favorite panties,
the ones with My Pretty Pony on them,
in the seldom-used utility sink,
promising repercussions and ice cream.

With Due Respect to Randall Jarrell

I also fell into the State.
Not its belly, but its bowels,
clenched and shaking like a fist
inside a basement holding cell.
My sentence was not douched oblivion.
It was life, bacterial,
until rehabilitation does me in.

The Selkie

You are unabashedly unpeeled,
bathing suit a tangled
sandy splatter,
a polychrome abandonment
spilled just beyond
the high tide's boundary
of shattered shells
and clumps of black-brown kelp.

Your bright plastic pail
is forgotten.
Instead, your sleek, sea-dark head
bends low as you painstakingly
decipher a sandpiper's
circling cuneiform.

Your own meanderings,
a chain of footprints
washed to phocine wedges,
could just as easily lead from
as to the sea.
I can't be sure,
seeing you pick your way
among black rocks,
your raw pink kinesis
constrained by uncertain footing.

Are you yourself, my girl,
or some fey creature
seeking her stolen sealskin
to slip it on and slip away from me
between the green strata
of the sun-warmed sea?

Patchwork Man

He read my body like Braille,
too simple for him to decipher.
Where I wrote runes,
he found road maps
and arrows saying,
"You are here."

I carry pieces of him with me,
so without protracted searching
I find that place where my tongue fits,
just behind his ear,
lapping up his alchemical, sweat-rendered syrup.

I still stumble on his clutter,
a thicket of cleats and clubs and cricket bats,
and, cursing, reel to see him
smirking at the discord he has sown.

I taste the clumsy meal,
uneaten then but savored now,
he prepared to comfort me,
soul-sick over our lost child.

He's more than just some APB rundown:
Brown hair, blue eyes, no distinguishing marks.
James is an amalgam of contradictions
hoarded in me like a Saxon trove.

I fuse the scattered facets of my love:
His knack for guessing birthday gifts,
the way he'd dangle Glo as she chortled,
the yin and yang of his contrition and his ire.

I assemble these within to make my quilt
while coldly I like longing in my bed.
My construct is not near enough to the truth,
but will, undimming, live as long as I.

Undoing Time

We are a prison of Penelopes
so busy at our looms
so full of weavings and unweavings

the strangling weft and warp
is plucked into dirging thrum
like fretful catgut
by our lanolined fingers,
greasy from the unwashed
wool we use, undyed,
gray as the ashes
of an apocalyptic sun

we're so busy
under official daylight eyes
dumb as sheep
bleating yessir, yessir
in our ungreen Ithaca.

We are equally busy in the night
dismantling our work,
using our teeth if necessary,
unpicking inches like reversed time
the tumorous wool
clotted and hirsute
uneven as stacked hourglasses,
unusable for tomorrows.
We snip it into tiny lengths
and fling it away
in a ghastly nocturnal
ticker-tape parade
celebrating one more dodging
of a resolution,
some unknown quota
still unreached.

Defenestration

When I was seven,
my sister and I
orchestrated our escape.
Kicking out the rusted fly screen,
meant to keep things out, not in,
we hurled ourselves like Br'er Rabbit
into the thicket of boxwood below,
then, glad-footed, careened
across the sun-sharp grass
till our trajectories were thwarted
by a heedful babysitter
who had pried herself away
from telephone and TV set
long enough to glimpse us
cannonball past the kitchen window.

Now my window to the world
is five by forty inches,
a sliver of normality
absurdly Constable in its composition:
a pond parasoled by a contorted oak,
a slew of bold and bickering geese,
and in the distance a bijou farmhouse,
all of this framed by flaking cinderblock
and fingernail-scarred putty,
gouged with tiny evacuations
and thick-furred with neglect.
No child's begrimed feet
can force an exit here.
The passage is too narrow.

John Corley

There is no portrait of the writer here because Burl Cain, warden of Louisiana State Penitentiary at Angola, refused permission for him to be photographed.

Angola. Even the name is evocative for anyone familiar with U.S. prisons, conjuring images of sullen prisoners working under an unforgiving sun and the unwavering stares of armed guards, eyes hidden by mirrored lenses. Sisyphus comes to mind, as I imagine the mindless, backbreaking labor, the equivalent of prisoners pushing stones up a steep slope, only to have them roll back down over and over until the men complete their sentences. Or they die.

The prison, all eighteen thousand acres of it, is the stuff of nightmares and executions, the location for Sister Helen Prejean's harrowing descriptions in *Dead Man Walking*. It is an intimidating place—intentionally so, I think, designed to produce compliance by draconian measures, both physical and psychological, and only a small step removed from the dungeons of the Inquisition. Fifty-two percent of all prisoners in Angola are incarcerated for life, and in Louisiana, life means until death.

When I selected John Corley's work for inclusion in *Exiled Voices* and began making plans to interview him, I didn't know how closely the prison would conform to those preconceptions. I didn't know if I would encounter the Angola of folklore, an antebellum plantation where the lives of prisoners have little value, or the more progressive facility advertised by Warden Burl Cain on the prison website.[1]

I was familiar with *The Angolite,* the prison's award-winning journal, and Wilbert Rideau, the former editor, recently paroled after serving forty-four years. I had read *Life Sentences,* Rideau's book, a collection of articles from the journal, which are powerfully written, providing a startling view of the prison experience in Angola and as riveting and wrenching as any writing about imprisonment I have ever read.[2]

As part of the material John submitted for my review, he included recent issues of *The Angolite,* in which I found lyrical, erudite pieces that many journals would publish. In one article, "Yesterday's Child," Corley provides an in-depth look at the issue of prosecuting juveniles in the adult system. In the article he urges us to remember that "when a 16-year-old takes a deadly turn, suddenly he's not a child but an adult who'll never see the prom because a jury of his peers—a misnomer since his peers aren't old enough to sit on the jury . . . are only too willing to echo the prosecutor's cry for 'justice.'"[3] He also reminds us that for a fifteen- or sixteen-year-old, a life sentence can be sixty or seventy years, something that is often difficult for a young mind to comprehend but is still deadly. John's writing illuminates the issues facing the prison system and prisoners. I therefore looked forward to meeting the man who was part of a program that fosters such excellence and dedication to the craft of writing and inquiry.

It took months for my phone calls and e-mails outlining my request to be answered, but my initial optimism was nourished by Burl Cain's approval. He granted permission to interview and photograph John Corley, with no restrictions on the content of our conversation. The warden's website proclaimed a devotion to rehabilitation and a firm belief in the perfectibility of the human spirit through hard work and redemption, and Warden Cain's philosophy articulated a mindset that completely contradicted the gothic model I had anticipated. It sounded too good to be true. And it was.

Relying on Cain's assurances, I bought a plane ticket and made hotel reservations. I contacted Lou Jones, and we coordinated our itineraries. Everything seemed set, but then I received an e-mail from Angie Norwood, executive management officer, public relations, informing me that the warden's permission to enter Angola had been revoked. The warden had asked me to make John Corley's submissions to *Exiled Voices* available; now he was playing the censorship card. I read the e-mail: "We do agree that in their pure form, the writings are of excellent quality; however, after further consideration, the decision was made to withdraw the approval previously granted to you for an interview [with] photos of John Corley." I was utterly disappointed. There was more. "We do not allow any inmate the potential for profiting from their crimes—either materially or through the enhanced status as a result of media coverage. Warden Cain feels the consequences of publishing these writings will not reflect positively on the prison or your project." The hopeful vision of Angola I had been encouraged to believe in became a caricature of the prison and its warden as avatars of the Old South.

In this ominous e-mail, which arrived the Friday before my planned Wednesday departure, I was informed that "Warden Cain would be happy to discuss the issues with you himself." When I contacted him the following Monday morning, I discovered a man comfortable talking about John Corley, the prison, and himself. He told me that he had reconsidered my request because he had read the pieces John submitted for publication in *Exiled Voices* and thought that John's writing was not sufficiently remorseful.

Burl Cain has a thick southern accent; Louisiana becomes *Loosana,* and John Corley, the man, is reduced to a boy, as is often the manner in the South. He told me, "I read John's story, and he writes well. It's a good story, but that boy's just not remorseful enough." He went on to say, "I've known the Corley family for a long time; I grew up in the parish next to them. They're good people, but I just don't know what happened to that boy." He took a breath, and I thought I might be able to say something, but he wasn't finished. He continued, "If I let ya'll come in here, the people of Louisiana will think I condone what that boy did, and I just can't let that happen." By permitting the interview, he thought the people of Louisiana would think that he, Burl Cain, was underwriting that lack of remorse—a personal criticism that he was not prepared to endure.

My response was to discuss the literary merits of the essay, pointing out that John Corley's submission certainly did reflect remorse for his crime. I invited the warden to become an active participant in casting Angola in a favorable light, emphasizing the positive influence *The Angolite* has on its staff and showcasing John as an example of the success of the warden's own emphasis on rehabilitation. I reminded him that I intended to publish the essay with or without the interview. He replied, "Oh, I know you will, but at least the people of Louisiana will know that I didn't condone you coming in here, and that is all that matters."

I asked the warden if he would be willing to speak with John about "Life in Four Parts." I asked if he would give John the opportunity to rework his memoir so that it more effectively showed the remorse that Burl Cain had admitted John feels, because, he told me, "I know John, and I know he feels great remorse for what he did, but this piece of writing just doesn't show it."

When our conversation ended that Monday morning, it was with Burl Cain's assurance that he would speak with John and call me Tuesday morning with his final answer. I was cautiously optimistic. But I quickly learned that having an award-winning author and journal in Louisiana State Penitentiary does not guarantee an enlightened approach to corrections. Tuesday came and went with no call. On Wednesday morning, two hours before my plane was scheduled to depart for Baton Rouge, I received a call from Angie Norwood, who told me that Burl Cain had refused my request for a final time.

Twenty years of dealing with prison authorities has taught me one thing above all: they are monarchs of all they survey. This point came crashing home on that May morning; meeting John Corley was out of my control. In moments such as these—and there have been quite a few over the years—I catch a glimpse of life in prison under the constant control of rigid authoritarians who impose their will as only feudal lords can do. However, I did not have to allow Burl Cain's attempt at censorship to reduce the artist that is John Corley to the level of anonymity.

John Corley has been living his life under the control of the State of Louisiana since 1989; a second-degree murder charge put him in the penitentiary. He is forty-five years old, and he will die in Angola if the state has its way. John and his family fight every day to find another solution. John's family has become very important to him during his incarceration; each year brings them closer, in spite of the distance between them. They correspond and talk on the phone (I am not permitted to telephone him), but because the family is so spread out, they visit only once or twice a year.

Given Burl Cain's intransigence, John and I were left with letters. In one of my first letters, I asked how he began writing. In his response, I was introduced to a man who works at the craft of writing out of love but discovered his gift for writing by chance. He offered a story from the past as explanation. He began, "I wrote my way out of an English assignment and a paddling from my high school princi-pal." I chuckled as I read the story. An English teacher had given an assignment to write about Chaucer's *Canterbury Tales*. John refused. He was sent to the principal's office, to see a man feared for his use of the paddle. John gave the principal all the usual reasons: it's boring, I'll never use it, it's a waste of my time and energy. The principal offered a deal. If John would write a paper describing why he shouldn't be punished for disrupting the class, the principal might consider letting him off the hook. He did just that. John wrote, "The paper worked—I didn't have to praise Chaucer and Mr. Salter didn't blister my behind. It was then I realized what a gift the power of the pen really was, and I had it."

In one letter he wrote about his status in Angola: "I am a

Class A trusty, and I have been a staff writer for *The Angolite* since 2005. I love writing; it's what I do best. It speaks to who I am." He wrote of a recent conversation with a college student during which he was asked which of his articles from *The Angolite* pleased him most. His response: "All of them." John pours all of himself into his writing; he has told me, "It is my craft and my joy." In that same letter, John wrote that writing "is what I want my future to be. It makes me feel I have worth." He writes because it is a part of him, because he longs "to produce something of literary merit that will outlive me."

In "Life in Four Parts," the reader accompanies John Corley on a journey through the life he once knew. We see him as a boy and a young adult, but through the eyes of the man; we wince at his pain, we hear his questioning mind, but we also feel the joy of childhood in the images he creates and the cadence of his language. We see and hear his regret. He writes, "I'm sorry for my many sins of the past, but the unfortunate thing about sorry is that its shadow falls only after the damage is done." His ability to examine his life-altering errors closely is startling; his words grab and force you to hold on to something solid when he speaks of the devastation left in the wake of his mistakes: "I was responsible; I effectuated the changes. I swept through a family and scattered it like the wind through parched leaves." As I read his eloquently crafted language, I contemplated what Burl Cain was thinking when he read these same words. How could he not see remorse? For John Corley writes that he is "bound, the ghosts of my sins forever pecking at my liver."

John told me that he has a file drawer filled with "a very bad first novel, two how-to manuals on public speaking, two short story collections, some four hundred poems, and short plays." He wrote that he "[sculpts] until at last [he] is satisfied it says what [he] wants it to say, eloquently, descriptively, and concisely."

His poetry is strong and vibrant, each word chosen for its impact, as in "Prison Rodeo: Guts and Glory," where he describes the age-old Angola tradition of the prison rodeo: "He stood panting/ sweat-soaked/. . . watched the beast/watching him." He writes about the rodeo because, as John told me in one of his letters, it has become "a focal point for the inmates and one of the largest moneymaking events in the region."

John earned an associate's degree in paralegal studies in 1995 from the Paralegal Institute in Phoenix, Arizona. From 1997 until 2005 he worked as an inmate lawyer, helping prisoners with litigation. He has also been active in the Forgotten Voices Toastmasters Club. He told me, "It was a great experience, and I met with amazing success, becoming vice president–public relations and editor of the internationally recognized, award-winning *Forgotten Voice/Articulator* club newsletter, 1998–1999 and 1999–2000." He has published articles in *The Toastmaster,* a monthly international magazine, competed in the Division Humorous Competition in 1999, and in November 2003 received the highest honor, Distinguished Toastmaster, one of only four Toastmasters in the world to receive that award while incarcerated.

"How has the prison changed during your incarceration?" I asked in one letter. John replied that Angola has calmed down since he arrived in 1990. He said, "Violence has decreased to the point that outbursts are viewed as shocking by the population." He told me that the present administration, which arrived in 1995, promotes a Christian environment, has hired more officers, and has brought in more vocational and educational programs, "but at the end of the day, it is still prison."

Many men and women incarcerated in this country live each day with the knowledge of what has brought them to these places of high walls, razor ribbon, and locked barred doors, of events they cannot change. John wrote, "There are things I would do differently if I could, and there are wrongs I might yet have a chance to right. There are things I cannot change, and these will haunt me all my days."

This is John Corley's existence; he is one of our many exiled voices.
                                                        —SUSAN NAGELSEN

Life in Four Parts

A Memoir

JOHN CORLEY

I

I sometimes dream of the old house. There the lilies along the fence bloom yellow and purple, the willow shivers at the slightest stir, the whitewashed cement birdbath sprouting Mama's miniature desert cacti dares me to climb up and have a look. I can smell the musty, rusty floor furnace that brands any foot brazen or careless enough to tempt its grating. I can hear the screen door slap its frame with startling suddenness.

I built matchbox cities in a long-dead flower bed under the blue room window, with outskirts invading the damp, dark, spidery nether region under the house. From this hidden metropolis, powerful in my invisibility, I watched the oblivious adults stroll by.

A young pin oak grew between the fence and sleepy Emery Street; from my perch in its branches I could see all the way down the hill to Hearne Avenue two blocks away, a prepubescent voyeur above the world, regarding everything and nothing at all. When you're a kid, it doesn't matter what you see; the mere sight of it feeds the hunger.

We had pear, peach, plum, apple, and pecan trees; fragrant camellia in the front, honeysuckle in the back, thick, deep, crisp St. Augustine green all the way around. In the spring, when everything bloomed and the grass was freshly mown, there was no finer scent to register in the catalogue of a boy's recollections.

After I was grown and my cycle of self-destruction began, I sometimes visited the old house when I needed nostalgia's soothing clarity. I shuffled through its rotting apartments and moldy halls with a beer in my hand and a pain in my heart. Each time I went, it all seemed smaller.

One day the house was gone. I walked over its cracked gray slab and felt a strange but strangely appropriate closure—rest in peace—to this most remote chapter of my life. After I left that day, I never went back.

At fourteen I moved to the farm. It was harder, quieter, with its own gods and devils. Toro Church was a step into the past, an isolated place in the woods a mile down the clay-gravel road from my grandparents' house. While I was still a city boy, Muriel and Otto let me drive them to church and back. I soon lived for Sunday. By fourteen I was an old hand.

With a marriage in shambles and whiskey for brains, I often drove to the church and sat out in the sandy lot across from the cemetery, drifting in the lazy streams of what could have been, surrounded by the pines. I'd hunted Easter eggs in my holiday finery there. I'd picked up wonderful arrowheads from yesterday's ambitions. I'd eaten dinner on the ground with the congregation and finger-painted "Men" and "Women" on the outhouse doors at Otto's request. I'd carried his casket across the road to its final destination, and many times I'd sat on his stone and begged him to tell me what the hell was wrong with my life. The church was my playground in innocent times, my sanctuary in troubled ones.

I don't dream of Toro Church as I do of the old house. I don't know why. There is a place in my heart where the farm lives as it was, before they cut the trees, before death and neglect transformed the sparkle into a charcoal memory. I close my eyes and traipse through the ash and ironwood along the creek bank, shoot water moccasins at the pond with Otto's antique .22, lose myself in the living room fire's marvelous, intoxicating warmth and smell.

They were innocent days. Responsibility was a big word for someone else to interpret, and I ran like the wind through stump-dotted pastures and beside the dusty road until the sun set behind the garden and crickets cranked up their orchestras and all country boys came in to bathe. Simple days, make-believe cities in the trees, air force jets from Alexandria screaming overhead and scaring the blue blazing hell out of a kid caught in the wide-open field. A cowhide rocker on the porch, an old man throwing up a leathery hand as he putters past in a decrepit pickup, summers hotter than hell's proudest pits, and creek water colder than a Montana snowman—these are my memories far from prison, the places I go when I need to, and I cherish them, the innocence and the pain, and will take them with me into that good night.

II

I got a letter from Mom one day. She asked, "So what's on your mind?" It was a blue day. What's *supposed* to be on my mind in this shithole?

A provocative inquiry. Simple, common, most often answered without contemplation of truth or detail, then forgotten. I wonder why sometimes it's so difficult. Why sometimes I'll spend entire days with the question raging through my scorched intellect, ranting, roaring, demanding attention and reaction. Very good question. Very good timing.

That's all it's about, isn't it? Timing? Maybe I wait for someone to ask because deep down I know it's time to admit the unthinkable, to shout the unutterable, or at least to consider the possibility. Maybe I need prompting to address what I long refused to entertain. Ah, the possibilities. So many, and none worth a fraction of the cells required to conjure them.

What's on your mind these days? She was expecting something profound? Casually tossing a question that struck a nerve in my nerveless consciousness?

Let me recall the statement preceding the question, a comment bearing extraordinary implications. Mom referred to me as "my son, the lawyer." I was not and am not. In my minuscule capacity as a jailhouse paralegal, I'm a cheat and a fraud. I despise the law, the procedural garbage of it and the insubstantial substance of it. You want to know the truth? I took the job so I could gain access to materials helpful to *me*, to work on *my* case, to look out for *myself*, and to hell with everyone else. But I was already battle-weary when I got here. Three trials with all the trappings had wrung me out like a rag.

Don't get me wrong—I'll help if I can. I refuse to give them my soul; I've always given my soul, believe it or not. Always my all for the job, for the cause, for the venerable institution I imagined my various efforts represented. Always the soul. Not anymore.

It's the blues, baby. When I get the blues, I get 'em in black.

When I worked for Legal Programs, I didn't care about other men's little battles. About their petty gripes and their grand schemes to sue the system and collect tons for injuries real or perceived. I didn't care if they didn't like the food or the sergeant slapped them sideways or whether they sued or not. I didn't care if the cancer floated like fog on the air, as most of us suspected. I was pragmatic; I couldn't change it, so I didn't waste time worrying about it.

When they opened their mouths, I shoved a form in them. Grievance form, post-conviction form, habeas form, clothing form, visiting form, fuck-you-in-your-ass form.

I had an associate's degree I earned through the mail, but I was a fraud. Men stopped me on the walk to ask my opinion or my interpretation or my advice, and I filled their ears with doublespeak just to get them out of my face, because I didn't care about their problems. "I'm in Forms," I'd say. "Check with Criminal Litigation." I had a life sentence. I didn't give a damn if their religion forbade the DOC's haircuts. Don't tell me anything about religion. Religion is no better than the law.

Sweet Mother, how I wish you could call me a lawyer and be proud, and I could hug you and dump loads of money on you and life would be eternally Rio in July! How I wish you could brag to your friends about me like other mothers brag! Oh, for a normal life—what would I give, I, whose entire existence has defied normalcy by fate or design? What would I give? Be real. What have I to give? Not much there to tip the scales, I promise you.

What's on your mind these days? War. The war I fight with myself as I age and become increasingly aware that my days are fleeting and I'm zooming toward complete ineffectiveness. Two decades later I'm the last one, the last holdout, the last irrationalist ballsy enough to insist I'll win this thing yet and walk out free and unscathed. But on the flip side I'm forced to admit things I've long considered inconceivable.

All around, the shells burst and men fall to the ground screaming, and blood runs over my state-issue shoes, and the smoke and stench of my life hang heavy, blinding, choking, stifling me. War. The war in heaven and on earth, Armageddon, and it's all being fought inside with an enemy unseen but very much alive: myself. This is what it's like to admit truths long known, long feared. Truth is wicked and painful. Maybe that's why we so frequently oppose it.

What was on my mind in those days was the possibility, no longer undeniable, that I'd never walk out of Angola. The reality loomed like a barricade against the sun. I woke with spite in my heart day after day, but there was something else. For the first time, I felt hope slipping away. I looked around at those whose lives in prison were measured in decades; I monitored societal trends that demanded retribution; I examined my own circumstances and felt hope sliding through arthritic fingers. It had been too long. The system, I feared, might beat me, might outlast me. It was an unnatural admission. I was aging, changing; there was war inside me.

I'd never been so close to admitting that I might actually live out my days here in this place I despise so much. It was happening. While the courts tossed my life back and forth in ultra-slow motion, my father was approaching seventy. My grandmother didn't remember me, where I was or how I came to be here. My mother had long since moved out west and taken a sister I hardly knew with her. My brother had fled north. Nothing of the outside world remained as I remembered. I was responsible; I effectuated the changes. I swept through a family and scattered it like the wind through parched leaves. Like a god. Prometheus, maybe. Bound, the ghosts of my sins forever pecking at my liver.

Nostalgia wields a heavy hammer for those who have longed for a purer life. I missed the trees I hid in as a child. I missed the creek, its fishy smell, its sluggish summer trickle, and its muddy winter fury when it swelled and swallowed the land. I missed the country folk I never slowed to notice. I missed what could have been. I felt sad.

I dreamed of the old house in Shreveport, of Grandma's in Plainview, of South Louisiana ports I worked from, and of the emerald Gulf peering back at Texas. Present was a pervading cognizance, an irrepressible undercurrent that cast a pall over every imagining, my anguish extending even to my depths: I was a prisoner, and I might die one.

Aristotle said that anything whose presence or absence makes no discernible difference is no essential part of the whole. He was talking about me, about all those whom society prefers to forget. I am no longer an essential part of the whole.

I once read a story in which four strangers sought refuge from a storm in a small cabin at the foot of a mountain. As the night wore on, each in turn revealed to the others his greatest fear. One was afraid he might die and no one would know, nor remember that he ever had lived. I remember thinking how horrible this man's fear was, and later recognizing how blatantly the materialization of that same fear withers the spirits of the damned in Angola.

I tried to identify my family's perception of me and saw myself fading. I saw the world outside changed and passing me by, the departure of friends, the disappearance of loved ones, the onset of a new age of despair. I saw a son whose single Father's Day card I keep in a Bible I never read. Life is grim, colorless, and cold in prison.

This is my reflection. I'm not a pessimist. I'm a realist. I'm analytical. I look at every angle before rendering judgment. In my second decade of incarceration, the angles were bloody sharp. What else could possibly be on my mind?

When you think about it, we're all prisoners in one way or another, but few of us can empathize with the banished. If we select our most appalling condition and imagine ourselves trapped hopelessly there for indeterminate years upon years, perhaps we can momentarily glimpse that hapless reality so many endure daily.

If you find yourself prisoner to dependents who consume your time and absorb your sacrifices and scream and demand more and again—if this is your prison—magnify it, extend it, visualize its perpetuity, hear the screams that never cease; imagine your bones that never rest though weary enough for the tomb. It is madness, is it not?

Madness, the hallmark of our ostracism. If you are a battered woman, imagine its never ending. If you are poor, if you are cheated, if you are a sufferer of any personal cataclysm, envision being enveloped by it, sealed in its festering womb, forgotten, damned. Then, my friend, you'll catch an inkling of what it means to be locked away in a prison, and you'll know exactly what's on my mind.

III

Roy always had something to say about the status quo and how he would rain down fire and brimstone on it someday. If I'd let him, he'd keep me standing in front of his cell for hours while he rambled on about the grand conspiracy and the illegality of the Louisiana penal system. He was serious, but we laughed a lot, Roy and I.

He lived on Isolation Block because he stabbed the life out of another inmate thirteen years ago over snide remarks and warnings unheeded. After that, men were careful not to offend Roy.

He was big in the porn rag network, buy, sell, trade, and when the DOC outlawed nudity in publications and ordered all porn holders to surrender their stock or suffer disciplinary action, Roy didn't take it lightly.

"I wanchu t' brang me ever'thang you gots on de Fust

Amenment in prison," he spat. "Dem muthafuckas think dey goan jes mess over me an' I's goan sit here an' take it, dey can think again!"

I told him he was fighting a losing battle. The courts had already decided the DOC could take the porn.

"Brang me a damn foam!" I took him a form. But he didn't have time to sue.

One day I found Roy sitting on the edge of his bunk. He lifted his shirt and showed me a golf ball under his arm. "Dey think it cancer." He shrugged it off, but there was cold, relentless fear behind his eyes, the kind we all hope never to encounter. Two weeks later Roy was officially diagnosed. The Big C. Terminal.

Before the week was out he was in the infirmary. I saw him a couple of times after that. The first, soon after he was admitted, was shocking. They had him locked in a dark room reserved for troublemakers because, they said, he was still assigned to administrative segregation. He'd dropped weight dramatically. He was wearing a morphine patch for the pain, and he wanted some books from his cell on Isolation Block. Drugs and disease disoriented him. He battled to form coherent sentences. I held his hand through the tray hatch and promised I'd get his books.

I took them with me the next week. Roy was a sack of bones under a flapping gown. Through the haze and gibberish, he pleaded, "Please, bro, jes git my mama. Thazall I want, jes git my mama." When the shit hits the fan, we all want our mamas, don't we?

I talked to the nurses, who didn't want to tell me anything but told me Roy could go any day, and I told them he wanted to see his mother. They said they'd try.

I cried on the way back to the office. Big strong prisoner, big inmate paralegal, weightlifter, shit kicker, cried big tears; that last day with Roy was my saddest in Angola. There he was, full of laughter and defiance, reduced now to a babbling husk whose only wish in the world was to see his mother one more time. I cried for him. I came in and told the office coordinator to go talk to someone about getting that man's mother down to see him. I don't know who was ultimately responsible, but she came and Roy spent time with his family, and a few days later he went away.

In the seven years prior to Roy's death, 196 prisoners died in Angola, an average of about 30 per year. Five were killed by the state, two were killed by other inmates, four killed themselves. The 185 others, average age slightly over fifty, died of a variety of ailments and diseases. Seven were thirty or younger; the youngest was nineteen. Nineteen were over seventy, the oldest eighty-three.

They died from the recklessness and deprivation of their pasts, the drugs and booze, the poverty leading to undiagnosed health conditions. They died because years of continuous incarceration sucked the very life from them, slowly, a day at a time, a torment worse than any inquisitorial persecution. They died in dark rooms behind locked doors calling for their mamas.

I don't want to be reduced like Roy. I don't want to be incoherent, or shit on myself, or be unable to function. I don't want not to recognize the faces of those I've loved. Debilitation is not for me. I'm too damned proud and too scared. I want to go quickly, knowing who I am and knowing I love those I love, and knowing I gave it a run for its money while I was here. Most of all, I want to die free.

IV

Back in the day when the work was hard and steady, the creek was the cure for all ills. It was good then, the icy creek, after a day spent hauling hay in the zillion-degree heat, straw stuck everywhere straw can stick to a body, sweat streaming. The whole crew made a beeline when the last bale was packed into the barn, pausing only to grab a bar of soap on our way.

We called it the Jackson swimming hole, so named, I was told, for my great-great-grandfather, who lived down that way ages ago. It was a pine-canopied bend in Toro Creek below my grandparents' house. The water was dark and cold.

On one high bank my older cousins set up a jumping board from a warped two-by-ten, which I never mustered courage enough to venture out upon. It disappeared the year I graduated from high school, the unmourned victim of an annual deluge.

To actually get into the water, you could leap from the high bank beside the board and risk spearing the creek bottom, or you could butt-slalom down a slick clay washout. I chose the washout.

No matter how hot the day, how hard the work, how many miles of fencerow, how many tons of straw that clung to my toothpick frame, the mere thought of submersion in the Jackson swimming hole was sufficient to dry the sweat and lower the temperature. Walking down the sandy pipeline, barefoot, sun beaming, anticipating that icy black water taking my breath, the dizzying rush—by the time I got there I wore goose bumps. But the anticipation of exhilaration, the very state of breathlessness for that long initial moment after sliding out onto the submerged ledge and then leaping into the frigid current, was an irresistible summons. Sweat-drenched or bone-dry, I went down to my underwear, navigated the washout, and cannonballed. Snakes and all other creatures beware, whole lotta splashin' goin' on.

And the silence of the woods was shattered by the exaggerated gasps, howls, and water-beating, the laughter and whoops of youth, and those were good times in spite of what would come.

Sometimes on Sunday afternoon Aunt Melba Rose would load us kids into Otto's '61 army-green Chevy and drive us to the Hardin swimming hole, the big kids' pool, off the Plainview blacktop. The muddy, cavity-pocked trail soon grew impassible, so we'd park and walk the rest of the way through the reeds, weeds, and woods, slender Melba Rose leading her line of ducklings eager for the pond.

Hardin was like an asteroid crater. It lay in a clearing ringed by pines, beside a cow pasture. On the east bank was a diving board, on the west a rope swing. Swimming from bank to bank was a challenge, and yes, when I was younger, the thought of running out of steam and drowning halfway across lurked in my mind every time I dared.

From time to time word circulated that one of Old Man Smith's alligators had escaped and was spotted sunning next to Hardin. Such rumors only fueled the need to swim there.

The rope was tied around a white oak's sturdy arm, and there was a runway through the woods where you could get a good sprint and grab the rope and hurl yourself out over the middle of the brown pool. It was the supreme rush. When you let go, you dropped like a meteor and *splash!* into the deep, dark cool. I never touched the bottom of Hardin swimming hole. I tried. Pushed myself so deep I got scared some creature would latch on to my foot and drag me into the abyss. Funny, the things we fear when we're young.

When I was in the world, I sometimes struck out alone to my woods and pastures and secret trails and the shadowy, gurgling creek beside which I've passed untold hours in private contemplation. Quiet time for the restless mind.

There was an old logging road between my grandparents' house and Toro Church. Otto took me there when I was a snip. It snaked into the woods, up and down hillocks and through trickly streams, darker as the pines grew denser. And then there was treasure:

petrified wood, a forest of it, sherds and bricks atop the straw and winking from the black soil. No one came here except Otto and me. And later, only me.

I miss that old road. I wonder what's become of it since I've been gone. There's a good chance I may never find out. That, and everything else I knew from yesterday, is merely a pamphlet I parse when I need to get away. The faces and places and songs and whispers—ghosts from a long-ago dream.

It could have been a better life, and I suppose it could have been worse. I'm sorry for my many sins of the past, but the unfortunate thing about sorry is that its shadow falls only after the damage is done. There are things I would do differently if I could, and there are wrongs I might yet have a chance to right. There are things I cannot change, and these will haunt me all my days.

I regret I didn't become a soldier; I would have made a fine one. I regret I failed to cultivate significant friendships throughout my life; we are enriched, or destroyed, by the company we keep. I regret I've lived without producing a work of note; every human being should strive to leave an artful testament to his existence, if only he alone derives satisfaction from the thing he has created. I regret I did not show love as I have felt it.

I've been a prisoner of the State of Louisiana now for nearly twenty years. Before that, I was a prisoner of my insecurities, a prisoner of love, a prisoner of the bottle, a prisoner of life. I suppose we're all prisoners of one thing or another, always seeking the unattainable, the *mobilis in mobile*—the freedom in a free world so elusive because it simply does not exist.

Maybe I should say more in defense of myself; maybe I should recognize more people who have influenced my life. Maybe I've said too much already. I've always been too analytical for my own good. The possibilities are endless. I think I'll just hang on to my memories, savor them, learn from them, and let it go at that.

Poems

JOHN CORLEY

The Changing

Summer came silently, suddenly, from an innocent night; unaware a
coup was stirring, springtime slept, in a hateful heated wave the green
season fell, supple leaves, sap-plump shoots caught guiltless lazing in a
bath of cool morning dew, honeysuckle perfume, gasped to a futile
defensive.

Fourteen, that magical age, barefoot again, digging slender
toes into moist dead sand death-scented beside the creek now
risen to its annual prominent pinnacle, seasonal savior,
haven to diamondbacks, possum, coon, deer, infinite
insects, cattle, and fantasies. Late import from the soulless
seasonless city, the surrealism of summer's naked blinding
glory thrilled me, filled me with fantastic strength and
sight: I didn't weep for spring, didn't care, didn't notice its
ignoble passing, the magnitudinous meaning of the
changing—content in reborn imagination, I played and
pretended.

Sleep, Jesse

They found her
in a double trash bag casket
knotted at the head and feet
covered with leaves
less than two football fields
from her bed,

the bed where she slept when the devil
came calling from the Homosassee
night, through the window, while her
parents dreamed.

It was poor,
this Florida home, but
it held love—
her rail-thin daddy with his
missing teeth and worker's cap
cried in the cameras three
weeks
when he wasn't searching,
woods walking,
calling, "Jesse! Jesse!"
hoping.

We all saw her smile on TV and
we loved her too and
we hoped too
although these things rarely
end well—
and the days passed.

He'd done it before,
preyed on innocence, the
defenseless ones,
got a little slap, did a little
time—
a little time
too little time
this time he took more.

This time he had her, bound, and
buried her alive, kneeling,
clutching
a stuffed purple dolphin—
and this is how she died.
She was only nine.

They found her twenty-three days later in a
double trash bag casket knotted at the
head and feet covered with leaves a glance
from her own bed.

Sleep soft my sweet sleep
sound at peace
until your soul returns;
most of us didn't know you but
we felt your touch, the
gift that woke us up
and somehow made us better
for caring
made us rally against the devils
made us aware too late
for you but
because of you in time to save
others.

Prison Rodeo: Guts & Glory

He stood panting,
sweat-soaked,
filthy in the heat of
an April sun,
and watched the beast
watch him,
focus on him,
snarl, drool
hate on him,
the antagonist
under twenty thousand eyes,
cacophonic roar
for either to outwit the other—
gladiators, man
& beast, prisoners each,
and neither
walking away with
a damned thing.

Charles Huckelbury

There is a touch of the southerner in Charles Huckelbury, "Huck" to me. You can hear it on the fringes of certain words or in certain intonations, and especially when he is telling a story from his years spent in Florida's East Unit or the Rock. When we sat down for our most recent conversation on a cold January afternoon at the New Hampshire State Prison for Men, it was in essence a continuation of a conversation that began fourteen years ago in a classroom.

I first met Huck when he joined a creative writing class I was teaching for a New England College program offered at the prison. I had heard other faculty from the college talk about him; after all, it isn't every day you have a student, any student, who wants to take statistics *again,* but Mr. Huckelbury was such a student.

At age sixty, Huck is now the old man on the pod; there are kids in his unit who weren't even a thought when he first went to prison. Serving a twenty-five-to-life sentence for first-degree murder, Huck is now in his thirty-third year of incarceration. When people hear that for the first time, their gasp is audible, and their eyes grow wide as I hear them say, "Oh my God, you have got to be kidding! How can anyone survive that?" Huck has done more than survive; he has earned two bachelor's degrees, one in English and one in human services. In fact, a faculty member at New England College once remarked that Huck had 320 college credits, far more than the faculty member, to which Huck replied, "Yes, but they are all at the under-graduate level."

Huck and I have worked together on many writing projects throughout these past fourteen years. We are both associate editors of the *Journal of Prisoners on Prison,* and together we edited and wrote for an issue on aging (vol. 14, no. 2).

Huck loves learning. "I am fortunate," he said. "I have had the opportunity to study and learn, and for a while, when I first got to New Hampshire, school was a full-time job for me." In 1991 the Pell Grants for prisoners ceased to exist. Postsecondary education pro-grams were killed, and most prisoners were no longer able to afford to go to college. But Huck sat on both sides of the desk. "I was fortunate enough to be able to teach in the New Hampshire Technical College program for a while, but that was killed too."

One of the main problems facing many prisons today is a lack of programs and productivity, and Huck confirmed that that is clearly the situation in New Hampshire. "All we have left is what passes for a high school. We used to have four different postsecondary programs out here. When I was teaching, I had students in my class who were reading on the sixth-grade level; this is the result of poor education on the street and in prison."

I asked Huck if he liked teaching. His voice softened, and there was a catch in his throat. "I loved it. I loved the give-and-take of it. I discovered that teaching is a learning process, and I discovered that the more frequently I taught, the more I learned. I got these marvelous texts, with wonderful writers. Overall, it was great for me. I loved it." When Huck spoke of teaching, a sense of wonder filled his face, and in those moments, there sitting before me was a scholar whose love of the written word, love of sharing information, was no different from that of my colleagues on campus. He was not just another number; he was not one of the voiceless or the warehoused; he was a teacher of minds, someone who has a wealth of knowledge to share and an enthusiasm that knows no bounds.

A writer in prison must constantly struggle against censorship, and Huck's experience has been no different. Every piece of mail that leaves the prison is marked with a stamp that indicates that the mail has been sent from a state prison and that its contents have not been evaluated. "The world out there is often intimidated by the stamp on the envelope," Huck said, "so it isn't really surprising when submissions are returned unopened with a red stamp on it saying *refused*. You get used to it. But you have to keep on writing. After all, rejection is a part of the game, isn't it? I was a contributing writer for a local newspaper for a while. The editor always identified me as serving a life sentence for murder, and as long as my pieces dealt with the prison environment he would run them, but when I tried to expand the scope of my columns, the same editor refused to print them. I was and would always be a prison writer."

Huck is now involved in a program called Pathways to Hope. This program brings dogs into the prison to begin training to work with disabled individuals. The men teach the dogs the basic commands, so they are prepared for further extensive training. Huck has a black Lab named Joey, who has taken up residence in the cell. "It's a little snug," Huck said. "But Joey's crate door is always open, so he can come and go as he pleases." Huck works with Joey every day on basic commands such as "Sit," "Stay," and "Down," but Joey can also fetch pill bottles on command and turn the lights on and off.

Joey is the star of the prison; everywhere Huck goes, people ask him about Joey. "Joey has brought a dynamic to both this environment and to me that I had long ago given up on. When he's sleepy, when he's just getting up, he's a hoot. Having something that sweet, it's just nice. I know he can reason," Huck said, chuckling. "I don't care what animal behaviorists say. It is almost like being a parent—it is such a responsibility, and it is so nice." A lightness came over Huck when he spoke of Joey. In those brief moments, I watched him shed the prison; his blue eyes danced with the tears of joy and pride that only a parent can know.

Connections are so important in prison—connections to family, to community, to the world from which these men and women are removed. Cutting people off from what can help them most, a world with opportunity and community support, is counterintuitive. Huck said, "All of us are damaged to some extent. The trick is to minimize that kind of damage. You do that by learning that an egotistical worldview doesn't cut it. Education, writing, family—all these connections make a huge difference."

Our conversation moved to "Riding the Tiger," a piece that is set in the late 1970s and brings the reader face to face with the harsh realities of what can happen when people are locked in cages twenty-four hours a day for weeks or months on end. Back then, Huck said, "there was a grudging mutual respect between prisoners and guards that we were all in a pretty nasty place. The guards had a thankless job, and we were in a spot where we didn't want to be either. There was the recognition that being in prison was punishment in and of itself. The staff and the personnel didn't go out of their way to make your life miserable."

Huck told a story about a time when he was trying to get to the law library to work on his appeal. He kept getting refusals. Finally he started holding on to his cell feed, the tray that is brought to the cell for each meal. It is passed through a slot in the door and passed back after each meal. Huck said that he must have had three days' worth of trays when the lieutenant came to see him.

"Huckelbury, what do you want?"

Huck told him he wanted to go to the law library.

The lieutenant said, "You know we could come in and take those trays if we wanted to?"

"I know" was his reply.

The lieutenant asked him if he would stop the nonsense if he got him a pass to the law library.

"Sure" was Huck's response.

The lieutenant said, "I'll get you the pass if you give me your word on the trays."

A deal was struck.

But now, according to Huck, things are different. "It could get physical, but now it is more psychological punishment. Being off the street doesn't seem to be enough. Now the staff seem to have taken it upon themselves to make it difficult for the men and women doing time." This has been particularly true with regard to visits. He told me that visits used to be used as an incentive for guys to go to school. If you went to school, you got an extra visit. But they decided that guys were "going to school for the wrong reason," and they took the extra visits away. To Huck, that just doesn't make sense. "School should be something they encourage. Education should be the main goal, because so many of these guys don't have the skills necessary to change their lives." But that is not the way things go in prison. "Once they take something away, you never get it back," Huck said. "Things in prison only get worse; they never get better." —SUSAN NAGELSEN

Riding the Tiger

CHARLES HUCKELBURY

"**H**ey, Stone, you think they're really gonna gas us?"

The high-pitched voice that came drifting over from next door belonged to Andy Reeves, aka Eighty-nine. Without looking, I knew where he was standing: at the bars at the front of his cell, arms dangling, face pressed close to the two-inch space where the wall that separated our two cells ended and the bars began. It had been the kid's favorite perch for the thirteen months he had been on the wing. I rested my book on my chest and looked toward the front of the cell, where a mixture of plastic trays, moldering food, dirty clothes, and black ash floated on an inch of stagnant water.

"Oh yeah, they'll gas us," I promised him. "You heard that lieutenant?"

"The one looked real mad?"

"That's the one. He ain't nothin' nice, and if he said he's gonna gas us, then it's coming."

Forty minutes earlier, Lieutenant Frank Lane had given all of us on Tier 2 North on P Wing an ultimatum to give up our food strike and eat dinner or else, the "else" being pepper gas.

Then he had ordered fried chicken for us as the ultimate temptation. He had certainly put the fear of God into Tiny Head, the runaround in cell one responsible for feeding us and cleaning the tier. Built like a bowling ball with legs and with a head the size of a golf ball, dimples and all, he bowed and scraped his way from cell to cell, sliding trays of fried chicken and mashed potatoes into the bean slot in each door. The food was even hot, and smelled so good that my mouth began to water. Funny how just a day without food can trigger certain responses. Rather than test my willpower, I shoved the tray back out,

---

dumping the load on the dirty concrete in front of my cell to mix with the other trash, which had started to stink.

The strike had started the previous day at lunch, when five guys found grubs in their macaroni salad. When you're locked in a cell twenty-four-seven except for a five-minute shower three times a week, it doesn't take much to crank things up just to relieve the boredom. Billy Royce in four was the first to toss his tray. That got the rest of us cheering and sounding like one of those soccer games in England, where the fans go nuts over the stupidest things, until the whole tier erupted. What started out as a protest quickly grew into a party, with food, trays, and anything not bolted down being tossed through the bars. Tiny Head, a veteran who knew the drill, went back into his cell, pulled his door shut, and waited for the response. First the wing officer tried to talk to us, but food and other material, some unidentifiable, some distinctly organic, flew through the air, driving him back through the barred gate at the end of the tier. Next came the wing sergeant, who had no better luck but ordered the hapless Tiny Head to clean up the mess.

At the evening meal, at four o'clock, all twenty guys dumped their trays outside, along with the red Kool-Aid that also functioned as either jelly or Jell-O, depending on the amount of water added to the powder. Nobody really led the thing; it was just an agreement that grew out of finding company in our joint misery on P Wing. Sure, we were yelling our heads off, and Taylor in fourteen and I started a contest to see who could throw our trays the farthest down the tier, but overall it was a group effort. Breakfast and lunch the following day brought more of the same, but boredom quickly set in once the initial novelty wore off. As a result, we started looking for more things to add to the detritus, so our state clothing soon increased the pile of garbage.

Next came newspapers, magazines, and pieces of mattress, all set on fire by arcing a wire from the single light fixture in each cell through the graphite of a number two pencil and touching the tip to the cell bars. The fires set off the sprinklers, which prompted the entire wing on the north side to flood out by jamming the cell toilets with clothing and continuing to flush them until an inch of water covered every bit of floor space. A few of the guys even fashioned paper boats and held the first annual Raiford Regatta. That's when Lieutenant Lane made his appearance, a little after three, when he should have been getting ready to go off shift.

Six-two and a tight two-twenty, Lane was so black he glowed, especially in the starched white shirt he wore. He ordered the wing officer to open the gate at the end of the tier and walked through the debris with no more concern than if he had been out for a neighborhood stroll, disregarding the damage to his spit shine, nodding his head at the clutter, and ignoring the acrid smell that still lingered. He stopped in front of each cell and asked the same question: "Are you refusing to eat?" He got the same answer each time.

When he got to the end of the tier, he turned around and walked halfway back before stopping in front of cell ten. "All right, listen up, 'cause I'll only say this once. I understand why you're pissed. If I'd found goddamn worms in my chow, I'd be pissed, too, but this bullshit"—he swept his arm over the area—"has got to stop. Now here's what I'm gonna do. I've talked to the kitchen, and they're gonna serve you a hot meal at four. Ain't no macaroni salad or green baloney; it's fried chicken and real mashed potatoes, not instant, and population ain't gettin' none of it. It's just for you, and it's the best I can do, men, but you gotta give this shit up."

He paused and looked up and down the tier. "The other side of that is what happens if you don't eat and throw the food on the tier again." He paused for effect. "And that's pepper gas and maybe cell extractions. Now I know some of you tough guys think because you're on close management status on P Wing that you got a gangster reputation to protect, and I know that ain't none of you was angels to get to this prison and this particular wing. Maybe some of you never had a whiff of pepper and don't know what it feels like." He shook his head slowly. "It ain't no party."

He paced until he was in front of my cell. He stood there with his hands clasped behind his back, rocking back and forth on his heels and toes. Frank and I had something of a history, and I think there was a grudging mutual respect at work, even though neither of us would admit it in public. I held his gaze until he motioned upstairs and moved down the wing. "What about your homies on the third tier? Ain't none of them goin' off like this. Same thing for downstairs, where most of the water ran off. You men are all alone in this, and that's why it ain't gonna get you nothin' but trouble if you don't give it up." He paced two more steps toward the gate. "So listen hard. I don't care about none of what's happened so far. We'll clean up and start all over again. But I swear on my kids that if you men keep this up on my wing, I'll gas every goddamn one of you personally." He looked up and down the tier again.

"Think about it," he said. "It's the chicken or the gas. Don't seem like a hard choice to me." He walked to the end of the wing and out through the open door, which slammed behind him.

At four o'clock precisely the food arrived, and Tiny Head served each cell with a smile, picking his way gingerly over the mess still to be cleaned up and sure that he wouldn't have to clean the tier but once more. He spoke to every one of us, urging a stop to the madness. "Smell this stuff, will you? Man, I haven't seen fried chicken in years. You believe this? Them potatoes so hot they steam."

My tray was the first on the floor, followed quickly by the one for the kid next door, in cell eight. I heard Tiny Head groan "Oh, shit." I stood at the front of my cell with my spook in my hand to see what the rest of the row did. Most cons stash a thumbnail-sized piece of mirror in our property just in case we get maxed. Once locked down, we use a dab of toothpaste to glue it to the end of a toothbrush that we can ease through the bars to see in either direction to keep the guards from creeping up on us. With this little piece of equipment, I could see up and down the tier.

I was looking down toward the grill gate at the guard's station when I caught a small glimpse of my face. Since I hadn't seen a reflection of myself in over three years and had never paid a lot of attention to it even when I could, the view gave me a little jolt: my eyes looked grayer, and so did my hair. My forehead had grown, but my teeth were still good. I guessed my weight at around one-eighty, and I could pass for Casper the Ghost, I was so pale. For a guy on the north side of forty in the state's worst prison, I thought, I was holding my own.

I watched the chicken dinners parked in the doors' slots, satisfied when they landed back outside each cell. With two exceptions, where they disappeared inside: number eleven, three down on the other side of the kid, and number five, two down on my right.

I yelled down the tier so everyone could hear. "Mullins and Geehan, you spineless motherfuckers, throw your trays out."

Mullins, a serial rapist with charges still pending in three other states, spoke around a mouthful from cell eleven. "Fuck you, Stone. You ain't runnin' nothin', and I'm goddamn hungry. I'm eatin' this chicken and don't care who don't like it. I ain't swallowin' no gas for you or nobody else."

Most of the other guys started hooting and hollering, but Mullins didn't say anything else. Geehan, the child molester in five, stayed silent, so I tried to get his attention. "Geehan, you baby fucker, stand up for once or you're gonna need another cell change when this is done."

That got the other guys going again, but Geehan stayed mum. I thought the fat bastard was probably too busy stuffing his face to talk. I still grinned, pleased that most of the guys had held up. I started to sit back down but the kid next door piped up.

"Hey, you two. This is Eighty-nine talkin'. We're all supposed to be doin' this together. That's the way it started out, and that's the way it oughta finish." He paused for a few seconds. "That's all I gotta say about it." And that's the way we left it until he asked me about the gas.

I put down my book and sat up. I leaned over to the combination toilet and sink bolted to the wall at the rear of the cell and pushed the button for water. A trickle came out, then stopped. I swung my legs off the bed and walked to the front of the cell. When I looked through the space between the bars and the wall, I could see the kid's face, pale like the rest of us and all planes and angles.

"They've shut off the water, so it won't be much longer—just as long as it takes them to get suited up and get the equipment from the armory. You ever been gassed before?"

"No," the kid answered. His one eye that I could see was wide open and wondering.

He had a spray of freckles across his nose that reminded me of Opie on the old *Andy Griffith Show*. He was a good kid with a lot of heart and hated anything that wore a uniform, but he was out of his element in this particular snake pit. I had already taught him a lot about max time and even taken him through the steps to make a zip gun in case somebody wanted to get cute on the way to the shower at the end of the tier, but gas was a new experience for him. I needed to take him to school. And in a hurry.

"Okay, here's what you need to do," I told him, leaning against the cell wall and watching the gate. "First, put on everything you own. Try to cover all the skin you can, because this shit gets into your pores, and you'll be feeling it a month from now every time you step under a hot shower. Then get a towel and wet it real good in your toilet and put it where you can get it in a hurry. Next, scoop all the water out of your toilet. Everything's wet anyway, so just throw the water on the floor."

"All of it?" Andy asked.

It was a good thing he couldn't see the look on my face. "Yeah, all of it. Once you get to the very bottom, take another towel and dry all the water that's left. When you're done, you'll have a pipeline you can breathe through. When the cops get to your cell with the fogger, stick your head as far in the toilet as you can and cover it with the wet towel. Try to plaster the edges of the towel on the seat to make a good seal. It won't stop all the gas, but it'll help. You got all that?"

"Yeah," the kid said, a touch of awe in his voice. "You been through this before, huh?" He sounded like he thought I was a combination of a Medal of Honor recipient and a World Series MVP.

"A few times," I confirmed. "I've been on this goddamn wing for nearly three years, and it's easy to get bored once in a while. But listen, when the gas starts getting to you, you'll have to fight the urge to pull your head up and go anywhere to get away from it. That's just natural, but you can't do that because there's no place else to go. The toilet's the best place to be, and you gotta remember that. Think, don't react. Just keep thinking that you gotta keep your head down, and it'll be over real soon."

"Okay, Stone. I'll try to remember. And thanks."

I could hear him working next door and saw the ripples in the water outside my cell as he emptied his toilet. He had only five minutes before the exhaust fans suddenly shut down, along with most conversation. Peaches, the sissy in fourteen, started singing an old Sam Cooke song, "A Change Is Gonna Come." Ten minutes later, the sound of heavy boots on concrete echoed through the wing. The main doors on the bottom floor burst open, and I could see about a dozen black-suited guards pouring in, most carrying shields and batons, one with a Taser. Two cranked the wing's windows shut tightly, while the others quickly climbed the stairs to the second tier. A few of the guys cursed them for the sorry bastards they were. One turned around as he was closing the windows—he must have been new—and said, "Keep it up, assholes. We're coming up there next." That's all it took to get us really charged.

"Bring your mother when you come, cocksucker."

"Yeah, and your wife and sister, the one who blew me in the visiting room last week."

"Never mind that," someone else yelled. "Just come up here naked so I can see how fine *you* are."

What the hell? We were getting gassed anyway.

"Here we go, kid," I yelled over to Andy, glancing back at my own empty toilet and towel draped across it. "Talk to you after."

I retreated to the rear of the cell and dropped to my knees beside the toilet, holding the wet towel in my hands. I heard the fogger crank up, followed quickly by the rattle of the gate being opened. Next came the shouted voices, only partially muffled by the visors and masks.

"ON THE FLOOR AT THE BACK OF THE CELL, SHITBAG! MOVE! MOVE!"

Tiny Head, in the first cell, was the first one to get it. Frank Lane, in jumpsuit, helmet, and respirator, had plenty of experience, so I pictured him inserting the fogger through the bars and discharging pepper gas until the six-by-ten cell was an impenetrable haze. Tiny Head's suffocating screams verified the scene but were drowned out by the whine of the fogger. Maybe it doesn't seem fair that Tiny Head got his gas along with the rest of us, but it didn't break any hearts on 2 North. A week before, someone had snitched out some wine Harris was cooking off, and it had to be Tiny Head, because he supplied the V8. What goes around comes around.

The response team made its way down the wing, filling each cell in order. I got an initial jolt as the pepper gas began to drift over the wing. The stuff literally hits you so hard it makes you jerk your head around like you've been punched. It stung my eyes and immediately started my nose running like a faucet. By the time the squad reached Geehan's cell, I was having a hard time keeping my eyes open, but I wanted to see Lane's face when I took the gas. Then I began to smile when I heard Geehan's voice over the idle of the fogger before Lane pulled the trigger.

"NOT ME! NOT ME, LIEUTENANT! I ATE THE CHICKEN. I SWEAR I ATE IT. HERE'S THE TRAY RIGHT HERE. YOU CAN SEE..."

I didn't get the rest of it. The two-cycle engine on the fogger drowned out everything else, but I thought I heard Geehan screaming before the coughing and puking caught up with him.

I waited at the edge of the toilet, squinting at the bars in front of my cell. Three large men, all dressed in black, complete with body armor, shields, and helmets, moved into view and blocked the light from outside. Frank Lane, in the center, held the fogger, a small canister attached to a long nozzle, the same kind of device pest-control people use to kill mosquitoes. Lane and I locked eyes through the lieutenant's visor. He nodded almost imperceptibly, a professional courtesy. "Run it," I told him, and ducked my head beneath the towel, sealing it as I did. I buried my face in the toilet and took a deep breath as the fogger's drone filled my ears.

• • •

Six months later, after four of us had been moved to population status, Lieutenant Lane's gas attack on the P Wing strikers was still a topic of conversation.

"Man, sometimes when the shower's really hot, I think I can still feel that shit on me." Travis scratched both his arms vigorously. He had been in the end cell and had gotten only a fraction of the gas the others ate because the fogger had run out. Lane had looked at him and shrugged. But I didn't mention that part of it.

I nodded. "They were supposed to shower us within a couple of hours."

The two of us were sitting in the bleachers in the gym. I was leaning back against the row behind me, legs sprawled out in front of me. Travis sat two rows down and was half turned toward me. "Bastards waited until the next goddamn day, gave it a chance to soak in real good." He scratched again. "Hey, what's up with Eighty-nine? Ever since we hit population, he's been hangin' with that M Wing crowd, and that's nothin' but trouble. Anybody talk to him?"

"Rudy tried, but he said the kid just blew him off."

"You can't do anything with him?"

I shrugged. "Tried a couple of times. Even talked him out of torching Sugar Bear for patting him on the ass in the chow line, but he likes the wing."

"Yeah, but then what? The kid gets more time, goes back to P Wing, and gets stuck here for five more years before they'll even look at a transfer." I sat up a little. "He's a decent kid, a little slow, but he's got a good heart. I just hate to see him jammed up, that's all."

Travis looked up as Eighty-nine came through the door and made his way carefully over the bleachers toward us. He waited until he sat down. "You playin' any ball this year?"

Eighty-nine shook his head. "Don't think so, not after Ray-Ray got stuck after that last game. And it wasn't even a foul."

Travis nodded slowly. "Yeah, that cost him a kidney. Guys get tense over nothing but a little ball. Next thing you know, someone's got a pipe or a knife and lookin' for a place to put it." All three of us were silent for a few seconds before Travis spoke again.

"Ask you something?"

Eighty-nine shrugged. "Sure."

"I've seen a lot of guys come through here with ninety-nine years, usually for a stickup, and a lot of them wanna be called Ninety-nine, and that's okay. But I never heard of anyone but you callin' himself Eighty-nine. How the hell did you get that number?"

"Didn't have nothin' to do with my sentence. I'm doin' twenty-two for a truckload of weed got busted down around Naples."

"Then what?"

Eighty-nine looked at me, and I looked at Travis. "It's kind of an interesting story," I said. "I heard it back on P Wing." Then I looked at the kid. "It's your story. Tell him if you want."

Eighty-nine got comfortable, and an almost smug look took command of his face. "Got the name when I was over in reception at RMC in Lake Butler. Coupla days after I was there, they gave me all sorts of these tests. Never did too good in school and ended up quittin' in the eighth grade, but I made nearly a hundred on the IQ test—that's a B+ if they gave out grades instead of numbers. Never done that good on anything before. Guys in the dorm couldn't believe it when I got the scores, couldn't believe I'd really scored eighty-nine, but when they saw the paper, they started calling me Eighty-nine." He picked at a spot on his hand and blushed a little. "It just stuck."

Travis looked at the name tag on the right side of the man's chest. "Your real name's Andrew?"

"Yeah, but my mom calls me Andy."

"Andy, huh? Sounds like some sort of TV character. I can see why you go by Eighty-nine." Nobody else said anything until Travis got up and brushed his pants off with his palms. "Must be close to lunch. You stayin'?"

I looked toward the recreation office, where my desk was. "Got a few things to clean up before my boss gets back—next week's schedule, the intramural list, the usual shit. And I gotta set things up for the movie tonight."

"Still that Clint Eastwood thing?"

I nodded. *Where Eagles Dare.*

"Okay," Travis said. "I'll catch you two later."

Andy and I watched him leave. Six guys at the other end of the gym played some half-court, and the clink of metal on metal drifted out of the weight room near the office. Other than that, the gym was nearly deserted at ten-thirty. After a couple of minutes, I asked Andy without turning my head, "What's up, and don't give me that bullshit about nothing."

"Nathan," the kid said.

"That thing with Sonny Boy last night?"

"Yeah, he told Sonny he couldn't make no wine on M Wing as long as he was there. Sonny Boy said something else, and Nathan slapped him. Right there in the dayroom, in front of everybody. Slapped the livin' shit out of him."

"What'd Sonny do?"

"Nothin'. Just stood there and looked at him, like he couldn't believe it happened."

I frowned. "That's not like Sonny. He's already stabbed three guys I know of. Figured Nathan would be cold and stinking by now." I looked at Andy. "So where do you fit in all this?"

"Well, Nathan's got his crew, and Sonny's got his, and everybody's takin' sides and talkin' about strappin' down and gettin' busy in the movie tonight." He pulled up his shirttail on the side closest to me and showed me a knife with the handle wrapped in duct tape. "Came down here to stash this just in case."

I sat up and turned to face the kid. "What do you possibly have to do with this? Nathan's crew are all doin' forever, and Sonny's are all crazy, and you're Snow goddamn White with a reefer case right in the middle of a war over selling wine. Which you don't even drink. If I didn't know better, I'd think you were Nathan's punk." I pointed to the Seiko on his wrist. "Nathan give you that?"

Andy flushed. "Yeah, but it's not what you think. He's just nice to me, that's all. You don't know him."

I shook my head. "I don't know him? Right. We came in about the same time twenty-three goddamn years ago, when you were still shittin' yellow. But you've been here a hot three years and got it all figured out. Since you already know every other damn thing, what do you want from me? And don't tell me it's nothing, because you've got that look on your face."

Andy stood up. "I don't wanna fight with you, Stone. I just wanted to know, you know, about what I should do if things . . . Well, if things . . ."

I looked up at him. "Sit down and listen to me. Have I ever told you anything that wasn't true?"

"No," he said.

"Then pay attention, because this time's no different." He did. "This is a train wreck waiting to happen, and they'll take you with them without a thought. If you think any of those guys—any of them— give a rat's ass about you, you're dumber than a day-old kitten. You wanna know what you should do? Forget about these assholes. Don't go to the movie tonight, and move off that wing. I think there's an empty cell on K Wing. Check in if you have to, but get as far away from those two as you can."

Andy stood up again and put both hands in his pockets. "I can't do that, Stone. I already told Nathan I'd be there."

I took a deep breath. I tried to remember when I was his age with the same attitude, until I found out that it was just more prison bullshit about a code that never was and never would be. So I tried again. "And because you promised this guy, who doesn't really care if you live or die, then you feel like you have to show up and maybe get your silly ass killed in the process."

Andy hung his head. "I know how dumb it sounds when you say it."

"Jesus, it *is* dumb." I let that hang a few seconds. "But you're still gonna do it."

Andy nodded without looking at me.

"Then I guess that's all there is to it." I got up and started down the bleachers, running over options on how I might be able to stop what was coming. I walked down two steps and turned around. "Park the shank by the stage over there. You can pick it up as soon as the lights go down." And then it came to me how to keep him out of this particular jackpot. I walked the rest of the way to the office with a smile on my face.

"Thanks," the kid said as I headed into the office. I tossed up a hand without looking back.

The prison ran out-of-date movies every Friday night for everyone in population. The gym doubled as a theater, and my duties as recreation clerk included setting up the projector, lowering the screen, and plugging in the speakers on the stage's apron, all of which got me into the gym earlier than anyone else. By the time I had everything ready to go, I had nearly forgotten about my conversation with Andy Reeves. When the rest of population began coming into the gym at seven, I had already moved my favorite chair to a good spot between the office and the bathroom and was finishing the last of a pint of fudge ripple from the canteen.

Everyone entering the gym for the movie had to undergo a pat search for weapons, which was silly as hell because during the day anyone could come in and hide anything, even a shotgun if you had one.

For that reason, the gym had a well-deserved reputation as a death trap. I had seen more people killed in the gym than anywhere else, one right at center court ten minutes before the start of a basketball game with a civilian team from Jacksonville. The game was canceled, and when the recreation director tried to reschedule it, the team's captain told him in no uncertain terms that they would never be back. Seeing people die was therefore nothing new for me, and as the lights went down in the gym, I settled back and prepared to watch Clint Eastwood kill dozens of Germans. Ten minutes into the movie, everything changed.

Sonny Boy and two of his crew slipped out of the bleachers and went into the bathroom first, followed by Nathan. I was surprised to see Andy right behind him. I was ten feet from the door and could hear heated voices, then the unmistakable sound of a slap. I swiveled my chair to the left just as Andy sprinted through the doorway. Nathan, bleeding from a gash over his right eye, was right behind him. Then came Sonny, long legs pumping and a ten-inch piece of steel in his right hand. Andy disappeared into the crowd in the bleachers, which parted like the Red Sea for Moses, but Nathan panicked and foolishly tried to outrun Sonny. He ran along the front of the bleachers, reached the equipment room at one end of the gym, and quickly turned right, Sonny gaining ground behind him. They made another right at the far wall and ran in front of the movie screen, two genuine warriors with real knives superimposed on fake German soldiers with phony guns.

When Nathan tried to make the turn at the weight room, Sonny got an angle on him just about where I was sitting, closed the gap, and stabbed him once in the back and again in the shoulder. Nathan staggered but kept running the same circuit, like some sort of bizarre relay race in which Sonny was trying to pass off the knife by planting it in Nathan's body. On the second pass, the guard by the door saw what was happening and turned on the lights. Then he ran out the door and locked it.

I watched with everyone else as Nathan quickly tired. Sonny, by comparison, looked as fresh as a marathoner after the first mile. He actually smiled when he finally caught Nathan's shirt directly in front of the bleachers at the same time Nathan slipped in his own blood on the floor. Sonny jerked him off his feet and slammed him to the ground on his back. He bent over him and screamed, "I TOLD YOU I WAS GONNA KILL YOU!"

Nathan held his arms up, but they were as futile as a New Orleans levee against a cat. 5 hurricane. Sonny was too big, too strong, and too much. He stabbed Nathan in the face and neck, then drew the knife back in a wide arc and plunged it into Nathan's chest just below the sternum. Nathan's body went rigid, as if someone had hooked up two thousand volts to him. A gout of blood gushed around the blade, then his body relaxed completely. Like everyone else in the gym, I sat transfixed by the killing. Then the double doors at the top of the stairs banged open and six guards ran in, but they stopped before they reached Sonny. Lieutenant Casey, a no-nonsense guard, prematurely bald and built like a block, was at the head of the column.

"Okay, Sonny, why don't you put the knife down and let us go ahead and take him to the clinic." He had his hands out in front of him. He knew Sonny and knew better than to confront a man who had just butchered another one.

Sonny sat down beside Nathan's body and looked at it. Then he shook his head. "Not yet, Lieutenant. Ain't sure he's dead." He stabbed Nathan in the neck and chest again and got no reaction. He lifted his arm and let it drop back down to the gym floor with a thump. He nodded once, buried the knife in Nathan's chest, and left it there. He got up, spit once in Nathan's dead eyes, and told Casey, "Now you can have the son of a bitch." Then he turned around and put his hands behind his back. The two guards who cuffed him tried their best to avoid the blood while Clint Eastwood was busy infiltrating the German high command in the background.

While the other guards cleared the gym and put crime scene tape everywhere, I looked for Andy. I saw the back of his head in the crowd of people near the door but couldn't get there before he was already in the hallway and headed back to his wing. He didn't look hurt, but I couldn't be sure from where I was.

Fifteen hours later, he was standing at the door to the equipment room in the gym. I looked up from my inventory when he called me. "Stone?" he said. "I'm in trouble." The Eighty-nine persona was gone, replaced by ordinary Andy Reeves, a skinny redheaded kid from Apopka, twenty-four years old with no prior record, a pot dealer who had never hurt anyone. He was a minnow who suddenly discovered that he was swimming with barracudas and was scared to death of being eaten alive.

I looked quickly around the gym. Five guys were playing hustle on one end of the court, and the usual crew of lifters was already hard at work in the weight room at nine o'clock. Little remained of the previous night's mayhem except for a few ominous stains on the floor, and the scuffing of sneakers would soon obliterate those.

"No shit. The investigator pull you in yet?"

Andy nodded. "This morning, right after count. I was about the fifth or sixth one in. He got pissed when I said I didn't know nothin', threatened to hang a snitch jacket on me and give me to the wolves. Then he promised me a transfer down south if I would roll over on Sonny."

I snorted. "Hell, he's probably got a dozen witnesses already and won't use all of them. Did he say anything about you and Nathan?"

Andy shook his head. "Nah, I don't think he knows much except what happened here. Didn't ask nothin' about what caused it, just what did I see, did I know either guy, stuff like that."

I indicated a private spot in the bleachers close to the bathroom. Andy looked once in the bathroom door and quickly looked away. Then he followed me over to the bleachers and sat down beside me. "First," I said, "tell me what happened in there."

Andy stared straight ahead and clasped his hands between his knees. "I lost it." I waited. Andy finally started talking again. "I was supposed to be carrying Nathan's knife for him, the one I brought in here and showed you." He looked up at me. "You know if he gets another DR for anything, he's maxed on P Wing for five." He was still talking about the dead man in the present tense, as if death were an abstraction.

"He doesn't have to worry about that now," I reminded him. "So you were supposed to hold his piece because you get only, what? Three years in max and maybe cased up on top of that?"

Andy's head bobbed. "I know, I know." I resisted the urge to ask why, but I waited until he was ready. "I went to get the knife from where I put it over by the stage, just like you told me, and Nathan told me to follow him into the bathroom. Sonny and some of his guys went in first."

"I saw them," I said.

The rest came out in a rush. "But the knife wasn't where I put it, and by then Nathan was already headed into the bathroom, so then I went in behind him, but as soon as we got inside, Sonny started yelling and slapped Nathan, called him a punk and said he was gonna kill him, cut him up so that his own mama wouldn't know him. Then Sonny pulls this huge goddamn knife, and the other guys try to block the door so we can't get out." He dropped his head again. When he spoke, his voice was scarcely a whisper. "Nathan yelled at me to give him the knife, but I couldn't because I didn't have it. Then I ran, pushed by the other guys, and left Nathan all by himself." He turned little boy's eyes on me. "I swear I couldn't help it, Stone. My feet just took off, like they didn't care what I wanted. I didn't think it would really happen, you know? Sonny with that knife. I couldn't tell Nathan I couldn't find his knife after he gave it to me."

I let the moment percolate there between us. Andy was clearly upset because his instinct for self-preservation had triumphed over his prison obligations to a guy who couldn't have cared less about him, and the only thing that would eventually make him feel better was putting some time between him and the murder. But he had bigger problems.

"Okay," I said. "What's happening on the wing?"

Andy shook his head. "Not good. Hit Man and Boonie won't talk to me, and Gary's acting like I'm not even there."

Gary was an Italian guy, one of the original cocaine cowboys out of Miami, and between him and his partner, they had twenty-three murders. He was Nathan's business partner and took his role very seriously. If Gary was acting like Andy wasn't there, chances were better than even that he soon wouldn't be. The other two might lump Andy up a little, but Gary would definitely punch his ticket. This was the same guy who, after killing a suspected snitch and burying him in the Everglades, got coked up and paranoid, went back to the grave, dug the guy up, put twenty more rounds into him, set the body on fire, and then planted a hand grenade under it and blew it up before reburying it. Yeah, Andy had a problem.

"You got two ways to go here," I told him. "But either way, you gotta get off M Wing, at least give you a little room where you won't be so open. You go to the wing officer and tell him you want to move. If he won't do it, ask for a sergeant, and if he won't do it, get a lieutenant."

"Which one?"

"Doesn't matter. Casey would be good, but you'll have to wait for shift change, and you need off the wing now."

"What if he won't move me?"

"Then you check in." I raised my hands before he could say anything. "Yeah, yeah, we had this talk already, and if you remember what happened, maybe you'll see I was making pretty good sense." For a young guy like Andy, going to protective custody was the ultimate insult, a violation of the code that demanded defending your honor with your life. Checking in was for cowards. Or so the legend went. "You check in," I repeated, "and then you ask for an emergency phone call. Get in touch with your mom down there in Orlando and tell her what's going on. You don't have to be specific, just tell her you're in a bind and you think it would be better if you got transferred to another prison, maybe someplace down south. It might take a while, but so what? Believe me, with the reputation this place has got and as often as it's in the papers, you won't have to say anything else to get her on the phone with the warden or Tallahassee."

He looked at me for a few seconds. "I'll think about it," he said.

He jumped when I slapped my thigh. "You don't have god-damn time to think about it," I told him. "As far as Gary's concerned, you got Nathan killed, and he's a very serious guy to have pissed at you." I resisted the urge to grab him by the shoulders and shake him, but I moved a little closer to emphasize things. "Gary will *kill* you, Andy, and no one on that wing will help you. You understand that?"

He chewed his lip while he thought about it. "Yeah, okay. I'll go do it now."

He got up before I could say anything else and made his way up the bleachers to the door.

He turned right and headed down the hallway. I blew out a sigh of relief and went back to the office. Andy's reputation might not survive a PC move, but if it saved his butt, he could live with it. It seemed a lot better than dying.

I spent the rest of the morning on the inventory and worked through lunch. I asked a couple of guys who came in after the noon count if they had heard anything about Andy. None had, which surprised me. Usually when someone checks in, it's on the prison telephone immediately, and the whole place knew that Andy was in a jam because of Nathan's killing. I lived on J Wing, three up the hall from Andy's wing, but he would have had to go past my wing to get to W Wing, the PC wing, on the other side of the hallway, and someone would have seen him. Could be he was locked in his cell waiting for the paperwork. I shrugged it off and got the uniforms and equipment ready for that night's intramural tournament.

By nine that night, when I locked in, I still hadn't heard anything about Andy, and I thought I had simply missed him while I was busy in the gym. I read until about ten and then turned out the light. I got up the following morning and did my usual routine before the doors opened for breakfast, still wondering about Andy. The wings are fed separately, so I didn't have a chance to check on him until I went to work after morning count. I had just sat down at my desk to type up next week's movie synopsis when Bill Van Perle walked in. He lived on M Wing, eight cells down from Andy's. He leaned against the wall by the door.

"Andy said to tell you that he had called his mom and everything was all right. She's supposed to call the warden this morning."

I slowly swiveled in my chair. "When did he tell you that?"

"About five minutes ago, right when I was headed out the door."

"On M Wing?"

"Sure," Bill confirmed.

"Jesus," I said, starting to get up.

Just then the king doors to the wings began slamming, sending echoes down the hall that could be felt all the way up to the gym. The prison's spine was a quarter-mile-long hallway, with the clinic on one end and the death house with the electric chair on the other. The wings run off the hallway like the legs on a centipede, secured by massive steel king doors. Whenever trouble erupts on one of the wings, all the wing officers leave their wings and secure the doors until help arrives. When these doors begin slamming, it's as if the gods on Olympus are having batting practice. My boss came out of his office and ran up the stairs to lock the gym doors. He took a look down the hallway as guards began rushing by him from the other direction to get to the trouble spot. I stood at the bottom of the bleachers when he came back down.

"M Wing," he said, and walked past me on the way back to work.

I ran up the stairs to the doors and pressed my face against one of the small, thick windows set into the door. Five minutes later, two inmates from the clinic hustled down the hallway pushing a gurney, followed by three more guards and a nurse moving at a more leisurely pace. That meant that the guy on the other end either wasn't hurt too badly or was hurt beyond anything they could do. I had a nasty feeling working as soon as my boss told me M Wing, and watching the nurse stroll down the hall didn't help things.

Fifteen minutes later, some of the guards who had responded first walked back up. One had blood painting the front of his pants and shirt and was gesturing to two more with him. Then he used his index finger and pointed to his neck three times and his chest twice. Then he shook his head, ashen under the black hair and mustache. I stayed glued to the window for maybe twenty more minutes before the gurney made the return trip.

The sheet was pulled up over the face, bloodstains marking it like the Shroud of Turin. One pale hand was exposed, but I couldn't tell anything by that except that one less white guy would be on the count. I was still hoping that anyone else but Andy was under that cover. Then I saw the sneakers protruding from the bottom part of the sheet. They were untied, of course, and scuffed on the toes from too many handball games, but they were so white they gleamed, and Andy always kept his sneakers immaculate. The clincher, however, was on the heel. On the thickest part, in careful calligraphy in wide red Magic Marker, "89" stood out like a beacon.

I watched Andy's body pass the gym, turning my face until his sneakers slipped out of sight, flopping loosely the way dead feet always do as the gurney bounced over the tile. Then I leaned my head against the window and blew out a long breath. I don't know how long I kept my face pressed against the cool glass. I didn't even realize I had closed my eyes until a harsh metallic tapping startled me. I looked into the face of the hall sergeant, who motioned me away from the door with a flick of his hand.

I walked back to the office and sat down behind my desk, next week's gym schedule partially complete on the screen in front of me. I stared at it for a minute or so until my boss asked, "You all right?"

I glanced over my shoulder at him and nodded. "Yeah, I'm all right. Just thinking, that's all."

He rattled the newspaper he was reading. "Don't get into the habit. Usually brings you grief in here."

He went back to the sports page, I went back to typing up next week's schedule, and Andy Reeves went down the ramp, out the rear door, and into the beige hearse that the local funeral parlor uses, usually after executions. In a few weeks, people would be sitting around telling Andy stories, reminding each other of the time he did something funny or stupid, like when Joe Greer talked him into smearing state-issue toothpaste all over himself to promote a tan and then lying in the yard in July until the stuff actually started to bubble on him. Or the time he thought he wanted to join the boxing team and got knocked out ten seconds into the first round of a sparring session. But Andy was gone.

Two days later, Gary was scheduled for arraignment for Andy's murder. We have a courtroom here at the prison to save the time and expense of transporting prisoners back and forth to town whenever someone gets charged with a felony inside. The judge drives out here with a court reporter and takes care of everything except the trial itself. That's held in town, and it's almost like a state holiday. All the locals come out to gawk and watch the guys being taken out of the van and into the courthouse. But all that was supposed to come after Gary's arraignment on Monday at nine.

He came down the hallway, shackled and cuffed to a belly chain, with a black security box over the cuffs as well. I figured two guards would be escorting him but thought they would run as soon as they saw the knife. They usually do, but even if they didn't, there was no way they were going to stop me from killing Gary. I had the same knife Andy was supposed to have had that night. After Andy stashed it, I went and got it. I thought that if he couldn't find the knife, the whole thing might not go anywhere, or at the very least he wouldn't follow Nathan around acting like he had it. Now it seemed like the least I could do, especially since it was pretty much my fault he got killed. I never figured him to go ahead without the damned knife. Dumb kid had more balls than brains. I also had a nice pipe with a fat elbow on the end of it to keep Gary from running. You'd be surprised how far a guy can run leaking blood, but crack his head and he usually drops right away.

It went down exactly like I thought it would. The door to the gym was open, so it was really a simple matter just to step out when Gary passed by and hit him in the head. That shot took him down and sent the escorts back down the hallway, reaching for their radios. I finished Gary with the knife right there, but I'm not sure he was even conscious when I killed him. I kind of felt bad about that, like he should have known why.

So now, in about thirty minutes, I'll be making my own trip down the hallway to my arraignment. I'll wear the same shackles, cuffs, and black box as Gary, but I think I'll have more guards as escorts. Plus the hallway will be locked down this time, so nobody can do to me what I did to Gary. Wouldn't make much difference if they did. I mean, I'm doing double life and sixty now, and I'll probably get another life sentence on top of that for Gary, which means this is my home forever. Maybe by the time I get off max in four or five years, they'll have cable TV in the dayroom like everyone says. Andy would have liked that. He loved *The Simpsons*.

Paul Moran

Paul Moran went to prison in 1986 and is serving a sixty-year sentence for sexual assault. He is incarcerated at Soledad in California. He is forty-six years old; his hair and beard are shot with gray, and he has dark circles under his eyes, a testament to growing old quickly in tough prisons. Paul is adamant that his life now is about trying to express the positive work he is doing to better himself. He told me, "I won't talk about my crime, because after nearly twenty years, I'm about talked out, and I don't believe it's relevant." He wanted to talk about the writing he has been doing seriously for twelve years, the play that ran eight weeks to rave reviews in a playhouse in Santa Cruz, and his work which has won honors in several competitions, so we talked about writing.

Paul has a wonderful laugh; it is deep and resonant. I asked him to describe a memorable writing experience, and he said, "I had this teacher who was wonderful. She made us write ten-minute plays. I told her that I really appreciated what she was doing, but I was working on a novel. She said, 'I understand, but do it anyway.'" Paul laughed.

I am always encouraged when I can see someone's humanity survive behind the walls, and there it was in a laugh that came from deep inside him. His play was submitted to the Louisville Ten-Minute Playwriting Contest and placed in the top one hundred, an honor that eludes most playwrights. This was not Paul's first experience with accolades for his writing; his first time came when he was twelve. "They had a statewide editorial writing contest, and I won, even against high school students. But then I played football. I left it all behind. I didn't even think about writing again until I came to prison," he said with a shrug.

We talked about the genesis of writing, especially in prison, with its dearth of stimuli, and Paul said, "A little seed will start growing and develop into something else." He told me that he got ideas from newspaper articles or stories on TV or even things he might see around the yard. "I am writing a horror novel now, and here in

Soledad there are cats on the yard. One day I was out on the yard, and I thought, *What if the cats were really inmates who turned into cats?* and it goes from there. Or I read an article about a guy who was charging a town to get rid of evil, so that might go into the story."

But he also said that there are limits placed on him because of his confinement. "I think about research. There are so many things I don't have access to. It is hard for me. I want to be able to see things, to be able to feel the wind around me." Writing becomes a much more daunting task when you lack the ability to experience what you are trying to write about.

Writing in prison has its difficulties, and one of the most challenging is dealing with security concerns that often conflict with writing. Paul talked about being able to write on a computer at his job as a clerk, a luxury that most prisoners don't have. Prison clerks, working in offices throughout the prison, keep almost all the records relative to the business of running a prison on computers, and in many prisons, once their work is done, and if their bosses are so inclined, the clerks are allowed to work on writing projects. Paul had been working on a novel and was two hundred pages into it when "security people came in and wiped it out." He sighed. "I didn't write for six months."

These setbacks remind Paul that "the humanness of the world doesn't exist in here." These difficulties have not deterred him. He showed me a magazine that was produced by the Arts in Corrections program at Soledad, called *Prose & Cons*. The work came out of a journalism class, and he had two pieces in the issue. In a piece titled "Recycling Humanity," his writing is powerful and heartfelt as he urges the citizens of the world to use prisons as a place to reeducate and rehabilitate for a better society for all.

Education is very important to Paul, and his respect for the men and women who teach in prisons is apparent, his appreciation boundless. He spoke to me about the college program that is making a comeback at Soledad. He talked about the losses relative to education in the early 1990s. "We lost the college programs, of course, but there is a wonderful woman here, an educational counselor, who against all odds has been instrumental in getting a two-year college degree program going for inmates. It's been so successful that she's now very close to getting a four-year degree program off the ground."

He was beaming as he talked about this woman and the work she has done for the prisoners at Soledad. It has been my experience that people who care don't usually last very long in the prison system; prison takes a toll on everyone, not just the prisoners. Paul confirmed this. "The staff that might care doesn't last in here," he said as he shook his head. "But she is different," he continued. "She is smart, proactive, and fierce when it comes to getting things accomplished."

However, there are also issues that surround the educational programs at the prison. "Most of the teachers here go above and beyond to help you with your education. But education is supposed to start at eight o'clock, per Sacramento, and a lot of times we don't get in here until nine. Security finds every way they can to cancel a program. That is a big problem here, and that is why guys get discouraged," Paul said.

In the twenty years Paul has been incarcerated, he has done the typical prison tour, having been moved to various prisons around California, and San Quentin was one stop on his way to Soledad. In "A Lesson on Dying" we get a firsthand look at life in a tough joint, and we are introduced to a number of prison survival lessons. We learn that "in the joint, fairness is a minor consideration," and when the COs are looking for answers to questions, "witness distance" is paramount in everyone's mind. Paul captures the essence of prison life by introducing us to a prisoner named Dirt and his stories on the bus ride to San Quentin, and we are engaged from the first line. These are difficult lessons, counterintuitive for most, yet vital for survival in the world of tiers and barred doors.

We talked at length about how things had changed since Paul had been in prison, and he said that he had seen things get steadily worse. We began our discussion with most inmates' favorite topic, food. "When I was at San Quentin, I was the food manager's clerk. He would let me decide whether we would accept the fruit from the vendor. The vendor took him aside and said, 'Why are you letting an inmate make these decisions?' My boss told him, 'He has to eat the food, that's why.'" Paul's eyes dropped for a moment, and then he looked at me and said, "It is almost like they want to take every bit of your humanity away."

Paul went on to say, "My boss told the guys that worked for him, 'You are professional cooks. If you don't want to be that, then find other jobs.' If you have a food manager that cares, that is great, but then I don't even know if that guy still has his job." It is not like that anymore. Most of the calories prisoners get are from starch, and even though the menu is set by a nutritionist in Sacramento, it is not necessarily what prisoners actually get to eat, because the vendors might not have the items on the menu when they get to the prison. Paul joked about trying to figure out what he was eating, because it was unrecognizable most of the time.

Paul has asthma, so medical care is something he also knows well. Along with his asthma come skin problems. "In this area you get skin rashes, and I get them really bad, especially because I have asthma and allergies. I tried to tell the doctor that I needed something for my skin. He told me to get lotion from the canteen. I told him that I needed something stronger; he told me to use Vaseline. He will not send me to a dermatologist." Paul laughed and asked me if I had any idea how greasy you got after using Vaseline. He told me he was going to keep pushing this time, and he wasn't going to stop until they sent him to a dermatologist. Should it really be that difficult?

California spent considerable time and money to revamp the Department of Corrections to put more emphasis on rehabilitation, but to date the only significant change is the name. Paul told me, "They worked really hard and paid a lot of money to change the name to California Department of Corrections and Rehabilitation, and that is a good change, but there is no money. They changed their name, and according to their new name they're really into rehabilitation now, but it is really the same dog." This serious lack of funding is negatively affecting the programming efforts at Soledad. A name change is not sufficient from the point of view of prisoners, who need to be productive.

Paul hopes that the name change is the beginning of something good. Maybe now that the focus is on rehabilitation, more money will be available for the Arts in Corrections program, which fosters writing and music and art for prisoners because it helps them gain self-esteem, become more introspective, and develop life-building skills—things that empower them to lead productive, capable lives in the free world. Programs such as Arts in Corrections provide a vehicle by which these men will come back to us in much better condition than when they left, and that is something we should all want.

—SUSAN NAGELSEN

A Lesson on Dying

PAUL MORAN

I was suspended above the polished cement floor, doing pull-ups from the second-tier railing, when the body hit. It made a cold, sucking sound, like a bag of melons being run over by a produce truck. Then I heard the scream. Its five-tier descent was apparently slowed by having to ping-pong back and forth from the housing unit's outer wall to the cell module wall, outer wall to cell wall, outer wall to cell wall, outer wall to cell wall, outer wall to cell wall to concrete floor. Then finally to me.

Suddenly hell was breaking loose all around: whistles tweeted, sirens wailed, and jackbooted feet sprinted. The jingling of heavy keys and the rhythmic clanking of aluminum riot batons on steel bars reminded me of where I was and that I had to move fast or risk getting caught near the body. That's something prison teaches you. When someone falls next to you, don't run toward them; run away.

I quickly pulled myself up over the rail and onto the second tier. Witness distance. Another prison thing: better to look like a witness than a perpetrator, although prison staff is rarely willing to make that distinction. In the joint, fairness is a minor consideration. The usual solution is to cart everyone in the vicinity off to the hole and let God sort 'em out, or someone who thinks he or she is God.

On the tier, with my back pressed firmly against the wall, I fought hard to control my breathing. I thought, *This is bad, really bad!* Still, it was the most amazing thing I'd ever seen. I mean, I'd heard all the prison horror stories about race riots, stabbings, and assaults of all kinds. I'd seen prison rape and other despicable acts played out on the big and small screens. But there is nothing, no thing, more eye-popping than having another human being's blood and stuff sprayed all over your brand-new Adidas like paint on the outside of a house.

Up to that point, my San Quentin experience, despite the joint's ominous reputation, ranked relatively low on the drama scale. A bit of a disappointment, really. But then, my expectations were high, mostly because of a character I met on my first day. I spent the earliest part of my first prison day on a San Quentin–bound bus, shackled hand and foot and waist-chained to a goaty-smelling shell of a man named Dirt. I kid you not.

Dirt was of indeterminate age. To my imperfect eye he stood about six feet six inches tall and carried barely more than one hundred pounds on his bony frame. As I regarded his spindly coat hanger of a body from as far back as our chain would allow, I took particular interest in his sun-faded, too-high head of brown hair and matching beard. The hair was completely dried out, making it look as if he'd stuck his weather-beaten face halfway through a tumbleweed. I wondered what he'd be more afraid of—a comb, a bar of soap, or a lit match.

Dirt wasn't what you'd call the picture of health. His sallow complexion, combined with eyes that pooled with some kind of cloudy liquid, made me think there might be something seriously wrong with him. Several minutes into the three-hour-plus journey, he fixed his rheumy eyes on me and told me what it was.

"I got me a lizard living inside my belly," he whispered. "It's eatin' me all up inside."

Say what? Before I could respond, he went on to explain that when he was alone, the thing would crawl down past his intestines, make a U-turn, then skitter along the outside of his rib cage until it reached his chest. Once there, it would poke its flat lizard head out through his left nipple, challenge him with those black, beady eyes that lizards have, then duck back inside his body before he could get hold of it.

He'd seen several doctors about his condition. Had x-rays, an EEG, and even a full-body image scan before accepting what he'd known all along. The lizard was meant for his eyes only. It was put there by Josiah Lee Evans, a Louisiana conjure man turned California wino. According to Dirt, ol' Josiah Lee had put that vexatious little critter inside his belly to worry him, to scratch at his stomach, to gnaw on his liver, to pretty much make itself at home in his guts, appearing and disappearing at will, until it finally worried him to death.

Supposedly, Josiah Lee killed Dirt with the lizard because of a fight over a half-empty bottle of whiskey. So Dirt killed him right back, by busting him upside the head with the bottle of contention. Then he shoved him in front of a bus.

As entertaining as the story was, I didn't for one minute believe Dirt's tale of sorcery and murder. That phantom lizard gnawing away at his insides was called cancer. It took me a while, but I recognized the culprit. I knew what cancer looked like. A few decades ago, it had looked like my uncle Ira, already a shell of his former self, wasting away on his deathbed. Today it looked like Dirt. I didn't tell him, though. I just sat there listening as he jumped from subject to subject, talking about anything and everything. I found myself admiring him for not allowing bad breath, or a complete lack of common sense, to deter him from expressing his opinions.

As the miles flew by, it became clear to me that Dirt knew a hell of a lot of people, mostly dead people. All of whom had met an untimely end in prison, many of them at San Quentin.

He told me about a convict they called Fast, who was caught buying Big C's punk a box of doughnuts at the canteen, supposedly for services rendered. This breach of prison etiquette ended up costing Fast his life when Big C finally caught up with him on the weight pile and dropped a seventy-five-pound dumbbell on his head before he could get out of the way. I guess Fast was more of a fast talker than a fast mover.

I also heard about Nissan, God rest his soul, who would borrow cassettes from people, pry open the casing, then use a razor to cut out his favorite tunes, creating his own "Best of . . ." collections. He was so good at his brand of thievery that he was caught only once. Unfortunately, once is enough when you're caught by the right person. Nissan's right person was a gangbanger called Rock, who found out that "Reasons," the long version, had been removed from his *Gratitude* cassette. The gangsta went berserk; then, using his razor, he proceeded to cut Nissan's throat.

And so it went for the entire ride up north, this modern Scheherazade telling me one harrowing prison story after another, right up to the moment we crossed the San Raphael Bridge and drove through the gate, past San Quentin's forbidding, concertina-wire-trimmed walls. By the time we pulled up to the Receiving and Release building, fear was playing wild and loose with my sphincter muscle control. Though I tried not to be affected by Dirt's stories or San Quentin's sinister reputation, I walked out of Receiving two hours later squeezing my bedroll like a childhood teddy bear and my butt cheeks even tighter.

I can vividly recall muttering the Twenty-third Psalm like a

---

mantra as I was escorted down a long, wide corridor, surrounded by manned gun towers and dilapidated multistoried buildings, my own Valley of Death, to West Block, the building where I was to be housed. Every step had me cringing beneath a barrage of bad vibes that ricocheted between the buildings, row after row of five-story-high concrete and steel keeps.

When my small band of inmates—minus Dirt, who had been taken straight to the infirmary—was finally ushered into the housing unit and the heavy steel doors swung shut, fight scenes from every prison movie I had ever seen flashed through my mind with Quentin Tarentinoish quality.

West Block's concrete floor was covered with several coats of state-bought varnish and buffed to a high-gloss finish. It looked like a frozen river of dark brown ice. Floating lengthwise in the middle of that river like a Mississippi riverboat was a five-tiered module composed of approximately four hundred nine-by-six-foot cells. The famed Gray Bar Hotel, except these bars were painted arctic blue.

Our escort officer, a petite, surprisingly attractive young woman with close-cropped red hair, happy green eyes, and an effervescent personality, allowed the steel doors' echo to fade before launching into her welcoming speech.

"Gentlemen, welcome to West Block," she began. "My name is Officer Boutay. Not Officer Booty or Officer Body, but Boo-tay. You will find me likable, witty, and relatively friendly so long as you can refrain from messing around with my last name. I've been working here for seven years. In that time I've heard every possible variation of my last name. None of them have been clever or funny. Yours won't be either."

For some reason she looked straight at me before continuing.

"Another thing—I don't care why you're here. I don't want to hear about your cases, about how you"—she made quotation marks in the air—"'didn't do it.' I'm not your lawyer, and I am not, nor will I ever be, your girlfriend. Respect me and I will reciprocate; disrespect me and I will reciprocate. Understand?"

We all nodded. But looking around, I saw a few clowns in the group. I was sure a few of us would try to come up with yet-unheard variations of her last name. And the brother hangin' in the back with the wavy, shoulder-length perm, a gold tooth, and a gleam in his eye would most probably take a shot at the "girlfriend" thing.

Bolted to the cell module's metal skin was a tortuously crafted wooden sign that had the words BAY VIEW and YARD VIEW carved into it, with arrows pointing to the west side of the unit and the east side, respectively. The sign was unnecessary. One glance out the forty-foot-high window panels, set a few inches into the two-foot-thick concrete walls, told the whole story. The view from the bay side showed San Francisco Bay; the yard side view showed the recreation yard. Simple as that.

Officer Boutay pointed a small, dainty finger to our left, and in her best tour-guide voice announced, "That's San Francisco Bay out there. On clear days you'll see windsurfers, jet-skiers, and ships, barges, and ferries. Those of you lucky enough to be housed on this side of West Block will be rewarded with a postcard view of nighttime Marin County; it's some of the country's most expensive real estate, and it's really beautiful."

It was beautiful, I thought. There was something ironic about California's best view for California's worst citizens.

Boutay waved her right arm like Vanna toward our right. "This is the yard side," she said dully. "Which can be interesting, too. For example, every two or three weeks a really good fight breaks out, and people get shot." She added a chuckle. When none of us responded, she shrugged and said, "Hey, to each his own, right?" Wrong.

At that point an inmate lumbered out of a glass-walled clerical office and handed Officer Boutay several white index cards before heading back toward the office.

Boutay said, "Hold up, Double R." When the inmate obliged and turned back to face our group, she said, "Gentlemen, this is West Block's lead clerk, Double R."

Some of us nodded; a couple of us offered the universal guy greeting, "S'up?" Double R simply stood there, unimpressed.

"If you need anything, just ask him," Boutay explained.

Double R's nickname could have easily been Double-wide. He was at least six foot four and weighed every bit of four hundred pounds; again, my eye is imperfect. And none of his girth was fat. He glowered at Boutay, making us all uncomfortable.

She asked, "Did I say something wrong?" But her tone and the way her eyes twinkled suggested that she knew exactly what she'd said.

Double R growled, "Hell, yeah. If you need anything, don't axe me." His speaking voice sounded like it'd been ravaged by years of smoking and drinking coffee. "Do yo' own fuckin' time." Then he turned on his heel and squeezed back inside the office. Conversation over.

"Don't worry about him," Boutay replied. "He's all talk."

"Yeah," Gold Tooth quipped. "He seems to have a real gentle soul."

The faux pas quickly forgotten, Officer Boutay began handing out the index cards. When my name was called, I stepped forward to receive mine. Up in the right-hand corner, typed in 12-point Courier, was *5-W-92*. Right away I knew that the *W* stood for "West," which meant my cell was on the west side. West side was Bay side. All right! But what did the numbers mean? The cell directly in front of me had *1-W-1* painted in three-inch-high black gloss characters over the door.

I thought. If 1-W-l was on the first floor, then 5-W-92 must be on . . . My eyes panned upward, five stories upward.

"Good Lord!" I said, much louder than intended. When everybody looked my way, I took a moment to calm down and said, "Excuse me, Officer Boutay. But I can't be up on the fifth tier. I have this thing about heights."

This wasn't true. I don't have a problem with heights in general, or as a concept. I just had a problem with that kind of height, the kind where the only thing between me and a five-story drop was a waist-high steel railing that wasn't gonna stop anyone from falling. It would just make sure he did a few flips on the way down.

Boutay's offhand reply was that I'd get "used to it." So off we went, up the metal staircase, toward the fifth tier. "Look at the bright side," she said cheerfully. "At least you're on the Bay side."

Yeah, there was that, I thought.

When we got to the third-tier landing she offered up another halfhearted pearl of consolation. "Besides, as long as I've been here, no one has ever fallen off a tier."

Officer Boutay's words came rushing back to me as I hunkered down on the second tier, waiting for the medical staff to come scrape the broken body off the floor. It occurred to me how she had stressed *fallen*. She'd said, "No one has ever fallen off a tier."

I found out later, through the prison grapevine, that the guy who screwed up my morning workout hadn't fallen either. He had been thrown off. Allegedly by a gangbanger called Do-low. I don't recall what 'hood he was from. It didn't matter to me then. It still doesn't. It mattered to Do-low, though. Enough to pick up a jailhouse murder by hurling someone named Andre off the fifth tier.

Supposedly before Andre came to prison, he was spending a lot of time in Do-low's 'hood. More specifically, in Do-low's house. With Mrs. Do-low, if you know what I mean.

It's funny: as terrible and exciting as the incident was to witness, what I remember most about it isn't the cruelty of the attack. I've seen so much brutality behind these walls that I'm no longer shocked or awed by the things inmates—or guards, for that matter—will do to gain respect from their peers or prove their manhood. The thing that has remained in my mind all this time is Andre's scream. I'd never heard a man scream before that. I mean, really scream. Once upon a time, before this whole prison thing, I thought women screamed like Jamie Lee Curtis in *Halloween* and men screamed like Sylvester Stallone in . . . well, just about every movie he's ever made. That's not true, though. Real screams, the I'm-gonna-die-and-can't-do-shit-about-it screams, have a shrill, high-pitched resonance to them.

My dad once told me that every experience, whether good or bad, teaches you something. If that's true, what I learned from this experience is the total absurdity of the cliché "Die like a man." Because when it's your time to go, you don't die like a man or a woman.

You just die.

William Van Poyck

There is no portrait of the writer here because officials in the Department of Corrections for the Commonwealth of Virginia refused or ignored requests to photograph him.

William Van Poyck is fifty-three years old but seems much younger. He has a full head of dark hair and his face is unlined; his frameless glasses are the only hint that he is not as young as his mind might let him believe. He has lived most of his life behind bars, and he is open about his life and his time behind the walls and circumspect about the death sentence that hangs over his head. Billy and I have written letters and talked on the phone for the past ten years, but we had never met face to face until I made the trip to Virginia, where he is housed, to talk to him about writing, his case, and life on the row.

I was looking forward to sitting face to face with Billy, and as I waited in the visiting area for his name to be called, I contemplated a conversation that would last longer than an allotted ten-minute phone call. It was a long wait, in a room filled with people who were also waiting. Billy is incarcerated at Sussex I State Prison in Waverly, Virginia, but he is a Florida prisoner. He is being held in Virginia for his own protection. I remember a conversation with Billy when I told him that he was a PC.

I wrote Billy a letter telling him that I was having difficulty getting permission to interview and photograph him for this book. I said, "When we called Virginia to ask permission to photograph and interview you, we were told, 'We have no Virginia prisoner by the name of William Van Poyck.'" When we tried to explain the situation to the officer on the phone, he kept repeating the same thing. Billy received my letter and called to see what was happening.

I said, "So apparently Virginia has no such prisoner."

Billy laughed and said, "This stuff happens all the time. They have turned visitors around, telling them I am not here. But what they were really telling you is that I am a Florida prisoner."

I told Billy that I had called Florida next and given the person in charge all of the necessary information to see if we could get permission to interview and photograph him. I said, "Billy, I told this man, I realize that Mr. Van Poyck is housed in Virginia, but we would like to have Florida's permission to interview and photograph him." Then I asked, "And do you know what he said, Billy?"

"He said no," Billy replied.

I said, "Well, actually it was worse than that. He said he couldn't tell me where you were because you were in protective custody."

"What?" Billy said, laughing out loud. "He said I was a PC!"

In Billy's world, being a PC means you don't stand tall; it means you are weak and you need the protection of the system. Billy would never "check in." In Billy's world, he is a stand-up guy.

In his memoir, *A Checkered Past,* Billy takes the reader on a journey that is doomed from the start, and when you turn the last page you are left with the unmistakable feeling that this is a story whose ending was a foregone conclusion.[1] I recall closing the book the first time I read it, the words "He didn't have a chance" echoing in my mind as I placed it on the bookshelf.

Billy's mother died when he was sixteen months old, and his father, devastated by the loss, was unable to participate in the rearing of his children; he passed his responsibilities on to a series of house-keepers until he finally married a woman who genuinely believed that her husband's children were "evil and corrupt," as Billy described it. Life for Billy and his siblings, Jeff and Lisa, became untenable. Jeff coped by staying out of sight and developing skills in burglary that would later land him in prison with a ninety-eight-year sentence and that he insisted his younger brother learn as well.

Billy makes no excuses in his book; he does not ask for un-derstanding, but it is all too clear to the reader that the expectations placed upon him by Jeff, a brother he worshipped, were to stand strong and fight through the pain because it only lasts for a minute. About a fight that his brother forced him into, one in which he was the smallest of the contestants but emerged the victor, Billy says, "It was a small and childish event, but I learned a timeless lesson that I will carry throughout my life—that a smaller man with a big heart will beat a big man with a smaller heart every time."

Jeff continued his younger brother's lessons, but the most important lessons revolved around what would eventually shape Billy's worldview: the code. "Never hurt women, children, or old people. Never steal from the poor or a working man, and only from rich folks and banks and insurance companies. And, above all, never, ever rat on your friends—you never talk with or cooperate with the police. The worst thing you can do in life is rat out and betray a friend."

From the first time Billy was caught up in the system, at the age of fifteen, when he was taken from his family and sent to the Okeechobee School for Boys "for his own good," the die was cast. From there it was a quick jump to Youth Hall for breaking and entering and burglary, and then the "big house" was not far off. By the time Billy reached the Florida State Prison in 1972 for armed robbery, his skills were honed; he was a burglar, an armed robber, and adept at escape.

"Will the following visitors please step forward when you hear the name of the inmate you are visiting?" I was snapped out of my thoughts when I heard the name Van Poyck. I was on my way. I was not granted permission to visit Billy through official channels. Permission to photograph him was also denied. I was visiting him today as a regular visitor.

Billy can add visitors to his list twice a year, in January and June; he can have only fifteen visitors on the list. "Don't forget to bring your copy of the visitors list with you. You never know when you might need it," he told me on the phone, for the third time, the day before I left for Virginia. Long-term incarceration teaches you to prepare for every possible glitch.

The visitors were escorted in groups of six. We were asked to follow the officers through a door and down a hall, and we were told to line up with our toes on an imaginary line that the lead officer pointed out. We felt the need to stand at attention; though the two officers were polite and professional, we stood erect nonetheless. An officer came around a corner with a drug-sniffing dog, and we were told that the dog would make two passes to be sure we were not carrying any drugs. We were all clean.

We were then taken into the foyer and told to go into one of two rooms, depending on gender, and we were pat-searched by an officer. I was told to lift my hair, to show the bottoms of my feet. Once I had passed this test, I was given the piece of paper I had filled out that indicated whom I was visiting and told to "have a good visit." I must have looked somewhat quizzical, because the officer looked at me and laughed as she said in a wonderful southern accent, "What's the matter with me, throwing you to the dogs when you haven't ever been here before?" Then she directed me to where I could visit Billy.

In the appointed room I saw the people who had come before me sitting, waiting once again. They smiled at me, and one woman said, "Just have a seat. Someone will call you and tell you when it is time for you to visit." I sat. A CO came out of a visiting room and called a prisoner's name. A woman stood and the CO said, "He refused the visit." Then the CO handed the woman a piece of paper and turned and walked away. The woman, who was probably in her late sixties, said to no one and everyone, "That's it! I am calling the warden. He hasn't had his meds in two months. He is a schizophrenic, and he was bad the last time I saw him. He didn't call this week, so I came to see what was going on." A woman sitting across from me asked, "How far did you drive?" The other woman replied, "Four hours." There was a collective "I know how that is."

The CO opened the door and, without looking up from the paper in her hand, said, "Van Poyck."

I opened the door to the no-contact visiting room, and there, sitting behind a Plexiglas window, wearing light blue scrubs and a smile, was Billy, a man who has become my friend, a man whom the State of Florida has sentenced to death, a man who has come perilously close to exhausting all of his appeals after spending nineteen years on death row. I smiled, picked up the phone, sat down, and said, "I can't believe I am actually sitting here with you after all these years. How are you?"

Billy, as always, was fine. First we talked about his case. Billy was sentenced to death by the State of Florida on December 22, 1988, for first-degree premeditated murder. The basics are uncomplicated. Billy and his codefendant, Frank Valdes, decided to break a friend out of prison. Billy had been paroled recently, and he would tell you that he wasn't adjusting to life on the outside very well. He told me, "I hooked up with Frank because if you are going to do crime, he was a good person to have your back." They worked out a plan to make the break happen while Billy's friend was being taken to a medical appointment, but things went wrong and a correctional officer was killed.

The state, in separate trials, insisted that both Frank and Billy were the shooter. They both received the death penalty. The state has since stipulated that Billy was not the shooter, but that has not changed anything.

Frank Valdes was stomped to death in his death-row cell. Reports indicate that many bones in his body were broken. The guards were tried and acquitted. Billy and I talked about that. He said, "Word came back to me that Frank was dead. But the official word wasn't out yet. That didn't come until later." The prison grapevine is a powerful source of information; there are too many people who see too many things for information to remain secret for very long. When the institution conducted an investigation, Billy was surprised that the investigators came to see him. He told me, "They started asking me all these questions about Frank, and I said to them, 'Do you know who I am?' I had to tell them I was Frank's codefendant."

Billy talked about the trial of the guards. "The prosecutor didn't even request a change of venue. How could anyone expect a verdict other than not guilty when you have an entire community that is supported by prison dollars?"

One day prison administrators came to Billy's cell with paperwork for him to sign. They told him to look it over and gave him five minutes to sign. Billy said, "The paperwork said that I was being moved to Virginia, and the whole time I was holding the pen above the paper I was thinking, 'What do I know about Virginia?' Then I said, 'Hell, it has to be better than Florida,' so I signed, and here I am, apparently a PC." Billy and I both laughed.

Billy spends his days on the row doing legal work: his own, or work for a lawyer friend he has known for years. He has prepared a certiorari petition for the U.S. Supreme Court, his last chance for relief. In the simplest terms possible, he explained the issue this way. "I am trying to get the Court to rule in my favor that if my jury had known during my trial that I was not the shooter, it would have affected the outcome of the sentence." Billy is also urging the Court to consider the fact that no mitigations were brought forward in his original trial. Mitigations are the factors that might have affected the behavior of the defendant, things such as poor home life, abuse, factors that would interfere with what members of society would see as normal development. Billy holds no illusions regarding his chances. "It is a long shot, but the case law is there to support these issues, and I am hopeful that I have worded them in such a way as to make them interesting to the Court." The petition was due in October 2007, and he will have to wait to hear what will happen. Billy has been waiting on death row for nineteen years; he is used to waiting.

Billy and I always talk about writing. When he submitted "Fake Identity," reality resonated from its pages. Billy knows from firsthand experience what it is like to pretend to be crazy; it can bring you far more than you expect.

"So," I asked, "am I supposed to bow in the presence of El Supremo?"

Billy laughed. "Oh, you know about that, do you?"

"I do, but I would love to hear the story from you," I said.

"I was in Florida State Prison and I wanted to escape, but I knew that I didn't have a chance from there. So I decided to play crazy on the hope that they would transfer me to the state mental hospital in Chattahoochee."

Billy told the story this way. He started writing threatening letters to President Nixon and his cabinet members, signing them "El Supremo." Before too long he was being visited regularly by the Secret Service.

Billy said, "Soon it was time to step it up, so I made a bomb out of matches. I even wrote notes all over it with instructions, such as 'Light fuse here.'"

Before long Billy got his wish; he was sent to Chattahoochee. But it was not what he thought it would be. There he was introduced to the world of psychotropic drugs and abuse, neglect, and human suffering beyond anything he had previously known. "Fake Identity" gives us an intense look at the world of the mentally ill from an in-sider's point of view, and we are shocked, saddened, and appalled at the punishment inflicted on human beings who are so terribly fragile.

The guard interrupted us. "You should have been gone by now," she said, her voice shrill with anger. She turned and left the room.

"Are you working on anything now?" I asked, standing, getting ready to leave, and not wanting the conversation to end.

Billy looked at me, smiled, and said, "Susan, I don't have much time for writing these days. I have a lot of legal work to do, both my own and for the lawyer in Jacksonville. It is how I make my money. Besides," he continued, "I have a stack of magazines I haven't gotten a chance to read yet, and I still have a lot to learn. I don't know how much time I have left. I need to learn as much as I can while I have the time."   —SUSAN NAGELSEN

Fake Identity

WILLIAM VAN POYCK

On a quiet, humid night framed by a rising gunner's moon, Percy Brown, of dark hair, bright eyes, and reasonable intelligence, formerly of sound mind and spirit, was questioning his judgment, if not yet his sanity. *Swish, swash. Swish, swash.* Back and forth, four strides to the stretch, Percy paced the concrete floor of the small room situated in the hulking red building, laid brick upon brick among the sprawling assembly of similar structures. The dark complex lay huddled like a sad story, deep in the pine tree forests skirting the Alabama state line. *Swish, swash. Swish, swash.* He felt his bare, callused feet rhythmically chafing like dry bark on the worn floor.

Percy paused, his eye catching one of the hundreds of lines of graffiti drawn, burned, scratched, and gouged into the concrete and stonework: *Today a rooster, tomorrow a feather duster.* His brief smile was interrupted by a noise.

Percy hurried to the solid steel door, cocking his head attentively to listen through the chest-level, steel-barred opening. Voices. The clank of heavy steel. The jangle of large brass keys. Leather soles squeaking on linoleum. Percy's gut leaped. It was almost time. He again checked the position of the towel on the floor at the base of the door. Surely nobody on the other side would be able to see it. He dodged to the rear of the room, banged hard on the wall several times, and scrambled up on the ancient, stained porcelain toilet, then up onto an equally ancient sink. Whispering hoarsely, he spoke into the grimy wire mesh welded across the air vent.

"Winky. Winky!"

"Yeah," came a muted reply after a long moment. "Who's calling my name?"

"It's me. Listen—"

"Is that you, Sheila? Sheila? Sheeeeila. Help me, Sheila." The voice was distant, lost, as though spoken from a deep well.

"Winky! Dammit, it's me, Percy. Listen to me!"

"Yeah." There was a long pause. "Percy." Another pause. "Okay! . . . Yeah . . . I know you, Percy. Is that you, Percy?" The voice was a monotone, flat.

"The cart is coming. Don't forget what I told you. When I give the signal, you do your thing. Don't forget. It's important. You remember what to do, Winky? You hear me, Winky?"

Percy balanced on the rim of the sink, stretching up, turning his ear to the vent, wincing as he felt his stitches pull taut.

"Is that you, Sheila? Help me, Sheila." The keening wail echoed from the well.

Percy cursed under his breath. It was time. His wrenching gut tightened another notch. As he climbed down, his foot slipped on the wet enamel and he lost his balance, falling backward, windmilling. He hit the floor hard. The cart slid up in front of the door, pushed by a heavyset, gray-haired female nurse shadowed by a very large man in a tight-fitting white uniform. Both stared at Percy.

"What's wrong with you?" the orderly wondered loudly. "Why did you jump off the sink?"

"I fell. I didn't jump." His leg hurt where it had hit the floor.

"You jumped. I saw you."

"So did I," the nurse added, nodding her head.

"You trying to kill yourself again, boy?"

"I fell."

"What were you doing up on that sink?" the nurse asked, pointing with her chin.

"Yeah. What were you doing on the sink?"

"Nothing."

"Nothing?"

"Nothing. Look, just give me my stuff. I wanna go to sleep." Percy forced a crooked smile.

"I think maybe you need a shot. To calm you down. You look excited. Doesn't he look excited?"

"Yes. Looks upset and excited to me," the orderly agreed, fingering his brass keys.

Percy's stomach knotted up even more. "I ain't excited. I'm calm as the goddamn Rock of Gibraltar. Now give me my goddamn medication so I can go to sleep." Percy did not want a shot.

"Don't you cuss me," the nurse said.

"Don't you cuss her." The orderly took a heavy step forward. "I won't take sass from you. You're excited. You need a shot."

"Look. I am *not* excited. I do *not* need a shot of Thorazine." Percy was breathing harder.

The nurse began pulling out drawers, searching for one of her preloaded syringes. Percy licked his lips. It was a salient moment, loaded with danger, and he stood still as a fence post, sorting his options.

> With thee all night I mean to stay,
> And wrestle till the break of day.

Percy blurted out the words in a singsong voice, even as he wondered where they came from.

Both the nurse and the orderly looked up, staring at Percy.

"Look, I ain't taking no shot. I'm not one of these lame-ass crazies you love to jump on, tie down, beat up, and shoot full of Thorazine." Percy backed up, spreading his feet. Thorazine shots were very painful and knocked you out for two days. His butt cheek still ached from the last shot. He was determined to take no more.

"You'll have to go get the goon squad, 'cuz I ain't taking no damn shot. I know damn well you aren't even supposed to be giving those shots without prior written authorization from a doctor. Ain't no doctor here." Percy paused, leaned forward slightly, and lowered his voice. "And let me tell you something, I don't have no public defender; I have a *real* lawyer, and if I get a shot I'll be reporting both of you, and my lawyer will be down here raising hell. I know what you two have been doing around here, and I'm just dying for an excuse to tell it all to the Department of Professional Regulation, the Inspector General's Office, and the damn newspapers. Just try me."

Percy stood firmly, feet braced, heart pounding. He was wary, upset, and angry. He was excited.

The nurse and the orderly exchanged glances. In the silence, Percy heard the nurse's labored breathing. Next door Winky was mumbling, talking to someone or something. This was dangerous, Percy knew, for he had seen what they could do. He felt as though he was posted at life's window, watching a scene unfold. Abruptly he thrust his hand forward, palm up.

Finally the nurse handed him a paper cup containing his prescribed psychotropic cocktail of Haldol, Stelazine, Mellaril, and grapefruit juice. Powerful drugs. He, like everyone else, was also supposed to receive Benadryl, to counter the horrendous itching, but it was seldom administered. Percy took the cup. The nurse and the orderly stared at him, eyes glittering in the fluorescent light.

"THANKS FOR MY MEDICATION, BOSS MAN!" Percy shouted out the agreed-upon signal, while slowly raising the cup to his lips. He waited for Winky to scream, the agreed-upon response to distract the nurse and the orderly, permitting Percy to spit the medication surreptitiously onto the towel. Nothing . . . The cup touched his lips . . . The nurse wrote something on Percy's chart, but the glaring orderly locked eyes, his face flushed red, neck bulging. Percy took the liquid into his mouth, feeling the bitterness wash over the back of his throat. He made an exaggerated swallowing gesture, tried to smile at the orderly. Silence filled the hallway as the orderly scowled back. Percy felt like a chipmunk.

"Swallow!"

The liquid burned all the way down as Percy reluctantly swallowed.

"Step closer! Open up!"

Percy stepped forward. He knew the drill. He opened his mouth, stuck his tongue out, and rolled it around in the standard fashion. He never saw the orderly's nightstick shoot through the door opening, only felt the impact at the base of his throat, driving him backward, leaving a choking gasp in his wake.

"Punk!"

When Percy, back against the wall, looked up, they were gone. He gingerly felt the soft spot just below his Adam's apple, swallowing tentatively. When he heard the cart leave Winky's cell, Percy crouched at the toilet and jammed two fingers down his throat. He gagged, coughed, sputtered — but did not vomit. After a time he gave up. Cursing to himself, he slumped down on the sagging bunk. The cold fingers of resignation pulled at his spirit as he anticipated the medication's inevitable course, flowing and whistling down the staircases of his body, through the corridors of his mind, seeping into his psyche like red-eye gravy on cat-head biscuits. Within an hour Percy would be unconscious. Tomorrow, after perhaps sixteen hours of sleep, he would awake, spacy, groggy, and lethargic. Later, the terrible muscle cramps and spasms would humble him further.

Percy's gaze slid around the bare cell, gliding over the cobbled graffiti, the variegated stains impregnating walls and ceiling, the naked, solitary light bulb defiantly clawing at the pressing darkness. Cast shadows abounded, mottled, leavening the air with a weighted, tangible scent of bleakness. Only the tired floor, worn smooth by legions of shuffling feet, remained free of blemish, save for the rough corner patch bearing the unmistakable marks of some desperate soul sharpening steel. Percy sighed.

At least, Percy reflected, it was not Prolixin. Six months earlier, following his arrest, when he first purposed to play crazy, he was strenuously warned by fellow prisoners to avoid Prolixin shots at all costs. When Percy was in fact given a shot, he learned why. Each shot, he was duly advised, lasts two full weeks. The first three days were uneventful, but on the fourth the drug kicked him like a government mule. At once Percy felt the change. It began with horrific muscle contractions and spasms, locking his jaw in a clenched position and pinning his head to his left shoulder. His arms drew up like a spastic's, and he drooled uncontrollably. Prolixin's side effects, he was told, were known to kill, and Percy became a believer. The prisoners called patients on Prolixin "crispy critters" or "bacon" for the way their bodies drew up, making them choke and gag like epileptic hunchbacks. Percy, too, drew up, slobbering and gagging on his thick tongue, certain of the nearness of death in that solitary cell. Sometimes the nurses would give him a shot of Benadryl or Akineton, bringing quick relief for a few hours; more often he was ignored, and occasionally mocked.

As terrible as the physical side effects were, the mental ones were worse. The drug changed the very way Percy thought, the mental process itself, shaking his concept of who he was in a manner impossible to articulate to others. Percy became agitated, restless, unable to sleep, unable to sit still, unable to concentrate on any task. A void filled his mind, crowding out all desire for anything, leaving behind only a frightened husk. Like a detached spectator observing a distant phenomenon, some part of him recognized that his mind itself, the most basic essence of who he was, had been altered. The fear that the change was permanent terrified Percy. By the tenth day he was debating suicide to escape the unbearable mental anguish. Only the faint, desperate hope that he might return to normal in due time kept him alive. On the fourteenth day, as sure as if a switch were thrown, he was suddenly normal again. He was back. At that moment he vowed to die before accepting another Prolixin shot.

Percy blinked hard, fighting the medicine. He ached for a cigarette. Slowly he lay back, stretching out his frame. His rancid pillow stank, even through the two T-shirts wrapped around it. But now it did not matter to him. At that moment the moon became visible in the small slit window high up on the back wall. Percy considered standing up on his bunk, stretching to take in the vast yellow orb. He had always considered the moon to be a friend, sharing his private solitude with a perfect understanding, devoid of judgment, eager to loan out its soft, limpid light to the whole round earth . . . Percy blinked again. He was weary. He struggled to keep his eyes open . . . Having feigned insanity with sufficient dexterity to secure a 120-day order of commitment to the forensic unit of the state hospital, he still had almost 60 more days to go. He wondered if he could make it, wondered if he should. The price was high.

Upon arrival, Percy had been placed in an open-bay ward with sixty other nut cases, mostly pretrial detainees awaiting competency examinations. Some were there for degrees of homicide, others for relatively petty crimes like Percy's—a drunken encounter with a convenience store clerk over some shoplifted pastries that had somehow escalated into a felony battery when Percy pushed and ran. Because it would be his third conviction, it was a very serious matter to Percy. At the hospital he quickly learned that prisoners from the nearby state penitentiary, called runners, ran the place with a casual brutality alarming in its arbitrariness. It was a zoo, raw survival of the fittest, pitiless and cruel for those patients who were genuinely mentally ill and unsophisticated in the ways of doing time. The rank scent of quiet desperation clung to everything.

Late one night, shortly after his arrival, Percy awoke with a start. He stared up into the darkness. He disliked going into the large communal bathroom after lights-out. Strange things occurred in there, and hearing them was bad enough. On that night, though, his bladder insisted. Treading through the dim dormitory, he stepped into the expansive bathroom, passed the gang showers, and stood at one of the urinals. He thought he was alone.

A low moaning cut Percy off in midstream. He looked around, saw nothing. He strained at the urinal, staring at the wall. The sound returned, sliding along the tiles, echoing off the porcelain, spiraling into a guttural, animalistic quaver that made his neck hairs stand on end. Percy wheeled about, eyes wide, searching the darkness. There, barely discernible in the corner, was a shadowy figure, hunkered down, squatting atop a toilet like a perched bird poised to lay an egg, one foot on each side of the rim. Percy strained to see. The figure appeared to be staring upward, as though lost in a trance.

As Percy watched, a long, horrible groan escaped from the figure's lips, a cry of anguish so wrenching that it seemed torn from his very soul. At that moment an orderly opened a door across the hall and a shaft of light fell through a bathroom window and across the tile floor, fully illuminating the corner for an awful instant. The horrific scene revealed to Percy would be forever burned into his mind. In that moment of terrible recognition, Percy saw Benjamin, a seriously disturbed young man charged with murdering his own mother. Percy's numb mind struggled to comprehend the scene. Benjamin's entire hand was inserted into his rectum, his face turned upward, twisted in torment. Before Percy's shocked eyes, Benjamin pulled out his hand, tightly gripping a handful of bloody offal and intestines. Benjamin's howl of agony pierced the night air, striking to the quick of Percy's soul.

Percy ran. He confronted an orderly, yelled, and pointed. No big deal, he was told. Benjamin had done this before. He was punishing himself. They took Benjamin away, and Percy never saw him again. Percy was not easily shocked, but he found no sleep that night, and for the first time in years he prayed.

The next week an elderly patient supposedly hanged himself, but the word was that the two runners who were terrorizing and extorting money from him had hung him up. The circumstances were very suspicious, but there was no investigation. Percy watched, saw, recognizing that in this place death was just a word.

A few weeks later Percy stepped into the shower, only to slip and fall. Bracing his hand on the floor to get up, he found himself covered in semicoagulated blood, a shocking amount coating the entire floor like a fetid varnish of claret putrescence. A patient, he learned, had castrated himself with a razor blade. The incident had not even caused a ripple on the ward.

For Percy, though, the denouement came several weeks later. In a semiprivate room attached to the ward lay Harold, a state prisoner who some years earlier had climbed inside an industrial soap-making machine to clean it. Somehow the machine had been switched on, mangling Harold, cutting off both arms and one leg and knocking a patch out of his skull. Harold was a mess. Invalid, a little bit retarded, he resided permanently at the hospital. One afternoon Percy was peering through the small patch of bare glass in the painted-over window separating ward from room. It was his daily custom to tap on the glass and call a few words of encouragement to Harold, try to make him smile. On that day, though, Percy was shocked to see Harold being raped by two runners, his feeble struggles for naught. Percy would never forget the forlorn look of resignation seared on Harold's turned face, the tears streaking his cheeks. The scene sent an arrow into Percy's heart.

Percy snapped. Picking up a wooden bench from the day-room, he threw it through the window into Harold's room. Before the shattered glass finished falling, he broke off a chair leg and charged through the opening, clubbing the runners with unbridled ferocity. Within moments Percy, too, was beaten down by a flood of orderlies and runners, bound in leather handcuffs, and injected with a massive dose of Thorazine. Then he was thrown into the solitary confinement cell, where the friendly lemon moon was smiling down through his narrow slit window.

Percy sighed again. The medication was on him. His eyes fluttered, closed. He was tired of fighting against the drugs. There was so much he was tired of. With a final effort he struggled to stand, looking up through his window, smiling at the broad-faced moon. Percy reflected on his situation, wondering how best to measure the value of this journey. The things he had seen were beyond belief, taxing his spirit perhaps more than he was willing to pay. Prison now seemed a reasonable alternative, a place he at least understood, not one beyond belief.

Percy watched the pine trees swaying in the darkness, rooted in red clay, reaching up to the bright stars. *Your heart decides what your head will believe,* he decided. *Perhaps the brightest and darkest lie next to each other in all of our souls.* For the second time in recent memory, Percy prayed, this time with sincerity so direct and strong that it cut itself, like the facets of a diamond, into the deepest chambers of his heart. Then Percy Brown stretched out on his bunk and fell into a deep yet troubled sleep.

The following afternoon, per his request, Percy was escorted to the office of the chief psychiatrist, a short, elderly, balding Vietnamese man wearing thick, heavy-framed glasses on a heavily scarred face. As Percy, in handcuffs and leg irons, entered the office, it occurred to him that in all his years in jails and prisons, he had never met an American doctor. He sat in the hard plastic chair. The conditioned air felt barely cool and smelled stale. A lone window, covered by a heavy-gauge, gray steel-wire screen, was tightly sealed against the dense rain silently sheeting down the glass. A low, leaden sky seemed to press its weight down upon the building.

Across from Percy, the doctor sat at his desk, ignoring him, reading a case file. It was very quiet except for the loud ticking of an unseen clock. The doctor's pen scratched as he wrote in the file. Percy glanced around, unable to locate the clock. The doctor, he noted, was absently toying with a pair of shiny stainless steel tweezers. The doctor looked up, staring at Percy as though surprised to find him there.

"I want to go back to the jail."

"Oh?"

The ticking expanded to fill the small room. Percy looked around again, uncertain of words or thoughts. He knew he was sweating. Where was that damn clock, anyway?

"I . . . I can't take this place anymore."

"I see." The doctor slowly twirled the needle-nosed tweezers while staring at Percy.

"Look," Percy said, exhaling loudly, "I don't belong here. I'm not crazy. Not at all. In fact, I'm just playing crazy, see? Playing. I fooled the doctor at the jail. I was just trying to beat my case."

"Fooled the doctor?"

"Yeah."

"Fooled Dr. Trung?"

"Yeah. I'm facing the third strike. Automatic life, you know? For a lousy box of Little Debbie snack cakes."

"So you fooled him, you think?"

"Yeah, I think." The clock ticked away. Percy wiped the sweat from his brow. His thigh muscle spasmed, and the leg jumped involuntarily.

The doctor eyed him closely and then wrote something on his chart. "No need to beat your case now?"

"Man, I don't care now." Percy vigorously rubbed his eyes with both palms. The medication made his eyes itch and water. "I'll go crazy if I stay here."

"Go crazy?"

"Yeah."

"Your medication will prevent that."

"Shit. I don't take that junk."

"Oh?"

"That's only for crazy guys." Percy's eyes itched terribly, and he rubbed them again. "I just told you, I'm not crazy."

"I see." The doctor scribbled something else in the file. "Why do you believe you will go crazy here?"

"The shit I've seen here, it's unbelievable. I've never seen shit like this, not even in jail or prison. This place is evil. Needs to be closed down, you ask me. Crazy shit."

"Crazy?"

Percy arched his back suddenly and then shook out his cramping leg. He ached all over. He was very tired. He wanted out. Now. So he told the doctor everything he had seen. Percy spoke of beatings and rapes, of nightsticks and cattle prods, and of runners amok. He told about suicides and castrations, of poor Benjamin and retarded Harold. He omitted nothing. He spoke of his friend the moon, with its perfect understanding. He told how he had prayed, really prayed, until the gates of hell itself felt the ponderous stroke, prayed with sincerity as certain as God's promises to Abraham and his seed. He explained God's promise that he was covered in mercies, a promise that now shone bright and perfect in its execution. And that, Percy explained, was why he could now return to the jail, shedding this fraud, this deception, like an old, ragged coat.

"And you believe all those things occurred here?"

"Sure. I saw them with my own eyes."

The doctor stared, toying with the tweezers. "And tell me, Mr. Nelson, do you still believe that your name is"—the doctor glanced at the open file—"Percy Brown?"

"Yeah. It is. I told you last time, I had fake ID. Nelson is just an alias, to fool the police. 'Course, it didn't work. Fingerprints, you know?" Percy offered up his hands. "Since they booked me under Nelson, Nelson it is."

"Fake?"

"Yeah."

"To fool them?"

"Yeah."

The clock continued ticking away, louder than ever. Percy's squinted eyes blinked rapidly. His leg jumped again. Sweat slid down his cheek.

"I see." The doctor scribbled more words, continuing to the next page. "And your suicide attempt?" The doctor nodded at the long cut navigating across Percy's neck like a black railroad track.

"Fake." Percy smiled weakly.

"Fake?"

"Yeah. Fake. Fake. Fake." Percy waved his cuffed hands like a conductor, emphasizing each word.

"To fool us?"

"Yeah."

"And last night, that was fake also?"

"Last night?"

"You dove off your sink." The doctor idly tapped the tweezers against a coffee mug.

"No. No, I didn't."

"I have the report."

"It's a lie."

"Both the nurse and the orderly witnessed it."

"They're lying. They just don't like me."

"Are they plotting against you?"

"Yeah, you can say that."

"I see." The doctor held the tweezers up, like a heron poised to spear an unsuspecting fish. "You may return to your cell, Mr. Nelson. Don't worry, I will arrange everything."

"That's it? I'll be going back to the jail?"

"I'll arrange everything—do not worry." The doctor smiled reassuringly.

"Thanks, doc. I'll be glad to get out of here, I'll tell you. Get visits. Cigarettes, canteen, telephone, recreation." Percy stood up, elated.

"Yes, I'm sure. Good-bye now." The doctor remained seated.

"Bye. Thanks again, doc."

Percy left the office, his leg chains tinkling and scraping on the shiny waxed floor.

The doctor stared out the window and then swiveled in his chair, turning on a tape recorder. After a moment he spoke into the machine, twirling the tweezers absently.

Patient is superficially persuasive, adept at faking sanity through innovative masking strategy of claiming he only feigns his psychosis. Diagnosis: patient is severely delusional, with confirmed identity crisis, demonstrating psychotic thought processes and exhibiting paranoid personality disorder. . . . Chronic suicidal tendencies noted . . . Probable psychoactive substance dependence. . . . Prognosis: poor. Recommend petitioning court for six-month extension of commitment order for long-term treatment. . . . Increase dosages of current medications, institute regimen of Prolixin injections.

Laos Chuman

When I first read "Diary of a Lifetime in Blue," my breath caught in my throat and I felt a shudder run through my body. I was moved by the power of the written word to convey the anguish and pain that human beings can inflict on one another. "Diary of a Lifetime in Blue" is a memoir. "I took a chance writing this down, but I didn't think anything would come of it," Laos Chuman said with a catch in his voice, but with his soft gold-flecked eyes holding mine. Laos is a writer with a startling story to tell.

I recognized him the moment he entered the room. I had seen him on a TV show with Kristy McNichol a long time ago. Laos looked older, but he was still handsome. His dark hair had streaks from the sun, and he looked fit and tan. He moved with grace, and he seemed comfortable in his body. He had a gentle handshake; he smiled and said, "I am so glad you finally made it here."

"Writing is a loner's craft," he told me as we sat down together on a beautiful California day at the Men's Colony in San Luis Obispo.

I had to ask, "What made you decide to write 'Diary of a Lifetime in Blue'?"

Laos took a breath and said, "I have been holding on to that story for twenty years. It seemed like it might be time for it to come out, and writing is the only vehicle I have. I never looked at myself as a writer at all. Once I got into prison, I found myself very limited, because the theater was my first love. When I am writing I am alone, and I start thinking about the past, and it can put me in a mood. I don't think of myself as a writer, because I only write nonfiction."

Thus on that clear but cool May afternoon we began our conversation about writing, his twenty-four years in prison, and how he has grown up in Folsom, Vacaville, Tracy, Soledad, and for the past ten years here at the Men's Colony. "I don't think I'm a writer. I just think I am in a place where I need an outlet. It is such a struggle for me."

I have heard that same refrain so many times from so many

writers, and when I said as much to Laos, he laughed and said, "Yes, but I struggle with your language. I grew up with so many languages. My mom speaks to me in Italian, and I spoke Spanish, so I struggle with English as well as writing." His accented English was melodious as he spoke of writing and his love for theater and dance and all things creative. His eyes lit up when he talked of the creativity that surrounded him when he moved with his family from Peru to New York City. His mother was a clothing designer and in the theater, and he told me, "I loved to sing and dance." He discovered at an early age that he was different from his friends. "When I was fifteen, my friends were looking at girls, and I was looking at guys." He is comfortable with who he is now, but that was a different time, when he was a naive young man moving in the fast lane, in over his head.

He told me, "I was young, gullible, and ambitious. I wanted to succeed. When I was twenty I got a contract to do a television advertisement for Coke, and they paid me $50,000, so I thought I was pretty hot shit. I was working a lot; I was getting acting jobs in television. Everything was happening very fast for me. All of my friends were pretty much like that. Everyone was surprised when my crime happened. I was the good boy. Everyone said, Not Laos." He talked about being twenty and living with Margaux Hemingway across from the French Embassy in New York. Laos said, "I was over my head. I was lying to myself."

Laos is serving a twenty-five-to-life sentence for murder. It was a sensational case, with headlines that might have read, "Opportunistic Gold Digger Kills Homosexual Lover in a Fit of Rage." The murder of Robert Gottschalk, the head of Panavision, stunned Hollywood in 1983. After Laos told me his story, he sat back, looked at me, and said, "I thought I knew it all, but I didn't know anything. I regret it. He was a nice man. I will regret it always."

Laos has learned a tremendous amount about himself during his time in prison. At fifty-two, he lives by the motto "Do all that you can, in the time that you have, in the place that you are." He is conscious of the fact that he has spent so many years in prison that he is out of touch with the world beyond the prison walls. "Your world is a world I don't know anymore. I live here. I know this world pretty well."

The prison world is something that Laos knows very well, and he has done noteworthy things within this system. In 1990, he was in the California Medical Facility, in Vacaville, where a number of his friends were dying of AIDS—alone. Laos and three friends wrote a proposal to the warden. The warden granted approval, and the hospice program was initiated. But that wasn't enough: "We got the legislature involved, and they gave us eight and a half million dollars to fund the hospice program. I was the coordinator." The program still exists, and Laos was able to start the same program at the Men's Colony. "No one here has to die alone. Before you die, there are no more pretenses; you get to be yourself." He went on to tell me, "These men who are dying have given me more than I give them, just by sitting with them and talking to them."

Laos was also involved in the first exhibition of a prison AIDS quilt, and he sewed it all by hand painstakingly, one stitch at a time, in memory of his friends. It was a massive undertaking at twelve feet by twenty feet, and it had the names of all the prisoners who had died of AIDS in Vacaville. "It is a rainbow flag, and there are four prisoners of different races dressed in prison uniforms standing behind bars," Laos explained. "We used actual prison clothes." Laos and his friends had to buy all the materials themselves, and it took about a month to complete this arduous task. It was an educational experience, and "it brought everyone together." Laos is the only surviving member of the group, and there is pride and sadness in his voice as he talks about the others who worked so hard to bring awareness about HIV/AIDS to the prison community.

His next project is already in the works: "I am writing a proposal right now to establish an art program that would be paid for by the prisoners themselves." Laos explained that prisoners can buy art supplies at the canteen using money earned by working. The money made by the sale of the artwork produced would be fed back into the program. He added, "Ninety percent of the money would go to a women's shelter, and ten percent would go back to the prisoners to buy supplies." He is hopeful that his proposal will be accepted by the administration.

Laos has a great sense of humor, and he laughed and said that he is good at putting together proposals, but he can't draw a lick. He does these things because he cares about people. Laos is a sensitive soul, something that is rare after all the years he has spent confined. "Some people change and become old and bitter because of doing so much time, and they feel that they don't have any hope anymore," he said. "And the way I look at it is, yes, I may spend the rest of my life here, but I used to pray, even when I was in the hole: please don't let me become old and bitter." Laos is anything but bitter. He was lively and fun when we talked; he was real and touching, and it was difficult for me to believe that he had been locked away from the world for almost a quarter of a century.

Laos seems unique in that he views the Men's Colony as his home and therefore something to be maintained with care. He refers to his cell as his house and told me that he waters the yard where they play soccer three times a week as a matter of course, because he likes it green. "I don't even lie down in the grass," he said. "I would never do that, but I like it green, and I love to play soccer." At this he laughed out loud, and it was nice to hear. His fellow prisoners do not understand why he would do anything to beautify state property, but Laos just shrugs it off and said, "This is my home, and I may die here, so I want it to be as nice as it can be."

Laos has found solace in his spirituality, which is very important to his well-being. He has tried several denominations, but nothing felt right until he found Buddhism. "My spirituality is so important. I am a Buddhist. As long as I am okay mentally and spiritually, as long as I stay centered, I am okay. I like where I am today; I like being fifty-two, and even though a lot of my experiences have been in prison, because I have been here twenty-four years, that's okay too. The outside world seems like a dream."

There is a strong Buddhist community at the Men's Colony, and there is strong support from the outside community. Laos has found comfort and support from the monks who come from San Luis Obispo once a month, and that is something that he was unable to find in the Christian denominations, where he was shunned because of his sexuality. "When we lock in and I can meditate for an hour, it is lovely. I can find peace," he said. There is a serenity about Laos; there is a sense of acceptance of who he is, of what he can and cannot change, and of the fact that he is doing the best he can to be all that he can, given his circumstances.

"In prison I have tried to accept that while I committed a terrible crime, it is not who I am. Yes, it is something that I did, but it does not encompass who I am," Laos said. "I learned in prison I can't lie to myself anymore. I regret what I did; I regret it more than anything." He was standing in front of a barred window, light pouring in around him, illuminating his face, talking to me about his decades of growth in prison. He looked ethereal. "I don't lose hope. Until the day I draw my last breath, I will have hope."   —SUSAN NAGELSEN

Diary of a Lifetime in Blue

LAOS CHUMAN

July 2, 1987

One tedious day follows another, identical, where I spend oppressive days searching for answers. But I cannot find them, and I tell myself perhaps it is better that way. It's been four years since I started my twenty-five-to-life sentence for a crime of passion. It's also been three years since I left, in the dark of night, the antiquated and infamous Folsom State Prison. Tomorrow once again I will be transferred from CMF (California Medical Facility) to DVI (Duel Vocational Institute) in Tracy. But not out of my own free will. Ha—am I delusional to believe I have any choices or any kind of voice? Let's be real, Laos. I'm just a number with a picture ID and a file. I'm somewhat scared of the unknown. Can you blame me? After all, we humans are creatures of habit, and for the most part, I don't want to leave this place where I've developed friendships. But who am I fooling, to believe or even conceive the notion I have an alternative? I've lost my precious freedom along with everything that ever meant anything to me. Nothing seems to make sense anymore, including my spiritual and moral belief system. I suppose I'm a pariah, cast out from the world and thrown on a ship without a rudder, destination unknown.

There are moments, though, when I fancy and torture myself that I will wake up from this nightmare—any time now! But reality is harsh. I have a new world now where life is cold and futile and earth is a sanctuary of sorrow. I don't think I'll ever adjust to this place, to this strange way of life. I must be in hell. I never imagined I had the capacity to feel the profundity of loneliness and despair. I ask myself, why didn't I see when they shut me out of the world? Because now I sit here despairing. I think of nothing else; this fate gnaws at my mind. There are so many unanswered questions. How in the world did I ever end up here when I had so many things to do outside? But it just happened so quickly. The beautiful life was brief, and destiny arrived in some haste.

I hate good-byes, but tomorrow with my face, my words, and my ways I shall offer them to those whose lives have touched mine, leaving smiles as soft as the wind, guiding me past the storms and sharing with me the sun. I will remember them, those happy strangers. If only I could have stayed here long enough to sweeten my life, but I just turned around and they are gone with the season, leaving behind a photograph and the memory of their laughter. I will remember them, those happy strangers, and I will smile, because I am happy that on my journey they cared enough to walk a mile or two with me.

July 3, 1987

Prior to daybreak, we were hauled into the bus like cattle, handcuffed and shackled. Swiftly we traveled through some dusty back roads, and I couldn't help but amuse myself imagining that, like a vampire racing with the night to avoid dawn, we were racing against daylight to reach our destination. God forbid society would have to take a look at the bus carrying the damned. Luckily, as the sun rose, it turned out to be a clear beautiful summer morning with no breeze. Just the warmth of a summer morning slowly rising. And in the distance you could see seagulls making their way toward the west. The anticipation had been overwhelming; after all, it had been three years since I'd seen anything other than these prison walls. The mere fact that I was about to get a peek at the outside world was exciting. I was lucky to get a window seat by myself in the back row and avoid the rest of the crew gathered up front, making a racket. I remained still, hoping I wouldn't be noticed by the inmates and have to participate in small talk. I tried to shut the noise out as I reflected on what I would do on a beautiful day like this. Most likely with my camera in hand I would get on my bike and head to the beach for the day. Those memories seem like a stranger I knew long ago. From my vantage point, I observed people going about their morning chores, oblivious of the bus. The visual spectrum of colors and people moving about was refreshing in comparison to my world of blue. But after some time I was overwhelmed with emotion and sobbed as I sat watching daily life pass before my eyes, trying to accept this life I did not want, when my soul searches and weeps for other things.

In other instances, some people recognized the twenty-foot-high Greyhound bus converted to the menacing black bus with its tinted windows. You could see the fear in people's eyes as they glanced at the bus carrying society's outcasts. The stigma is quite apparent. I wanted to shout, "Please don't be afraid—I'm not a monster. I'm a human being." I was glad when we were in close proximity to the prison.

Inside the new prison's boundaries, the outside world's discernment quickly dissipated as my awareness shifted to the familiar stench and monotony of prison life with its rules and regulations, strip and cavity searches. I'll never get used to the humiliating strip searches. I expected to be housed with another inmate for the next ten days, until Classification reviews my file. I don't get it—why ten days? After all, my file arrives with me. But I don't make the rules. A lot of these rules have no logic behind them. They seem like they're decided on whims, because they last for a short while at the very most.

I was apprehensive about a cellie until an Indian guy who arrived with me on the bus asked me to cell up with him for the duration. I didn't know him but had seen him around CMF. In fact, he lived on the same tier I did, but we never spoke. I agreed without any further thought. But for some reason, once the cell door was locked, I was overcome by a premonition that I had made the biggest mistake. It was the way he looked at me. I'd seen the glare of lust and desire in people's eyes before but knew well enough to stay away from certain people and predicaments. Unfortunately, I couldn't walk out of the room; I was trapped.

My solution was to alert the CO, but on second thought, I would be labeled a snitch, and that is a dangerous label in prison—it follows you, makes your life miserable, and puts you in danger. I didn't know what to do. I was alone and scared. We were like two animals in a cage with no resolution other than to confront each other.

I had to think fast. The cell smelled and was filthy beyond words. The temperature was over 100 degrees outside and in the cell. Regardless, I did not want to shed my clothes. He wasted no time and took everything off but his underpants. He attempted to get my clothes off with the notion of how hot it was in the cell. I couldn't agree more, but I resisted his argument. He was persistent, and when he couldn't get me to take my clothes off, he confessed his lustful desires for me.

I was terrified, didn't know what to do, and I was unable to respond. Fear does that to me sometimes. So instead, I ignored him and attempted to climb up to my bunk, but before I got the chance to put one foot on the rail, he grabbed me by the neck, pulled me down against the wall, and continued to press my neck while he declared what he wanted from me. Frightened by his sudden outburst of fury, I managed some courage and got a few words out and vehemently refused to comply with his orders. This didn't make it any easier for me, because each time I rejected him, he punched me all over my body. This went on until I could no longer bear the pain and could actually feel the life go out of me. I tried to scream for help, but when no one came to my rescue, I had no choice but to give in. When it was over he patted me on my head and fell asleep on his bunk. Sobbing and lying on the floor, bleeding from my rectum, I felt filthy beyond words. I hated myself for my weakness and for not being able to resist his force and abusive demands.

July 14, 1987

Wallowing in my own misery, I lay on my bunk all day and refused to eat. I tortured myself with the knowledge that life is cold and futile, wanting a life I couldn't have. For the next ten days I hardly ate or slept, and the few times I went to chow to seek help, I failed; I remained silent and helpless. I had no voice among strangers in this friendless world. I was alone. All I knew was that I wanted to live beyond the ten days. When I did get some sleep, it was out of exhaustion. In spite of it, he never felt pity or compassion for me; rather, he threatened that if I told anyone, he would find a way to kill me, and he continued to beat me each time I refused his advances until I submitted. He was ruthless.

On the morning of the tenth day, I felt nothing; something had died inside of me. Nothing mattered to me anymore. I couldn't reason or fathom how another person could treat a human being like a disposable Dixie cup. When the cell door opened, I walked out without saying a word or looking at him. I got in line and waited to be called for my cell assignment. A few minutes later, I felt his presence and smelled him behind me, whispering into my ear, reminding me what he would do if I told anyone. Without acknowledging him, I walked away, got into another line, and waited for my turn. After I was interviewed, I was given my new house number. I looked around, but he was nowhere to be seen. I asked the clerk for directions to RSR (Receiving and Release) to pick up my property. With my property in hand, I headed to my cell.

Unlike CMF, which had individual floors, DVI had three floors with open tiers. To my surprise the cell was empty. Great! No cellie, or so I thought until a few minutes later. While I was cleaning the cell, the same clerk who had given me directions earlier appeared at the door with a box in hand.

"Hi, my name is Steve. I'm moving in with you. Wait a minute—didn't you ask for some directions a moment ago?"

My first reaction was to reply, "Why are you moving in here?" but instead I said, "Yes, I did," and shook his hand as I introduced myself. I was doubtful and trusted no one, but I kept my composure and told him to wait a few minutes until I finished cleaning. He was very talkative, took no for an answer, and immediately started helping me and asking a lot of questions. He appeared to be a happy-go-lucky person without a care in the world. But I knew better than to rely on appearances. Or did I? After all, I didn't want to make the same mistake, but how will I know other people's real intentions? Nonetheless, he was a blessing in disguise, because his cheerful chatter kept me out of my head, out of my emotional turmoil.

August 7, 1987

I've been living with Steve for over three weeks, and I've concluded that I don't have anything to fear about him. He's respectful, witty, and considerate, and most of all clean. He's your typical twenty-eight-year-old, born and raised in Northern California, with long brown hair, and in prison for possession of drugs. He tells me that he feels bad for me because I have a long time to do. I told him to spare me the pity, and to alleviate his sympathy I added, "What is time, anyway? Isn't the moment, the now, what really matters most, for tomorrow may never come?" He somewhat agreed, but I think it was too deep for him. Anyhow, I need to document a funny story.

A week and a half ago, about 2 A.M., I woke up for some reason and saw Steve sitting on the toilet. Upon seeing me he said, "I'm sorry, I didn't mean to wake you up but I had to take a piss."

"It's okay, no bother, you didn't wake me up," I responded. Then I wryly asked him, "But tell me, do you always sit on the toilet when you take a piss? I don't recall seeing you do that before."

"Ha-ha—that's very funny, Laos. No, of course not, silly, but I make it a habit to do so late at night when you are asleep so I don't wake you up. I hope you do the same for me," he answered.

I wasn't surprised by his thoughtfulness and replied right away, "Promise I'll do the same for you."

Steve has taken it upon himself to be my guide, always by my side and introducing me to his friends. I'm beginning to feel stronger now that I'm eating and sleeping regularly. I'm trying my best to forget what happened, but I can't. It haunts me, and it makes me feel angry and helpless. I don't know what other people see when they look at me, but when I look at myself in the mirror I feel angry and ashamed.

August 10, 1987

I've been forgetting to write down that a week after classification I got a job sweeping and mopping tiers. But after a few days into the job my boss told me that he had reviewed my file and confirmed what he had suspected: I don't need to be sweeping tiers, because I have a college background. He asked the assignment office to reassign me to a suitable position. What could I say? I wanted to tell him I didn't want a new job, that I was happy sweeping floors, but I had no choice but to comply with the order. Within a few days I was reassigned to the captain's office as a clerk. The offices are clean and air-conditioned, and only the chosen few get to work there because there's a lot of female staff. I'm lucky to be away from population most of the day and in a different environment. I've learned that staff are clueless about this place, even though they spend five days a week here. Their rules and belief systems don't apply in here. As far as I am concerned, they are naive, but they think they know what life in here is like. I can't deny that in comparison to my arrival, my living and working conditions have improved dramatically. But then again, I'm not surprised because my life has always been one extreme or another, never in between. Odd but true. I am content for the time being, but the reality of being raped continues to haunt me. Sometimes I can't sleep at night, and I think that perhaps I should have a doctor look at me or find someone to talk to about it. I need help.

August 15, 1987

I am so happy today! I received tons of mail; okay, about ten pieces. Still, in comparison to the majority in here who get mail, it's a lot. I cried when I read letters from my mom, sister, and friends. I miss them so much. I miss my life with them. I wish I could speak with my sister to tell her what happened—not that it would change anything—but I better not because it will only burden them, so I won't tell them. She wants me to call her up ASAP, but I'm not sure when because she always knows when something is wrong with me. I've never been able to hide anything from her. I have to get stronger before I call her. Meantime, I will write immediately to her and my friends.

Steve continues to be a solid friend. I am so grateful for his friendship. DVI has an enormous yard. In fact, it's bigger than Folsom and three times bigger than CMF: twelve handball courts, two tennis courts, four basketball courts, a running track, four separate areas for each race (black, Mexican, white, and other) with weights to work out, and to top it off, an Olympic-size swimming pool below an officer's tower at one end of the yard. Steve says that unlike other prisons, this place has these amenities because it used to be a youth authority institution. In other words, I suppose, this is not your typical prison. I couldn't believe it until I saw it with my own eyes. I was beside myself, since all I could think of was that it had been four long years since I'd been in a pool. I dove in and tried to forget all my sorrows. Day after day, Steve, his friends, and I play tennis after work and then go swimming at nighttime until closing time. His friends are protective toward me, and when Steve is away they never leave me alone. I appreciate their friendship and company, especially John, who is burly and stands six feet five inches tall. He is very witty and calls me "little brother." He's taken it upon himself to school me on prison etiquette. I trust him and pay attention to his advice. All of these guys have been down for a long time and know the tricks of the trade. I feel safe around them.

Regardless, I'm a fool to believe I can run away from this knot inside of me that perpetually haunts me. And although the yard is enormous, the distance is never big enough when I see the Indian lurking in the distance, watching me have fun with my new friends. Each time I see him, I get angry, especially when I see him look in my direction and laugh. Each time I want to hide, but instead I act as if his presence doesn't bother me. Steve by now knows me well enough to suspect something is bothering me. He's asked me numerous times, but I always conceal it from him. John has noticed it, too, but he's been more direct and inquired if anyone has done anything to me. I've said no, because I'm not ready to speak to him about it. I'm ashamed.

August 26, 1987

How time flies! It's been a hectic day at work in the captain's office, full of drama. I get to read a lot of info I'm not supposed to and learn about prison politics between administrators. I must have typed ten reports today and done just about everything anyone asked me to do. I've always been quick to respond under pressure. My boss is a nice lady, middle-aged and petite, with blond hair and a wonderful motherly disposition. I can tell she likes me; she is always asking all sorts of questions. I don't mind. I'm told that this job is considered a "juice" job among the prisoners. However, to me it's just another prison job, and my way of thinking is like the Buddhists': whether you're sweeping floors or in a high position, do it mindfully.

The other day I decided to use my juice and look into files for any information concerning the Indian. I found out where he lives, works, and some other nonconfidential information. He is a lifer, and he's been down for a long time already. I'm curious now about his crime and whether it resembles his characteristics. It will take longer to find out. I've also noticed that he rarely goes anywhere and mostly stays in his tier, where he works as a porter. Mind you, I'm not complaining, because I detest seeing him. I don't trust him. What bothers me most is that when I see him on the yard he's been hanging out with two Spanish guys, and when he thinks I'm not looking his way, he points in my direction. I'm scared, but I refuse to let him or my fears govern my life.

September 1, 1987

I can't believe it, but today is the twenty-first anniversary of the day my mother brought my brother, sister, and me from Lima, Peru, to live in West New York, New Jersey, right across from New York City. We were so young, full of hope and dreams. A time when we enjoyed another life. But that seems like a dream now, because I have a new world now.

September 25, 1987

Lately Steve has been sharing his personal life. I was curious why he never gets any mail. He says that his family has cut him loose for doing drugs, but that he no longer has the need and wants to clean up his act. I hope so, because he's a nice person. He feels bad because he doesn't contribute to the household. I told him that he shouldn't worry about money, and to make him feel better I told him that sometimes people contribute more in other ways, that money isn't everything. I don't mind sharing what most people hold of value: money and material things. In any case, he keeps the cell spotless and does the laundry to compensate for the food I bring in the cell.

October 1, 1987

If September was an Indian summer, it extended to October. The temperature refuses to let down. Sure would be nice to get a cool breeze, but so much for wishful thinking. These cells are so hot; it feels like being in a kiln, cooking between stones. A lot has happened lately; my life continues to be one extreme or another. But first I'll start with Steve and his passion for TV.

I've never met anyone who loves to watch television as much as he does. I don't object to anything he wants to watch on TV because I prefer reading a book. However, that was until last week when I got back from work. As usual, Steve was sprawled on his bunk watching his afternoon shows. He greeted me without taking his eyes off the TV, at which time I saw what he was watching as I sat on my bunk to undress before taking a shower. Alarmed, I couldn't think of anything to say fast enough and instead reached for the TV and changed the channel. By the look on Steve's face, he was surprised yet annoyed, and protested, "Hey, I'm watching this movie! What's wrong with you?"

In my defense, all I could think to say was, "It's my TV, and I have the right to watch what I want, since I never object to anything you want to watch."

"What is it with you, Laos? What's so important that you have to watch right now?" he retorted. I didn't know what else to say and remained silent. "That's what I thought, nothing! What's wrong with you lately, anyway?" he inquired. "Come to think of it, there's a guy in the movie who looks just like you." I stood fixed in place without saying a word as he reached for the TV and turned it back to the movie. At exactly that moment, the guy who looked like me was on the screen, and it took Steve but a second to realize who it was. "It is you!" he exclaimed. "Why didn't you tell me you are an actor?"

I gave up and said, "It's not a good movie anyway. You don't want to see it."

"But I do," he responded, and lo and behold he got up and yelled through the cell door window across the tiers to his friends and for everyone else to hear, "Hey, guys! Turn to channel twelve. My cellie is on TV in a movie with Kristy McNichol." By then I thought it was useless to object to anything, and instead of showering, I sat down with Steve to watch the rest of the 1980 CBS Movie of the Week, *Blinded by the Light,* the movie I appeared in with Kristy McNichol, who at the time was at the height of her career.

Ten minutes after the 4:30 P.M. count cleared, the tiers were released for chow. Instead of following the standard routine of forming a line and making their way out of the wing to chow, a mob of inmates gathered in front of our cell, while others leaned against the rails to get a look at me. Needless to say, I felt threatened at the sight of the crowd, because in prison the only time you see a crowd is when there's a riot or something is about to happen. In this rare situation, I was the instant celebrity. *Nightmare on Elm Street,* I thought to myself as I looked at

Steve and sought his help. Two guys reached out their hands, introduced themselves, and expressed how much they enjoyed the movie and how they had always wanted to get into movies.

By then the commotion and the look on Steve's face said it all. "I'm sorry, I didn't know it would be like this," he whispered into my ear, and then he announced out loud that interviews would be scheduled later, but right now they had to make room to let us go to chow before it closed. I was nervous when the crowd booed him while I excused myself through the would-be inmate paparazzi.

October 10, 1987

Wow! I can't believe it, but ever since Steve announced to the tier I was an actor, the news has spread like wildfire to the rest of the wings. But then again, we live in a small community. I can't go anywhere without strangers introducing themselves, wanting to know about the movie business and how I got started; others simply want me to join them in sports. It appears they want to be my friends. For the most part I have been courteous, but I decline invitations to meet them at a later time. I don't think so! For all I know, they may have good intentions, but I don't trust many people yet. I'm grateful to have Steve and his friends as my support system. Especially big John; he's really cool, funny, and makes sure to warn me who to stay away from. I can always count on him to go swimming with me when everyone is busy. People respect him, and in many ways they know that if anyone messes with me, they mess with him, too. It's a good feeling.

The other night while Steve, John, and I were stargazing, John asked me, "Why didn't you tell us you used to be an actor? Why are you so secretive about your past life? If you don't know by now that we are your friends, you will never know."

In silence, I continued gazing into the venerable silence of the stars and realized how selfish and absorbed in my own sorrows I have been without considering their feelings. "I am so sorry! You guys are right—you have been my trusted friends ever since we met, so I'll tell you what: ask me anything you want to know about me, just ask. No more secrets."

I was certain I was ready to answer their questions but changed my mind when I heard John say, "That's good, Laos, that you are not afraid to open up to us, but we don't want to know anything you're not ready to tell us of your own free will. We know you are different from most people in here. We can see your awkwardness and know you don't belong here, and that's why we have taken you under our wing so no one harms you."

In response, I said, "Thank you. I really mean it. I'm really sorry for having been selfish, but this strange way of life is not easy for me. I'm suffering, and right now I'm not able to tell you any more than what I've said. I wanted to a few minutes ago, but after hearing John, I realize I'm not ready yet. I need more time, guys. Thank you for understanding. You have no idea how grateful I am for your friendship."

October 28, 1987

After all these months, I still can't shake the repulsive feeling I get whenever I see the Indian lurking in the shadows. I feel heat surging through my body, and I know it is anger. I can't take enough showers to get his filth off me. I feel dirty beyond words. I'm concerned that his two friends have moved into the tier. I don't like having them nearby. I don't trust their deceitful smiles, and I wonder if they know. They have already attempted to introduce themselves, but luckily for me, John happened to walk into the wing, and they immediately scampered away. John told me to stay away from them; he doesn't trust them and calls them shady characters. I couldn't agree more. But since then they have been brazen-faced, hanging around within a short distance of us.

November 20, 1987

Another catastrophe I never imagined fell upon me without any warning after my last entry. I knew I feared those shady characters for a good reason. A week ago I was let out early from work—rare—but I took the opportunity and left before they changed their minds. Most of the tier was at work around the time I got back, and the ones who weren't working were out in the yard. The tier was silent. Normally I shower with Steve, but I felt brave that day and decided to take one by myself. The first- and second-floor showers were closed. They were being painted, so I had to go to the third floor. I didn't like the idea of going upstairs, since it was away from everything, but I ventured anyway. The showers were empty, and in many ways it felt good to shower alone for a change, a rare occurrence in prison. But halfway through my shower, the two shady characters walked in, fully dressed, without their toiletries.

I knew there was something wrong, but before I could run away they rushed me. One of them held me while the other put a knife to my neck and forced me to get on my knees and perform fellatio on them. I refused, yet he kept pressing the knife, telling me that he would use it if I didn't comply. *I don't want to die!* was the only thought running through my mind. All at once, I felt helpless and had no choice but to comply. After it was over, they laughed at me as they wiped themselves with my towel, threw it on the ground, and walked away. I sobbed, sprawled out on the tile floor with the water running over me. Somehow I managed to get back to the cell without being noticed. Steve had already returned and greeted me as he pointed out that I was bleeding from my neck. I was unaware of it until he questioned me. In a quick response, I said that I had cut myself shaving in the shower and thought the bleeding had stopped.

December 1, 1987

Twenty-four more days before my birthday; I will age and grow gray in this desolate house. There is no future, no road or hope for me. My body, heart, and spirit ache, and winter is within me. My tears are colder than the ice and snow. In this little corner, I am an alien who resides in an unfortunate land.

December 7, 1987

Although I have tried, I haven't been the same since November 13. I haven't been convincing, because Steve and John are persistent and want to know what's wrong with me, but I can't tell them. I don't want them involved, because I'm somewhat aware of prison politics and I know what will happen if I tell them: a riot will start up and I will be the cause of it. I don't want any more blood on my hands. I can't allow them to fight my battles, and the possibility of someone getting hurt on my behalf is more than I can stand.

To add to my agony, a few days ago my sister sent me a short note on her way to Peru, relating that our grandmother is on her deathbed and that all of our family will be there except for me. I was given their phone number and am expected to call. I did and was told that Grandma had passed away but not before calling for me. I am devastated and disappointed that my family refused to tell her I was in prison, so she died not knowing the real truth why I couldn't be there. I will never forget Grandma, for she was my beacon of light, the one who insisted on teaching me our ancestors' (the Incas') original language. I remember her long silver hair, especially when she let it loose down to her waist at night. I will treasure the moments when she kissed me good night, saying, "Mima kuigi" (I love you), in Quechua. I'll never forget when she took me to Sacsayhuamán, the mighty fortress brooding breathless over Cuzco, navel of the universe, where we stood in awe watching ten-ton megaliths that had been rolled there from distant quarries; we marveled at the three-tiered giant serrate walls built a thousand years ago and due to stand for thousands more, defying flood and ice and wind and sun and quaking earth. She pointed out and we looked in admiration at the perfect fit of every joint, so closely formed, and she lovingly laughed at me when I tried to pry a stick into a crack. I will never forget Grandma and the last words she said to me the last time I saw her: "My little Peruvian prince, never forget where you came from, your roots."

December 23, 1987

I'm in the hole, and now I sit here despairing in this filthy, dark, and dingy cell with green graffiti on the walls. I suppose I should start from the beginning. Yesterday was the Christmas staff party—no inmates allowed, of course, but we lurked in the distance, hoping there would be some leftover scraps thrown away so we could rummage through the garbage and hope to find something worth eating. Hey, don't frown; people do it all the time. Mind you, I never thought of it until I came to prison. In any case, during the festivity, my boss pulled me aside and took me into one of the empty offices. At first I thought, *Great! She is going to break a rule and sneak some food to me,* but it wasn't the case. Instead she said that she was very concerned about my behavior and just knew that something was wrong. She caught me in a vulnerable moment, and her motherly concern and persistence overwhelmed me. I broke down and told her everything, from the first day to the recent shower rape. I emptied my heart on her shoulder, an act prohibited by prison protocol.

In spite of it, she didn't object and said how sorry she felt for what had happened to me. Afterward, she told me to stay put and excused herself for a few minutes. It was only when she came back with the captain that I realized the repercussions that would follow. She told me that she was sorry but it was her duty to alert staff of an incident and that I needed to repeat my story to the captain. I regretted telling her everything, because I knew what would happen to me: I would be locked up under protective custody for my safety. To this day, I don't get the logic after the fact of the incident. What about prevention, so it doesn't happen to anyone? But as I've said, some of these rules seem to be decided on whims. Simultaneously, while being handcuffed and escorted to the hole, I thought of my friends. I wouldn't get the chance to say good-bye. However, I knew for certain that eventually they would find out. After all, there are no secrets in prison; it's just a matter of time before information leaks out to the population.

December 25, 1987

Every day, and especially today, I remind myself to keep love in my heart alive, or else how shall I live through the day? Today's my birthday. I am thirty-three years old in this dark and dingy dungeon with its wire-mesh and barred window. I wish I could see some daylight or the night sky, but you can't see a thing but diffused light through the filth. When a window opens, it will be a consolation, but who knows when. I haven't received any mail, but maybe it's on its way. I hope so! But then again, does anybody really care anymore? The way I feel, sometimes getting mail is like flowers on a grave.

Tomorrow is my sister's birthday. It's been four years since I saw her or we shared a holiday. I miss my family. The things I gave up so lightly seem to be the ones I crave the most. Well, that's what I was thinking this afternoon when one of the tier officers opened the latch and said, "Your paperwork indicates that today is your birthday. Would you like to make a five-minute call to your family?"

"Yes, thank you." I was excited with anticipation, but it quickly dissipated when I was handcuffed and shackled and escorted to his office; the harsh reality of prison life is unavoidable. I looked around his office, searching for anything to define his personality, but couldn't find anything as he dialed the number I gave him and waited for an answer. When someone answered, he placed the phone on my ear, which became a balancing act.

Immediately I recognized my sister's voice and said, "Hi, sis, it's me!" And in the same breath my sister screamed and yelled, "It's my brother on the phone!"

Her enthusiasm almost made me drop the phone off my ear, but I managed to control it. In the background I could hear laughter and music. After we exchanged "Happy Birthdays," she asked how I was. At the time she didn't know my latest predicament, and I wasn't about to tell her and ruin her moment. "I'm fine, sweetheart. In fact, any better, it would be just like being home. However, at the moment I'm a bit tied up." She laughed out loud, and it was just as well that she didn't get my meaning. I changed the conversation, and continued saying that I had been given a five-minute call and just wanted to wish her a happy birthday, and before I gave myself up, I ended the conversation and thanked the young officer for his kindness.

January 25, 1988

Yesterday I went to Classification and was put up for transfer to CTF (Correctional Training Facility) in Soledad, so it's just a matter of time now before I leave this place. It could be weeks or months, who knows? I will go to another place; a better one than this, perhaps. There is no hope or road for me, as I have destroyed my life.

March 12, 1988

I'm still in this darkened room where I've learned to live contented with little, driving out the yearning and desires from my heart, forever weeping like the wretched ones. I know now what Wordsworth meant when he said, "Suffering is permanent, obscure, and dark, and has the nature of infinity."

Michael McLean

Michael McLean strode through the door, his hand extended, a smile on his face, and clearly prepared, with a folder under his arm filled with pictures and papers that were to be the visual aids to accompany his time with me. If not for the prison uniform, this could have been a job interview, but Michael has been incarcerated for thirteen years, and we were in a tiny room set aside for our interview at Fishkill Correctional Institution in Beacon, New York. Michael was sentenced in 1994 at age twenty-seven to fourteen to forty-two years for arson and burglary.

Even at six feet four and 248 pounds by his own admission, there was a boyish quality about Mike, especially around his eyes. "I'm a big guy, but I can carry it," he said. "My wife makes sure that I have plenty of food, so I eat well. I always have a good eating partner." His Brooklyn accent leaves no doubt that he is a native of the city.

Michael is all about family. He began our conversation with pictures of his wife, Crystal, and his family. He and Crystal have known each other for eighteen years and have been married for seven. He met her before he went to prison, when Crystal was working at a day-care center his cousin was attending. Crystal and Mike became friends, and she stuck by him throughout his arrest, conviction, and long years of incarceration. They were married in the prison chapel. Mike's praise for Crystal's work with children and his undying respect for her love and devotion to him was in every word he spoke. "She is my angel," he said with reverence and that ever-present smile.

Mike is involved in the family reunion program, and he and Crystal had just spent two days together. Prisoners can earn this time every sixty to ninety days so families can spend time reconnecting in a way that the prison environment rarely allows, and Mike had pictures of him and his family playing board games, making breakfast, and just playing around, as families do when they gather for holidays or reunions. Connections to family are essential to the development and well-being of prisoners and their ability to reenter society, and that is clearly the case with Mike.

He spoke with love about his parents, who died during his incarceration. "I thank my father for teaching me good manners. I have learned to be respectful, to never forget where I am." Mike has great respect for all that his parents taught him and for all that they did for him during their lives, even while he was incarcerated. "It was difficult for them, especially toward the end, when my parents were both so sick." There is no easy way to lose a parent, but the death of a loved one brings a prisoner profound regrets. Mike spoke of his parents' deaths as a result of smoking. "They just quit smoking too late," he said with sadness and resignation. He started a smoking cessation program in the prison as a way to honor his parents; it is just one of the many ways Mike reaches out to other inmates.

Another of his talents is as an amateur magician, and he has always enjoyed working with children. "People have always told me I should work with kids. Whenever we have programs in here for families, I am always in charge of entertaining the kids."

As an inmate grievance representative, Mike learned to mediate and work with both inmates and the administration. He helps prisoners work through the system to solve problems, to try to get some relief when the burden of being a prisoner gets too heavy. "I developed a streamlined grievance form to make it easier for prisoners and for the administration," he told me. He developed the form because prisoners were getting turned down because they didn't know how to file a grievance. Mike works with prisoners who have fears about the process and are illiterate; he helps them find a voice in a system that is beyond caring.

Mike is a natural storyteller, so when I asked him what writing had done for him, he looked at me and said, "Can I tell you a story? I wrote a poem called 'Phone Monkey.' I was still waiting for trial, and I was moved to a new floor. Now, sometimes you are moved, and some houses are good and some are buck-wild, as they say. But I have always been blessed with good houses. Now you have to understand that I have seen with my own eyes a lot of slashing, people getting cut up with knives over access to the phone. So one of the guys in the house comes over to me. He takes me over to the phone and he points to the phone and he says, 'You got to read that.' I looked at where he was pointing, and there on the phone pole was my poem, 'Phone Monkey.' So I say, 'I don't got to read that.' I take my ID out of my pocket and I say, 'I don't have to read that because I wrote that.' I got a phone slot right there and then."

The phone is power; it is the key to the outside world, and when there is only one phone for thirty men, problems are guaranteed. "In Brooklyn House there is one phone in the unit. I have seen people sliced over the phone, bashed with mop wringers," Mike explained. He went on to tell me that he has been very blessed, because he has had very few conflicts since he has been in prison; he has a clean slate. In fact, the only issue he ever had was for sending a wishbone home in a letter to his wife. The guards thought it was voodoo, and they wrote him a disciplinary ticket, but Mike was able to get it reduced to a minor offense.

Mike and I began talking about how writers get ideas for their work, and that led us to "Jaundiced Jeopardy." "We were in Rehabilitation Through Arts, and there was this guy who was a diehard racist in the class, and the teacher was encouraging a dialogue between two guys, this racist and a black guy. When the class was over, she told me to go write." He wrote a poem called "That Ain't Me," which condemned racial stereotyping. He read it at a poetry reading to a crowd of fifty people. His words reached deep; they were heard. Mike gained respect that night, not just because he wrote the poem, but because he had the guts to stand up and read it in front of everyone. "I had gang members come to me and give me a hug and say, 'I never looked at it that way,' and that was wonderful. They could see me as a real person."

His poem "That Ain't Me" morphed into "Jaundiced Jeopardy." "It took on a life of its own." Mike talked about the words tumbling out of him at such a pace that he found it difficult to keep up, and we laughed about writing taking on a voice of its own, leaving the writer as a conduit for the words that flow through the fingertips and onto the page. Mike has earned respect through his writing. Whether essays or poetry, prose or drama, Mike shows the reader prison from his point of view.

What evolved from that poem is a piece that looks at racism in America's prisons at the dayroom level, with all bets off. We see prisoners with little to lose and everything to gain by maintaining their perceived reputations. We are introduced to Mr. Teaps, who commands respect easily and from everyone, to TJ, who demands it, and Doug, who is a different breed of prisoner. "Jaundiced Jeopardy" is about respect. In this vivid piece, filled with intense emotional interaction, we are asked to consider the human spirit rather than the package and urged to renounce alliances with stereotypes based on race. Mike asks us to see the human for who he is, for that alone is how he should be judged.

Mike has learned through his many years of incarceration how to get along with people; he has his faith. "I am Doug. Doug doesn't care. I am not going to condemn someone because of their prejudices—that's just not who I am."

Michael McLean is someone who still has dreams. He dreams of working with kids and walking with his wife, Crystal, and he still has hope. "I am so lucky. I have family who support me. If I need help, they are there for me."

As I listened to Michael, I wondered whether he could be as sincere as he appeared. He seemed too in love, too nice, maybe even a bit too prepared, but those doubts disappeared when the topic of parole surfaced. His face flushed; he spread his large hands on the table, body width, trying to hold back his emotions, his longing for freedom, and his fear. He took a breath. "I admit I am nervous about parole. It will be my first time seeing them, and I don't know what to expect." He went on. "It is scary to think that the parole board will spend just a few minutes looking over my file before they make their decision, but I have faith. I know who I was then, and I know who I am now. I hope I am blessed when the time comes." Michael knows the pitfalls of the system; he has lived it far too long not to have his eyes open about what may lie down the road.   —Susan Nagelsen

Jaundiced Jeopardy

MICHAEL MCLEAN

This is a story of how a racist KKK man discovers how polluted he is in mind and heart. His journey to understanding begins with a connection with the very thing he has hated his entire life, the black man. His reconstruction begins with a relationship formed through letters exchanged with a black state prisoner, who has promised his mom that he will reach out to this young man who is facing prison time. Ronnie's jaundiced beliefs are the perfect recipe for death and conflict in the prison society, and Gregory has learned a lot about conflict in his many years of confinement. Gregory can "keep it real."

June 8, 2006

Oh, Ronnie, I had to drop you another letter, because I'm sitting here hyena-laughing out loud. I'm thinking about the irony of this whole backward arrangement. Here you are, at the bottom of your life, in the dungeon of your existence, and you're still falling deeper! Who is it that you're reaching out to for help? Who is it that you want to throw you a lifesaver as you stew in your prison predicament? Me! Yeah, this nigger. Where are your supremacy brothers now? What would your KKK Grand Wizard say if he knew you were asking a nigger for help? Think about that when you make your bed and try to resist putting that white pillowcase over your head. Think of all the niggers' heads you kicked for kicks as you read this letter from your black savior—me! Yeah, that's me, 'cause I'm going to save ya from yourself. Your worst enemy is you. I'll inform you again: I am not your friend. I am not helping you for you but for the people who went to bat for me, for those who dared to help me change. I'm the man I am today in part because of them, their faith in me and the human spirit's ability to overcome. You see, son, you aren't the only one who's been in the dungeon of dire circumstance. Remember that!

Oh, and you're right, you are going to do exactly what I say, because if you don't, I'm out of here. The person writing this letter is a man who has spent too much time in jail, behind bars and walls, twenty-five years on this bid alone. I have no time to waste. If there's only one lesson this prison time has taught me, it is that life is short, that I have but so many blinks and breaths in life before I receive my morgue toe-tag. If you think I'm going to waste any of those blinks on you, you're crazy. These moments that I'm writing to you, that I'm reading your scared, whiney letters, I will never get back.

Check this out, Ronnie: based on the responses in your letters, I smell some things burning. One is growth. Perhaps you've reached some sort of an awareness (that's yet to be seen), but I also smell a tinge of game. I'm warning you now, don't game me. It won't work. I realize that some dudes, even those you warn not to game you, still think their game is the game. They cleverly convince themselves that they're going to get over. Check this out: this is not baseball; you don't get three strikes and you're out. One strike, one lie, one hint of game and you're out, and I'm out, too. See ya, and I'm going out with a Kool-Aid smile on my face, and you can kiss my black ass good-bye.

Do you have any idea how much sleazy game I've been around during the years I've been in prison? I can smell game before it turns the corner. If this sounds like a cautioning, your hearing is fine, because it is. The best thing you can do is be honest. That's it. Picture me as your lifesaver; you are stuck in the middle of that white supremacist ocean, and you're sinking. *News update!* The sharks haven't even begun to smell your racist blood. Wait until you get sentenced and travel upstate to real prison, when you're surrounded by men doing twenty-five, fifty, seventy years to life, men who have no hope of seeing the streets again. Then they spy that "White Supremacy" tattoo on your neck, and the seeds of hate in them germinate and grow into a plot to slash your neck. It becomes their mission, the reason for their existence—to savagely murder you.

Ronnie, you can be killed for a carton of cigarettes. With your racist label, dudes may do it for free, for the thrill of the kill. You may think I'm making this up to scare you. I wish I were. You need to be scared. Your fight-or-flight response better have a tune-up. That's why you need me, or some guide, to help you negotiate the prison minefield before you get there. As long as you KEEP IT REAL, you'll have me there to help. Not just me, Ronnie, but the army that is standing behind me, my network of friends and support. They are standing in the wings waiting to hear from me about you. Yeah, your white behind. I can tell them, "Ronnie is changing, send him this or that," or "Ronnie is gaming; he's simply not worth your sincere compassion and time." The choice is yours, Ronnie.

Don't be afraid to make a mistake; you won't get negative feedback from me for that. I made mistakes, and I'll make some more before the Grim Reaper comes knocking at my door. Mistakes are inevitable; growth is optional. Just don't even think about lying or gaming me; that is what will sink your life preserver.

If you veto your get-over-game urges, then one day you'll look back on today and see what a racist fool you were. If destiny blesses us, then you will be able to call me friend, and I'll consider you one, too. But we're a long way from there, Ronnie Racist, a long way. I'm still a Kunta Kinte nigger to you. You're just desperate now, looking for a way out from the quicksand. That's cool for now, 'cause I've seen loads of people like you, and now you are pitiful. I also see past your hate, and you will, too, if you stick around for the ride, if you do the work to find out the truth, and that truth lies past skin color and is in the heart.

Hey, listen, at the same time there are tons of black people who are just as racist and ignorant as you. There are plenty of people who hate whites just because they are white. I bet some are in there with you now. They are looking at you in the yard, in the shower, just itching to stab you in the neck or fuck you in your ass. That "White Supremacy" tattoo you sport on your neck is the billboard that validates their hate. Hate, not just for your sorry ass but for all whites. Yet we're not focusing on them, but on you. Ask yourself how you want to go to the grave. What will RIP stand for on your tombstone? Will it mean "Racist in Purgatory," "Racist Ignorant Person," or "Rest in Peace"? Think it over. When your tiny cell gets even smaller at 3:00 A.M. and realization seeps in and an epiphany is knocking at your soul, ask the universe how you should spend the remainder of your existence. *Think it over* before it's all over and the dirt's tossed over your coffin.

Later,

Greg

June 27, 2006

Dear Gregory, listen, this is the last time I'm opening a letter to you with "Dear." "Dear Gregory." It sounds like I'm writing to Ann

Landers or an old friend from the neighborhood. Anyway, from now on it's "Hey Gregory" or "What's up, it's me." Dear? Nahh, just doesn't sound right. I'm not aiming to offend you, dude, but you ain't dear to me, not in this present day anyhoo. Hey, you preached to KEEP IT REAL with you, right? What's with that phrase KEEP IT REAL? I hear that shit a thousand times a day in here, along with NO DOUBT! Is that some mandatory phrase you gotta say once you get locked up? "Keep it real, no doubt, son!" What language is that, Prisonese?

In other news, I did your little exercise, as you called it. Yeah, that deep-introspection, look-into-the-deep-recesses-of-who-I-am bullshit. I feel like I'm your big white rat, and you're experimenting on me. Oh, you were right, I needed to look up "introspection": "The art or practice of looking inward to examine one's thoughts and feelings; self-examination." BLAH-BLAH-BLAH. I know I'm being sarcastic, but you said not to lie to you, remember? You told me our relationship is not baseball; I get only one strike and I'm out, and you're gone. I'm just pissed, because you're so fucking right, and I can't figure out why that shit is bothering me beyond measure.

I'll just explain my flashback from your little Freudian exercise, and you can dissect it in your next letter. I tried reverting back to an early childhood memory, a traumatic one, like you suggested. At first I thought, "What's this ni—," but shit if I didn't catch myself. I didn't say it. I didn't say the *n* word. I know, I thought it, but heck, I didn't say it. Just three weeks ago I wouldn't have blinked about saying the *n* word. It was automatic and encoded in my DNA. You said change comes in increments, so I guess your psycho-down-in-the-dungeon-rock-bottom-babble speech is working on my cracker ass. (Ha-ha.)

So there I was, yoga-sitting on the end of my cot in this piss-tank jail I now call my home. I started getting fed up with this exercise of yours, and BAM-BOO-YA! I got a breakthrough—a parting of my cerebral waters. Damn, it was like some shit out of a *Matrix* movie. My brain unlocked and as clear as one of those techie plasma TVs, I observed myself when I was eight years old. It was freaking spooky weird; I felt like I was inside my eight-year-old body, but at the same time I could, like, see the whole scene as if I was looking down over a movie theater balcony. I'm walking with my dad, and I know it's Sunday, 'cause I'm wearing black patent leather shoes and a yellow short set that my grandma only let me wear to church. He's holding my hand as we cross the street to go to this mall shopping place. Except he ain't holding my hand caringly, like, he's pulling me like some mutt on a leash, 'cause he's bothered by my short stride or something. I could feel the wart he had on his hand; I hated that fucking wart! It was gross and black, yuck. He was smoking his stinky cigar and had been drinking his Johnnie Walker Red—of course. In the back pocket of his greasy Lee overalls was half a bottle of J. W. Red; Mr. Johnnie Juice is what he called it when he was drunk. We crossed the street, and I remember an ice-cream truck in the shape of an ice-cream cone parked there. The rusty loudspeaker spit out a recorded jingle: "Ice cream, we all scream for ice cream . . ." Sheepishly, I asked my dad for a cone, and he told me, "No, I ain't got the money!" The prick just bought a cigar and a beer ten minutes ago. What did he think, that I didn't see that roll of cash he pulled out of his pocket? Whatever.

Next thing I know, my dad is gone! I'm lost! I started to panic, but I couldn't scream out for him. I took off running, my eyes scanning for him, and I slipped on a waxed Dixie cup. I scraped my knee, saw blood, and that was it. I started bawling my eyes out. I whirled around and was frozen by what I saw. Fear coursed through me, yet strangely, I was calmed at the same time. This was spooky shit, reliving this memory that had been dormant for decades. In front of me was an angel, a black angel in a cream paisley dress and fancy yellow hat. Not a real angel, Gregory. I just mean a lady that was angelic-looking. Her eyes were so tranquil, reflecting velvet kindness. Her love-filled eyes captivated me. I know this may sound racist, because it's coming from me, but I don't mean an ounce of disrespect. She looked like the Aunt Jemima lady from on the pancake box. You know, with a smile that would calm killer bees. Her voice, it was like a merry bird serenading me. She had a scent that was heavenly but not a perfume. Her fragrance was sort of like a fresh after-the-rain smell. My knee was bleeding; she whipped out a tissue, kissed it, and said, "Put some sugga on it, li'l man." She wiped my knee, and magically it was better.

"Are you lost, li'l man?" she asked.

I couldn't talk. All I could hear were the echoes in my head of what my dad always said: "Boy, stay away from dem niggers; they'll kidnap and eat ya."

She asked me if I wanted an ice-cream cone. I still couldn't talk. That was it, I reasoned—she's being nice to me to kidnap me.

Run, Ronnie! Run, run now! my inner voice screamed. I didn't run; I couldn't. It was . . . was like whatever that lady had in her spirit, the love, was stronger than all the poison and hate my daddy fed me.

"Li'l man, you want Miss Betty to get ya an ice-cream cone? Li'l man, the silent kitten don't get fed."

I said, "Ricky Rude."

"What, li'l man?"

"Ricky Rude," I repeated.

"Rocky Road—is that it, li'l man?"

I nodded. She asked the ice-cream man how much a scoop was. He snapped, "Fifty-five cents." Even at eight years old, I could tell that he didn't like black people either. His tone was like . . . well, it was like his ice cream was too good for her.

Miss Betty didn't flinch; she chuckled and said, "Give Li'l Man two scoops of Ricky Rude, please."

I couldn't believe my ears; I'd never had two scoops before. She took out an itsy-bitsy change purse that had purple and yellow flowers sewn onto it. She gave the man two dollars and an honest smile, then said, "Sir, you keep the change and have an ice-cream cone on Li'l Man and Miss Betty."

He was shocked and seemed almost to feel sorry for his nasty attitude toward her earlier. He tried to put a Band-Aid on it by saying, "No, ma'am, I—"

But Miss Betty wasn't having it. She said, "No, you have a nice day and a nicer night, sir."

He politely handed her the cone, and then we walked to a nearby fountain. Cool mist pelted our faces, giving us minor relief from the sweltering Detroit sun. She handed me the cone and said, "Before you eat your cone, li'l man, I want you to make a wish. Here's a penny— not any penny, but a lucky penny. Now, you make a wish and toss your penny, but don't tell your wish or it won't come true."

Gregory, I had a lucky penny in one hand and a double-scoop Rocky Road sugar cone in the other. If Miss Betty had told me she could sprout wings and fly away, I'da believed her! I closed my eyes, made a wish, and then took the longest, sweetest lick of an ice-cream cone ever.

I wished that my dad would stop beating on my mom. That wish later came true, when me and my two brothers kicked my dad's ass. He knew we were ready to die that night. We were terrified of my father, but that night there must have been a full moon, 'cause we couldn't care less. Me and Robby had bats, and Junior took the batteries out of his toy robot and put them in a sock. We were only ten, eleven, and thirteen, but we crept up and whacked him upside his head anyway. My dad was in the kitchen smacking our mom around extra-hard. After we whacked him, he recovered a bit, but he couldn't believe his eyes when he realized we were the reason his head was bleeding. He saw past our eyes to our souls. Instinctively he knew he would have to kill us to stop us. What he didn't see behind him was my mom. I saw her looking at the big butcher knife, one of those *Friday the Thirteenth* big knives. If he came at us that night, she was going to snap and drive it into his back. The bastard bully never hit Mom again, but he stepped up his mental torture. He became so evil I think my mom preferred the beatings instead.

That's what I wished for at the mall fountain. Then I remember my dad yanking my hand and dragging me away from Miss Betty and the fountain. As we turned the corner, I looked back at Miss Betty. Her face was now as sad as it had been happy before. She looked like she had just lost her entire family in a car accident. When we turned the corner, my dad slapped the cone from my hand and then slapped me in the face so hard it loosened my tooth. Blood trickled out of my nose. I was too scared to cry; I peed in my pants instead. I was staring at the Rocky Road melting on the scorching asphalt. All I could think of was Miss Betty. Miss Betty, with the eyes of love, would buy me another cone and put some sugga on my cheek to make the pain go away. I was glad Miss Betty couldn't see the ice cream melting on the sidewalk.

I squinted up at my dad, the sunlight assaulting my eyes, and he was dazed because I wasn't crying. I guess Miss Betty's mojo love was still doing something to me. We were standing by the curb, about to cross the street. There was a garbage truck barreling down the road. A big truck, bigger than the one that killed our dog, Chase, I mean squashed him bad, puppy blood and guts everywhere. I wondered if this was the answer to my wish. I seriously thought about trying to shove my dad in front of the truck; then I thought about jumping in front of it myself. Instead I went home, and I got beaten with a black extension cord for accepting nigger charity. Gregory, my dad taught me two things: to hate, and how to pronounce "Rocky Road" or get a whipping.

Okay, by now I'm sure you've noticed the shiny penny taped to the bottom of this page. I'll explain. I bought this penny on the prison black market, no pun intended. It's amazing what you can get for three packs of cigarettes. The brothers thought I was crazy to pay over $15 for a penny, but they took this white boy's money with a smile. I hustled up this penny because I want to make a wish with you, Gregory. I ain't got no fountain to throw it in, so you're my fountain—of hope. I'm breaking one of Miss Betty's rules. I'm telling you my wish; I think she'd forgive me. I wish . . . I wish my eyes had the look Miss Betty's did, the look of compassion, of love. I want, I need some of whatever she had in her that made her eyes give off that love. If this is a tall order for you, oh well. Look at the date on the penny, 1971, the year I was born. That can't be a coincidence. That's my lucky penny. I know you said there are no coincidences, only circumstances, but screw that fortune-cookie crap. Something spooky is happening over here in this crusty jail.

"Yo! I said on the count, Ronnie Cracker! Get your punk ass up and on the gate. Yeah, I said Cracker; this is your lucky day, Mr. KKK. I's the *po-lice,* and my cousin's doing a shift with me, and lookie there, the control captain on duty is my brother-in-law, which spells B-A-D, bad news for you, punk-meat. I can and will do what I want to you. Don't make me call you for the count again, boy."

Shit, Gregory, that exercise you gave me pulled me so deep into a trance that I almost scored a beatdown from the biggest, blackest officer I ever saw. But your ass was right—again. What's my next assignment, Sensei?

Penitentiary Pen Pal Ronnie

P.S. How many officers does it take to push my Klan ass down the stairs? None—I fell.

July 9, 2006

Yo, Gregory! Attention! It's your racist pen-pal person, pouting a prison pity party parade, paa-leeze! (Ha-ha.) In your last scribe, you suggested I attempt to find and keep a sense of humor—even in this dungeon. Once again I thought you were crazy. Ain't nothing funny about this shit-pit-jam I'm in. But once again your black ass was right. What? Your ass ain't black? Just kidding. If it makes you feel any better, my ass is Casper Ghost white. (Ha.) You're not going to believe the madness I witnessed in the rec room three days ago. Damn, who am I kidding—you've probably seen all this, and a case of beer, with all the behind-the-wall time you've logged.

It was Sunday, and on Sundays it's mandatory that you gotta go to recreation after the lunch meal, or the riot squad comes and drags you out. It's some rule about fostering good cohabitation relations, shit. I think it's just so the jailers can bunch us all together to increase the chances we'll kill each other.

Anyway, it's Sunday and it's hotter than the devil's armpits, ninety-something degrees, and there are thirty of us caged up in this shoebox rec room. There's one TV, one fan that a ninety-nine-year-old asthmatic with a dash of emphysema can blow harder than, one deck of tattered cards, and a chess set with most of the pieces made from soap. Oh, and picture the grossest I-95 gas station bathroom you've ever seen; multiply that by ten. That equals our shit-and-piss tank. Okay, the place is not Auschwitz, but it's the pits. The TV is the key, Greg-o. Without the TV, that hypnotic noise keeping people distracted from the reality of where they're at, it would be chaos. Well, whatta ya know, the TV and the fan go off! "Ahhh, whoa!" The usual grumbling happens. "Yo, CO! The TV is off!" God forbid we miss the end of that rap video we've already seen a hundred times this week. No answer from the Man. In fact, it was probably an officer who cut the juice off. Gregory, not even two minutes after that idiot box shut off, the hypnotizing effect wore off. Eyes started roaming, realization began dawning, and egos started Humpty-Dumpty cracking. I'm in the corner thinking to myself, *This is* un-*freaking believable. I'm trapped in this zoo, and soon dudes are gonna be lookin' at me as rec food.*

That's when I heard a raspy voice. No, not like the voices in my head I've been telling you about. This was a dude, Doug, another white guy that came in here. He was extradited from your stomping grounds, New York City. He even wears a Yankee hat. He's about two inches taller than me, and I stand six feet. The dude's got a dirty-blond crew cut and a boxer's or swimmer's build, pushing a lean two hundred pounds, I'd guess. I hear him say, "What are you looking at?" to TJ, the top dog who runs this unit.

TJ's no newbie New Jack. He's got three state bids in his past and a perpetual chip on his shoulder. He reminds me of Apollo Creed from *Rocky* in build and looks, minus the mini-Afro. TJ sports corn-rows and a thick goatee. TJ's also from New York, someplace called the Bronx or Bronco, the Boogie-Down Bronx? Shit, you New Yorkers actually have a town called Boogie-Down?

So anyway, TJ barks back, "A cracker, that's what I'm looking at." TJ and his gang laughed. Like pit bulls, TJ's crew waits for a command to attack Mr. Cracker. But TJ's in no rush; he knows it's twenty brothers against this Lone Ranger white guy. Truth is, I'm glad the attention's on this dude and off of me and my white supremacist tattoo! But what the white dude said next stopped all their laughing like a VCR Pause button.

"Who wants to die first?"

He didn't scream it, didn't direct it at anybody specific. He just said it as a matter of fact, like it was some established law of physics that couldn't be broken. That's what froze everyone; our souls registered he wasn't bluffing. It was as if he were some lion that, yeah, we could overpower if everyone attacked at once, but someone was gonna have to die before he did. The first person who came close to him was destined for the morgue—not the jail box but a pine box.

TJ sensed it, too, but this is TJ, ruler of the cell block. He has to do something—"represent," as you all say. I think TJ realized that if he sicced his posse on him, crazy motherfuckers as they were, they probably would have backed out, 'cause nobody wanted to be that first one dead. And that fate, having his posse not obey him, was worse than the alternative to him, or to his shaky ego. Mr. Nitwit did what any half-baked fool would do. He challenged a man who has nothing to lose and who's ready to die—over what?

TJ said, his tone masking subtle fear, "Okay, whitey, I'm already in here for a body; what's one more cracker corpse?" Then he removed the gold chain from his neck. The white guy just cracked his neck the way Bruce Lee always did before he fought. I could see a tinge of the unknown rimming his eyes, too. At least then I knew he was human.

One of TJ's thugs offered him a shank, a big one with a blade about ten inches. TJ refused it and made a point of letting everyone know he didn't want the weapon. He was dueling gladiator solo, sans weapon. The white guy saw that, too. TJ took three steps toward the white guy, but Mr. Teaps stood up and placed his hand on TJ's chest. Not forcefully, just out of concern.

Mr. Teaps was an old man, a Pops or OT old-timer like you explained to me a few letters back about prison nicknames. Mr. Teaps was pushing seventy, but he had the silent respect of everyone here—even me. Not only because of his age, but more for the way he carried himself. Though he was two tons of cobwebs past collecting a Social Security check, the OT could handle himself. He's about six feet, cocoa skin, and has a powerful walk; he could be ex-military. Weird thing is, the guy has no eyebrows, at least as far as I can tell.

About four weeks ago we were in the rec room eating our lunch—chicken legs and mashed potatoes, with a strawberry ice-cream cup for dessert. Well, this young buck about two whiskers over twenty-one just arrived in the cell block. Only been there an hour, tops. He's an easy six-six, 260 pounds, dark-skinned, with a shaved head. He has slash zipper scars on both cheeks; he's no Denzel Washington, put it that way. I'm no Einstein, but this guy's IQ had to be in the minus digits, somewhere around negative sixty. He was big, black, and brawny. I wanted no part of him or his nitro temper. He walked over to Mr. Teaps, Mr. T, as we affectionately call him, and said, "Yo, Pops, gimme dat chicken and I cream. Don't call the Man and I won't pound you out." TJ and his crew saw this go down, and one of TJ's boys was about to step to the giant about picking on the old man. TJ grabbed his arm and told him to chill.

Mr. T wiped the corners of his mouth with his handkerchief and simply said, "Son, I'm asking you, please, let me eat my meal in peace."

The giant said, "I ain't your son, Pops. I said I want your fuc—"

Yo, Gregory, I don't know what happened next, and I was there! Mr. T sprang up like a cobra; you couldn't see his hands! He punched the giant in the throat and sat back down before the dude collapsed to the floor in a coughing fit. Mr. T's facial expression looked like he was sorry he had to do that, to reach back to the violent side of him he hated visiting.

Then Mr. Teaps stood up and with one hand grabbed the giant by his collar and dragged him to the officer's gate as easily as if he were a crash dummy. He said, "Officer, this guy is choking on something. I don't think he likes the accommodations here."

It took two officers to drag the giant out. Even the officers respected Mr. T; we never saw the giant again. Mr. T walked back to his seat, but not before stopping by the giant's tray, taking his chicken legs and ice cream, and putting them on his own tray. Yep, the old dude had heart and brains. TJ stopped out of genuine respect for Mr. T.

Mr. Teaps had a fatherly, Yoda tone when he spoke. His words penetrated you without assaulting your manhood. He told TJ, "You want to set it off in here, TJ? You know the goon squad will bum-rush us all, after they drop tear gas through those ceiling slots." Guys looked up at the slots; most had never noticed the slots before.

"It's ninety-eight degrees in here now. I don't want to imagine what it will feel like in here with five canisters of pepper gas going off, plus a few lumps from the guards to this busted old body. I'm no Napoleon to command you to do what I want you to do, but I will ask for a time-out from your who's-going-to-be-alpha-male game. At least wait until they let us go back to our cells before the gladiator games begin. I think I've earned that reprieve. Absent that scenario, I pose a challenge to you, to both of you. I have two and a half bags of commissary goodies in my cell. If you cowboys duke it out with words, I'll give the winner the two bags and the runner-up the leftovers. How about it, TJ?"

"Mr. T, I'll pull back on taming the cracker here, but I ain't got nothing to say to whitey."

"Bock-bock," the white guy barked.

"Yo, sucker, don't push your luck. You must want your wig split!" TJ said.

Mr. T told him, "TJ, if you truly have nothing in your arsenal to say to this man except 'cracker,' then you should examine that. Socrates said, 'The unexamined life is not worth living.'"

TJ thought for a sec and then said, "Uh-ite, I'm down. All I gotta do is tell this sucker what a sucker he is, and if I slam him I get the commissary?"

"Yeah. It's like a debate," said Mr. T.

"You mean like the president debate shit every four years?"

"Yeah, sort of, but the only vote that counts is mine. You can't lose, TJ—even second place gets half a bag of goodies. And no one loses their life, at least not today."

"Uh-ite, let's do it," TJ challenged.

Yo, Gregory, you can't make this shit up! One second death is in the air; blood is gonna be spilled—damn if I didn't see the Grim Reaper cheering on the sidelines. The next moment a debate is set. It was as if we were in some Harvard auditorium about to debate *Roe v. Wade*. *Un*believable! Mr. Teaps reminded me of Moses speaking on the mountaintop.

Mr. T said, "Okay, TJ, you're up first. Just tell him what you think, feel, whatever—it's your floor."

At first TJ was nervous; you could tell public speaking wasn't his forte. Then he pushed his nervousness aside and said, "*Yo, yo, yo!* We got a new whitey in the house!" A few laughs came from his crew. "Yo, check it, we got not one but two—count 'em, two—crackers in da house. Mr. KKK White Supremacist over there." He pointed at me, and I wanted to jump out of a window! "And his twin, Mr. Yankee Hat. The crazy cracker." More laughs from his posse rats. "Now, I know what you all are thinking. Just how high can two crackers jump? Don't even think that; you know white guys can't jump! Heck, the only time whites jump is when they see a black dude next to them." His crew was rolling. "But this cracker's got a death wish. Ain't that right, Yankee Hat? He's either crazy or a fool or a crazy fool. Who else would stir up twenty pissed-off blacks in this closet with the heat pushing a hundred degrees? Yep, we gots a crazy fool, and we got a recipe for crazy fools like you—but that's gonna marinate.

"I know you, cracker. I see it in your eyes, like this demon over here." He pointed at me, Gregory. "You're just another cracker whitey-white boy, hiding behind your mask. Drop your mask, and I bet we'll see we're all spade moolie jungle-bunny spear-chuckers to you and your family tree. We're just niggers to you. You'd put a rope around my neck if you could, like your ancestors did to my ancestors. You'd love to whip me raw, back bleeding, mind wishing for a quick death—I know your kind. You're keeping quiet now, hoping we won't pay you no mind until your daddy bails out your rich behind. You think you're better than me, than us, 'cause you got a few bucks or 'cause you think there'll never be a black president or whatever shit you need to feel bigger than black people." Gregory, he was spilling his heart up there; he had people's attention.

"When the media pimps out the stories in the 'hood, on the five o'clock news, on exploit TV, you get a hard-on. Another crack war has taken the life of a two-year-old boy. A drive-by shooting took his life. Blah-blah-blah. You eat that shit up over bagels and lox at breakfast. As if that's the face of every black neighborhood or person. You don't want to see white incest babies and trailer-park trash on the TV on the eleven o'clock news before you go to sleep. No, after turning in and tucking in Junior and kissing the missus good night, you want to sleep tight. Nope. Seeing that shit would rock your reality. That your kind, that whites have a dark side besides eating people and the other serial-killer shit you guys do. Awesome, dude! That's you, your pedigree. You may not have tattoos on you like Ronnie Racist here, but your tats are on your mind and in your heart, where all hate starts.

Martin had a dream where you and I could chill and drink a beer or two. But that ain't my dream; that's a freakin' nightmare. In my dream you're pumping gas into my red BMW and then you go back to your trailer park . . . and die. By any means necessary, as Malcolm would say. And this is where I say *ta-ta!* See ya, definitely wouldn't want to be ya!" TJ bobbed over to his seat as his boys whooped it up for him and his bigoted speech.

Mr. T, his face full of glistening sweat, sitting between two and a half bags of commissary, merely nodded over to Doug, who was already on his feet. Doug gingerly removed his Yankee cap and set it on the table like a surgeon placing his scalpel down.

Pointing directly at me, Gregory, Doug said, "*That* ain't me! In case you didn't hear me or think I stuttered, *that* ain't me!" To Doug, I wasn't even a person. I was a "that." I felt like a "that," Gregory. As if I were some alien you'd see on the SciFi Channel.

"Listen, this debate is a declaration to people who lie to themselves. It's an ode to those pretenders standing for equality for all people who are really closet racists themselves. I speak to the peeps who smile in my face but who'd love to stab me in the back for no other reason than I'm white. This oration's for chameleons who can't differentiate between the color of skin, my bark, and the person, the man, and the human inside the skin. This diction is for dudes who refuse to see past skin, for people who get bent-out-of-whack ballistic when I consistently refute their preconceived notions and images of the white man, the cracker. It's for mortals whose reality would crumble if even one white person were actually proven to be human, who would rather lie in the face of fact than submit to truth. You know who I'm talking about. Perhaps I'm talking about you. If not, cool.

"I asked you, 'What are you looking at?' 'A cracker,' was your reply, TJ. Great answer. I sense where you stand; your veil's off as you gawk at me like I'm the one who put you in jail. Hating me instantaneously just 'cause you see white. Don't know jack about me, but white's enough to feed your resentment fire. Scoping me and seeing some slavemaster who whipped your ancestors, conjuring up pictures of me running a slave ship through the Middle Passage. Wake up, dude! That ain't me, no more than your black behind is the guy who knocked my mom down and stole her purse. Yeah, I got a mama dukes too. Tell me, what else do you see, TJ? Do you see me with a white sheet on my head as a KKK Grand Wizard? Can you smell the pizza sauce on me from Bensonhurst Brooklyn? 'Ayy! Do the right thing! Yo, Tony!' Ha,

I'm not even Italian, TJ. That's merely more of your clouds of confusion, like the white judge who sentenced you, the slave ship captain, and the Klan man. They're just conjured-up images in your mind that you see when you see me, and you've been fed a line and took the bait like a trout. The hook of hatred is in you. You're programmed to hate, not differentiate. Yeah, those events took place, no doubt, straight up they happened, all of it, and the oppressor is still oppressing. I don't deny it, never did, but that ain't me, even if you see it as me. You thinking I'm to blame, that I'm responsible for your rage, doesn't make it so, TJ.

"When you peep me as the guy with rich parents, as white corporate America gobbling up ghettos with high-rise exclusive penthouses, 'exclusive' being a phony code word for 'no blacks or spics allowed,' that ain't me. You're thinking I live on Easy Street, always get the promotions, and get the job over the black man. TJ, what you're imagining is an illusion in your mind. That ain't me—I'm me! What? They're all the same, dem crackers.

"Funny, isn't that what they said about blacks: they're all the same. Of course that evil happens—whites get passes while blacks get a bone, get oppressed—but that ain't me, and that's who I'm talking about man, me. I'm here, and I ain't about that crap. My cosmic journeys landed me here in this part of space, traveling at warp speed having to face you. TJ, you can't see my spirit, hear my soul. You don't want to, and that's cool. You don't have to. I'm not here to get acceptance from you. That's not my mission, to get your okay to exist, to knock down your walls of ignorance, the barriers you've placed between you and me, before you and me ever got to see who we are.

"Oh, and TJ, I hear your venom, when you're kickin' it to your man on the gate when we're locked in. Yeah, not that I crave hearing your dribble-drabble, but I hear 'cause I got ears, and that's what ears do. You spew, 'Get yourself a fat white bitch like I got.' Like you reeled in some trophy. Yeah, you think you're cool when you vomit that, 'cause she sends you packages and creams your account. You're thinking you're elevated to big-playa status 'cause you've preyed on her insecurities and poor self-esteem, the lack of love in her life. You're a player, true indeed, playin' your soul, kickin' that crap, thinking you're only messin' with white trash. You're the garbage and need to be taken out, kicked to the curb. You're not elevated by that, TJ. You slink from under your rock to the slimy basement of humanity, to Parasite Hotel! Yeah, I know, it's the white man's fault!

"Your eyes still broadcast that all you see is hate, in flesh, and all that happened before me. If looks could kill, you would've slain me the first time you laid eyes on me, what you thought you saw in me. But I'm still here, still going like the Energizer Bunny. TJ, all you see is 666 on my forehead. You think I'm wearing a White House and Mr. Oppression Man mask. Sure, I have some semblance of a mask, we all do. Because I don't leak all of me for everyone to witness at once doesn't make my mask a hatred mask, or a racist nigger-hating mask. Yeah, I hate niggers, but niggers don't have to be black; they come in white and in all colors of the human rainbow. TJ, you can't see the real me. Glasses won't help you. No prescription is strong enough. A Seeing Eye dog could piss on your leg and it would do no good, 'cause you only wanna see what you wanna see, and you ain't tryin' to see me. That's fine by me, TJ, 'cause I see past you. Yet a part of me wants you to see me, even if you're lost in hating me, 'cause I'm human, and that's what I want you to see.

"Another part of me says forget you and your hatred disguised as a movement or a cause, as if your hating me is not an injustice, as if it's your right. Now, Garvey, Malcolm, King, they were movers, and no, the X-hat T-shirt combo you wear don't make you down with the plan. Because you knew King said, 'I have a dream, deeply rooted,' don't mean you're living the dream. So wake up from the fantasy you're in, TJ, thinking I'm your nightmare. You don't even see what it's doing to you, TJ, where you're headed if you don't get a grip on that runaway train you call your mind. You're only repeating what you've heard and not thinking for yourself."

Yo, Gregory, after Doug finished, TJ stood, picked up the two bags of commissary, and took them over to Doug's table. Then they both exchanged fist pounds as if they were buddies forever and not close to killing each other earlier. Now TJ and Doug play chess all day. Doug, it turns out, was a big brother to two of TJ's cousins when he was a lifeguard in the Bronx. Small world, huh?

By the way, I'm in the infirmary. I'll be okay—I got an infection on my calf, in the place where I had that tattoo I told you about. Yeah, the one with the little black baby hanging by a noose off a tree. After Doug and TJ had their battle of words, I finally had one of those epiphany things you said I'd have. I realized that "*That* ain't me!" is me in the flesh. I feel ashamed, Gregory, and this is a foreign feeling to me. I scraped off the baby tattoo with a razor and a green scrubby pad. My calf is swollen and infected with greenish black pus that oozes onto my sheets. The putrid stench wakes me up at night. I'll live, the doctor said, but even alive I feel dead inside. I can see it now, you'll be telling me I have to die in order to be reborn. Greg-o, is . . . is my heart as infected as my calf? Where's my cure for a poisoned heart?

TJ and Doug are comrades now, and Doug even has his own phone time slot. That's a big deal in here, because no one dares use that phone without TJ's okay. Oh, but everyone here still hates me. The cockroaches get more respect here than me. But at least I'm starting to understand the hate, from them, and inside of me.

See ya,

Ron

P.S. I have a secret I need to tell you.

John "Divine G" Whitfield

When the door opened, John "Divine G" Whitfield came into the conference room at Sing Sing like a supernova filling the room. His uniform was freshly pressed, and there was an aura about him that told of his personality, for Divine is a man of discipline, a man of strong beliefs and opinions, and a man who contends that love is at the core of everything. He is a jailhouse lawyer, a philosopher, an actor, a writer, an ombudsman, a mentor to younger prisoners, and, as I quickly learned, a determined and articulate self-promoter.

Originally Divine came to prison on a "skid bid," or a one-to-three for selling drugs, and as he described his life before prison, he said, "I made one of the biggest mistakes of my life. I ventured off; I sold some drugs to try to pay some bills. I thought I could sneak in and get out. I was wrong. I got caught." Divine said it was ironic because he had planned on being a New York City police officer. He had passed the civil service exams and the physical, but his family begged him not to take the job. There had been too much death in Divine's family; he had lost a brother during heart surgery, his father and two uncles had died, and his mom and his siblings couldn't bear the thought of him in a job that would be so dangerous. Divine's voice took on a serious tone as he said, "I wanted to be a cop, but I understand that my family asked me not to do that out of love."

Divine's difficulties didn't stop there. In 1988, at the age of twenty-four, when he had just begun serving his sentence for selling drugs, he was arrested for murder. He was convicted on snitch testimony and is serving a twenty-five-to-life sentence. "I have been telling anybody I can find that I did not commit this crime, and it has been my mission to try to prove that I did *not* do this crime." Along with help from the Legal Aid Society, Divine found evidence in the form of an eyewitness and a taped confession that exonerate him, but he has "gotten no rhythm from the court." For nineteen years he has been fighting. In 1998, Divine's legal efforts forced the district attorney to surrender the taped confession that clears his name; yet he has had no relief.

"How have you kept from becoming angry?"

"Oh, I get frustrated; I get plenty frustrated. But angry? No, not angry. I do get tired of telling people I didn't do the crime. I mean, I have the evidence—what else do they want?"

Recently Brooklyn Law School's Second Look has been helping, and the students on the case want to take the evidence and present it to the district attorney again. Is Divine hopeful? "No, I don't think it's going to help, but if that's what they want to do, then I'm not going to stop them."

"How have you kept the disappointment from getting to you?"

Divine was adamant. "I refuse to allow the bitterness to consume me. At one point I was totally frustrated. My writing is my way of hanging on to that one piece of me that I don't want this place to take from me. Writing can help me reach that level of tranquillity in myself, and I am going to hang on to it."

He began his writing career as a way to tell his story to the world. His first recognized piece was *The Whitfield Files*, which won an honorable mention in the PEN America Prison Writing Program in 2004. "It illustrates my prison journey, the discovery of the evidence of my innocence, and that is what inspired me to write," Divine explained. He had never written before prison; in fact, he almost laughed when I asked him if he had. "I didn't care about writing. If you asked me ten years ago if I would ever be a writer, hey, it was the furthest thing from my mind."

We talked about the first thing he had written, and Divine smiled. "Actually, believe it or not, I love sci-fi and fantasy. I would write it, but nobody could relate to what I was trying to do." When other prisoners read his work, they said, "Oh, you have a gift." Divine said he didn't see it that way; he saw it as therapeutic. "The process of getting my built-up frustrations out through my stories was wonderful."

Divine told me, "I am always pushing the element of love. I promote the question of love, so some people tell me that my stories are a little contrived." These comments do not faze Divine. "I think we need people to promote elements of love, especially in a mean-spirited environment like prison."

Divine reads voraciously to fill the prison hours, whether it is Socrates, Jung, or Asimov; they have all played a role in his development. "I have done more legal reading than anything. I used to sit up and read case law after case law trying to figure out how this happened to me. I have had lawyers tell me that they would hire me as a paralegal if I were out there. They tell me my briefs have flair." He is fascinated by the philosophers, especially the Greeks. "In my journey of writing, you will find heavy elements of love. The Greeks felt that the ultimate love was altruistic love, the ability to show love while helping someone else. That is profound."

Divine is a disciplined writer. He writes all the time. "I feel uncomfortable if I am not doing something related to writing." He said that what really helped him evolve as a writer and as a person was a group called Rehabilitation Through Arts (RTA). He got involved with the group in 1996, as one of the founding members. The pride is visible when Divine talks about RTA; his smile is wide, and his hands, though always in motion, dance even faster as he talks of the "elaborate costumes and sets" and the "joy of seeing prisoners work together." He loves the collectivity of the group, and he believes that prisoners reach a point at which they can benefit from working together.

Divine recently finished his bachelor's degree in behavioral sciences from Mercy College and has applied to the master's program at New York Theological Seminary. I asked him to help me understand his view of God. "God is keeping me focused. I see God as the ultimate spirit of goodness that exists within all of us." Divine told me that he sees the "G" in his name as standing for good, grand, great, and he believes that these are attributes of God that we have within us: "We have that little voice that tells us what is right and what is wrong. That is God's voice, and it can guide us. But it can be subtle; you have to listen carefully and act accordingly." There was such sincerity in his voice when he said, "If someone does wrong, it is wrong. It is just that simple. Wrong is wrong." He believes that the vast majority of people will side with what is right. Oh, he recognizes that things in prison can spiral out of control quickly, but on the whole, Divine believes in the goodness of people to "be right."

Divine is an accomplished writer; whether it is legal briefs, short stories, novels, or drama, he has developed the philosophy that "writing is a craft that is designed to inspire." *Peakzone* is indicative of his success as a dramatist. As I was reading the play for the first time, I realized that in all the years I had been working with prisoners, I had never stopped to wonder what would happen in the event of a disaster. I was chilled and ashamed. I was stunned by my lack of awareness.

"*Peakzone* is about crisis bringing out the best in some people," Divine told me. This is something that he knows at firsthand. He watched prisoners help each other out in the aftermath of a riot on Rikers Island. He had just been arrested; it was his first time in prison. "It was a humbling experience. I was scared out of my mind during the riot. I was scared to death, but it was touching because guys who hated each other were helping each other out."

In a larger sense, *Peakzone* is about giving people chances. In a strange way, Sing Sing has given Divine a chance; he has risen to the challenges placed in front of him, and he has proved himself successful. Divine has found a way to build his life behind the walls into something productive and meaningful; he has been able to use his talents as a writer, jailhouse lawyer, and thespian to keep his case alive, fighting in the only way left to him—with words.

—SUSAN NAGELSEN

JOHN "DIVINE G" WHITFIELD

This harrowing tale of prison struggle and subsequent perseverance asks the question, what would it be like in a prison environment if terrorists struck a nuclear plant? Although some of the scenes in this play are constructed to ensure that certain characters confront other characters, this story attempts to proffer an idea as to what it would be like, at least from the perspective of the main character, Jakwan.

Cast of Characters *(In order of appearance)*

Rusty
Bones
Drama
Da'ud
Rashien
Jakwan Robinson
Kev
Shondu
Dondi
Mel
Ziggy
Blackjack
Sara Barns, deputy superintendent of administration
Eric Blair, deputy superintendent of security
James Caldwell, deputy superintendent of programs
Will Wilkinson, superintendent
Gripper
Rondu
Primo
Bob, civilian
John, civilian
Males #1–4, Board of Pardons
Females #1–3, Board of Pardons
Three corrections officers

Act I

SCENE I

The curtain rises on a busy prison recreation room. Upstage right are a TV on a stand and two prisoners, Da'ud and Rashien, sitting at a table, peering at the screen. They are watching a talk show. Upstage left, three prisoners, Jakwan, Shondu, and Kev, sit at a table with law books in front of them, talking among themselves. Downstage center, two prisoners, Mel and Dondi, are playing a game of Ping-Pong. Directly next to the Ping-Pong table downstage left is a weight bench with three prisoners, Bones, Drama, and Rusty, working out and talking.

RUSTY: I tell ya, Bones, I don't think them chumps are gonna show.

BONES: This is the last time I'm gonna say this, Rusty. All you gotta do is keep that hardware ready. *[Looks at Rusty suspiciously.]* You brought them thangs with you, right? Lemme see 'em.

RUSTY: *[Pulls three huge homemade knives and secretly shows them to the others.]* Yo, Drama, this them new pieces I picked up. *[Smiles.]*

DRAMA: *[Looks around covertly, sees everything is cool, and then snatches the knives. He slides and pokes his thumb across the dull points.]* These are bullshit pieces, you stupid motherfucker! *[Shoves them back to Rusty.]* I told you to get the ones stashed in the yard!

BONES: *[Places a hand on Drama's shoulder.]* Be easy, Drama. *[Notices the others looking at them.]* Don't worry; I brought some backup. *[Lifts his shirt, showing the knives tucked in his waist.]* We ready if they show.

[Bones, Drama, and Rusty resume their workout.]

DA'UD: *[Stares at Bones and the others, then looks at Rashien.]* I think Bones and his crew are about to act up again.

RASHIEN: *[Looks over at Bones and the others.]* Bones and those fools are always up to no good. As long as they keep that bullshit over there, everything's fine.

DA'UD: When are you gonna start taking the stuff going on around us more serious, Rashien? What they do affects us all. Just last week they shut the jail because—

RASHIEN: *[Interrupting.]* If Bones and Gripper want to stab and kill themselves over dumb shit like who's running the phones and TVs and all that other nonsense, I'm not putting myself in the middle of that. I keep telling you, Da'ud, cats who stick their nose where it don't belong usually get it cut off.

[Da'ud sighs loudly. He and Rashien look back at the TV.]

JAKWAN: I wouldn't chance it! I'd file the petition as soon as possible. If they turn over something as a result of your FOIL [Freedom of Information Law] requests, that's Brady material. You can always do a motion to the feds to have your habe held in abeyance.

KEV: I'm not saying he should hold his habe beyond the one-year time limit. I just think he should wait about a month. The DA is going to answer that freedom of information law request within that time because we won that Article 78. If they try to play games, he can have them held in contempt of court and have sanctions imposed for violating the judge's order.

SHONDU: I gotta side with Kev on this one, Jakwan. I got four more months before my year runs out. A month ain't gonna make a difference.

JAKWAN: Hey, it's your call, Shondu. We here to help you lay this thing out the right way.

[Suddenly, three additional prisoners, Gripper, Ziggy, and Blackjack, enter stage right. Their hands are stuffed in the front of their pants. Everyone in the room jumps to their feet in a state of panic. Bones, Drama, and Rusty pull their shanks and head toward Gripper, Ziggy, and Blackjack. Dondi and Mel stop playing Ping-Pong and get in between the two groups.]

DONDI: Hold up, Gripper. Y'all ain't comin' in here blowin' up the spot with that bullshit!

MEL: *[Blocks Bones's path.]* Why you spazzing out on each other? I don't never see y'all fightin' the fuckin' police.

BONES: *[Stares angrily at Mel.]* Get the fuck out of the way!

[Before things can jump off in the recreation room, there is intense commotion offstage. Everyone in the room stops. They look stage right with shocked expressions. Their heads move, trying to see what's going on. They all stop abruptly and their eyes grow wider.]

DONDI: What the hell is this?

ZIGGY: *[Excitedly.]* They just locked us in here! They probably setting it off somewhere else.

BLACKJACK: Naw, this is something bigger than that. They would never lock us in here and run off. Even the area CO left with them.

SHONDU: This violates every rule in the book. *[Shakes his head nervously.]* Ah, man, this is real serious, whatever it is.

[Everyone's attention is captured as an irritating, shrill hum screams through the TV. They all move toward the TV with urgency. Bones and his crew are still apprehensive about Gripper and his crew. Blackjack and Rusty attempt to attack one another, while Ziggy and Drama do the same, but Mel and Dondi stay in between the two, shoving them away from each other.]

MALE VOICE: This is the Emergency Alert System. Be advised, this is not a test. This is an actual emergency. All residents within the Westchester County region and surrounding areas are urged not to panic. The Indian Point nuclear power plant has been struck by an explosive device. This is believed to be the work of terrorists. The Nuclear Regulatory Commission and FEMA are urging citizens to proceed with extreme calm. Citizens who plan to leave the area are advised to leave as quickly but safely as possible and to travel in a southwesterly direction, away from the radiation cloud . . .

[As the emergency broadcast continues, all thirteen prisoners look at each other with shocked and terrified expressions. The lights go down rapidly.]

SCENE II

The lights come back up on an office with a woman, Sara Barns, sitting behind a desk while three men in civilian clothing, Will Wilkinson, James Caldwell, and Eric Blair, are either pacing or sitting in nearby chairs.

SARA: *[Looking at monitors in front of her.]* Where the hell are they running to? There's nowhere to run.

ERIC: *[Sits down with both hands to his head. He's visibly distraught.]* That's so easy for you to say! Imagine if we weren't in this underground radiation-proof bunker—what the hell do you think we'd be doing?

JAMES: *[About to fall to pieces.]* Oh, God, this can't be happening! My wife and daughter are not far enough away. I have to call them. *[Heads for the phone.]*

ERIC: *[Places a hand on James's shoulder.]* We have got to hold it together, James. Debby knows what to do. This is something we saw coming. Thank goodness we've all talked about it and made plans for this day. *[When he sees James starting to relax, he turns to Sara.]* I thought you said they would secure the inmates before they left the facility?

SARA: How was I supposed to know we weren't going to be warned before word hit the airwaves? The procedure says we would be informed first so we could implement the prescribed contingency plans.

WILL: *[Shouts, almost panic-stricken.]* We have got to stop bickering! *[Pacing.]* I need to think, damn it! *[To Sara.]* What did Albany say about evacuating the inmates?

SARA: They told us to follow Executive Order 65. This is obviously a state of emergency. The prisoners will remain on the prison grounds until we're instructed otherwise.

JAMES: Why are we spending all this time talking about inmates? We need to discuss our own evacuation from this area.

WILL: We're talking about it because they are in our care, custody, and control, and we did not provide them with those pills . . . Think! *[Taps finger on his head.]* When the smoke clears and all those prisoners develop radiation sickness and cancer-related ailments, and dead bodies start piling up because they weren't given potassium iodide, who do you think they are going to blame?

[James, Eric, and Sara look on with concerned expressions.]

ERIC: *[Clears his throat loudly.]* Not to sound mean-spirited, but who's gonna care about murderers, rapists, and criminals when so many law-abiding citizens are dead or dying?

WILL: *[Shakes his head.]* You just don't get it, do you? What the hell does it make us when we consciously fail to carry out the law and our behavior kills other human beings?

[They all look at each other as the lights go down rapidly.]

SCENE III

The lights come back up on the recreation room. The prisoners are in the same positions as at the end of Scene I. They stare at the TV screen as the emergency broadcast continues.

MALE VOICE: This emergency broadcast will return every twenty minutes with additional information, instructions, and updates. Please stay tuned. *[Static blares from the TV as the broadcast ends.]*

[There is an intense moment of silence as all thirteen prisoners stare at each other with wide-eyed terror. Several prisoners get up and pace with trancelike movements. Rashien turns off the TV.]

BONES: Rusty, go check that damn door. Ain't no way in hell they left us locked up in here.

[Almost everyone mutters in agreement as Rusty exits stage right.]

JAKWAN: You're wasting your time. You heard the broadcast. Radiation is sweeping across the land. Anyone in his right mind would haul ass away from that cloud.

KEV: There's an unwritten law that says us prisoners are stuck in here, no matter what type of disaster happens.

ZIGGY: *[With rising terror in his voice.]* But . . . but they can't lock us in here to die! That's murder!

DRAMA: *[Laughs sarcastically.]* All that shit you was talking like you the ultimate thug. Now look at you. You sound like a cold-blooded bitch!

ZIGGY: *[Lunges at Drama, but Dondi grabs him.]* I'ma fuck you up! Let's bang out! Me and you, one-on-one!

[Rusty reenters and instantly starts fighting Blackjack, while Bones and Gripper are engaged in a standoff, sizing each other up with knives in their hands. Jakwan, Kev, and Shondu rush toward the commotion.]

SHONDU: *[Screams at the top of his lungs.]* STOP IT!

[The shout startles everyone. They all freeze. They all cut their eyes at Shondu, glaring at him as if he's crazy.]

SHONDU: What the fuck's wrong with your ears? A nuclear plant has been hit, and radiation is headed right at us!

JAKWAN: For those who don't know what that means, in simple language, we're about to be exposed to deadly doses of radiation. Once exposed, we could be dead within forty-eight hours. I did the research, and believe me, radiation sickness is a wicked way to die.

SHONDU: We got two choices here. Either we work together and possibly live through this situation, or we die fighting and killing each other over some bullshit nonsense.

[The prisoners slowly pull separate, staring at each other with smirks and frowns on their faces. Ziggy takes another swing at Drama. The blow drops Drama to the floor.]

GRIPPER: Maintain, Ziggy! You throw another shot and I'll personally wipe your bitch ass up with the floor.

[Drama staggers to his feet and is about to rush at Ziggy, but Bones grabs his arm.]

BONES: Chill, Drama! Let it ride!

DRAMA: *[To Bones.]* He stole on me, man. *[To Ziggy.]* The last motherfucker who snuck me—

BONES: *[Shakes Drama aggressively.]* I said let it ride!

[There is a moment of silence as the prisoners resume their staring match, struggling not to continue fighting.]

SHONDU: *[Excited.]* The first thing we need to do is see if we can get out of this rec room. *[Looks around, causing everyone else to do the same.]*

DONDI: Naw, I think the first thing needs to be done is to have Gripper and Bones shake hands or something and give us their word that they gonna work together.

DA'UD: Yeah, 'cause what y'all do from here on can hurt us all.

JAKWAN: I say they all should shake hands and give those knives to a neutral party.

[Gripper and Bones lock eyes with each other as the silence intensifies. They reluctantly shake hands. Drama sucks his teeth while sighing in disgust. Gripper and Bones look at the others, instructing them with nods to go along. The two rival groups shake hands while giving their weapons to Mel and Dondi.]

SHONDU: Now we can check this place to see where we stand.

DA'UD: Me and Rashien will check the windows over here. *[Da'ud and Rashien exit stage left.]*

GRIPPER: We'll check the police booth. *[Gripper, Ziggy, and Blackjack exit stage right.]*

JAKWAN: *[Tugs at Kev's and Shondu's arms.]* Come on, we'll check all the doors down here.

[Jakwan, Kev, and Shondu exit stage left. Drama pulls Bones and Rusty downstage, looking around suspiciously. Before he talks, he looks to see what Mel and Dondi are doing. When he sees they're not paying any attention, Drama whispers.]

DRAMA: That shit he just pulled ain't going down without being dealt with. Just follow my lead.

RUSTY: We should just air them out right here and now. I still got two bangers and a razor.

BONES: Hold up. I know that chump violated, Drama, but right now we need to focus on gettin' the fuck outta here. After that, we do whatever.

DRAMA: Naw, man, we gotta bust our guns now.

BONES: Well, I'm pulling rank. I'm crew chief, and we do it my way.

[The groups return to the stage with depressed looks on their faces. As Bones heads toward the group, Drama and Rusty whisper to each other. They break from their huddle, nodding as they join the group.]

SHONDU: The doors are dead.

RASHIEN: So are the windows.

GRIPPER: There's nothing in the booth either.

JAKWAN: We should talk about this as a group. Do some brainstorming or something. Come up with a plan of action.

[All the prisoners pull up seats, forming a circle. Da'ud and Rashien re-arrange the seats near the TV stand, while Shondu, Jakwan, and Kev retrieve the chairs from the table they sat at earlier. Dondi, Mel, Gripper, Blackjack, and Ziggy lean against the Ping-Pong table, while Bones, Drama, and Rusty sit at the weight bench.]

SHONDU: *[Looks at watch.]* Not to scare anyone, but I think we better keep an eye on the time.

GRIPPER: The bottom line is, we gotta get out of here.

BONES: If we ain't got keys or hacksaws and a damn tank, I don't know how we gonna pull that off.

RASHIEN: Even if we get over the wall, the radiation is going to be everywhere by then. That broadcast said the wind is blowing that stuff toward us. Shit, we're probably exposed to it already.

[Almost everyone shifts nervously in his seat. A nervous silence grips the room for several seconds.]

MEL: Since you put it that way, then maybe it might be wise for us to stay put.

KEV: *[Nodding.]* That might be a smart move. I heard one of the ways to deal with radiation is to go down inside a basement and seal up all the windows and doors with tape.

JAKWAN: *[Shakes his head.]* And what about air? If air can get in, then so can the radiation. What you talking about is a strategy for dealing with a biological weapon, and even that is suspect.

GRIPPER: *[Rises to his feet.]* I don't know what the hell y'all talkin' about. Stay put? Man, this is an opportunity. All the COs left. That means the ones in them gun towers, too. We could walk right out of this place, free men.

RUSTY: *[Eyes light up.]* Yeah! We should be talking about gettin' the fuck out of here!

SHONDU: If that's what we all agree to shoot for, we better do it before help arrives. We can start—

RUSTY: *[Interrupting.]* How you know help is gonna come? The way all them COs broke out, we the last thing on their minds.

DA'UD: Shondu's right. It might not be the COs, but someone will come here. They'll probably be dressed in radiation suits.

KEV: After they get this thing under control out there, they comin' up in here. How many of us'll be alive by then is another issue.

MEL: *[Heads for the weights.]* Let's get these weights together. We can use them to break open these gates.

DONDI: Let's break up some of these tables and use them as well.

[Everyone goes to the weights, picking them up, examining them closely.]

SHONDU: I ain't trying to badmouth this here, but I don't think this is gonna work.

DONDI: Well, let's try it out first.

GRIPPER: *[To Shondu.]* Man, I don't know what your problem is. This shit is gonna work.

[As the lights go down, all thirteen prisoners are moving the weights and the tables.]

SCENE IV

The lights come up on the bunker/office. Will, Sara, James, and Eric are counting boxes of supplies.

WILL: That's six boxes of bottled water—about two months' worth for the four of us.

SARA: I counted ten boxes of canned goods. With twenty cans in each box, I would say we have enough food for three, maybe four months.

ERIC: Medical supplies are at standard levels, with standard materials. There are more than enough potassium iodide pills.

WILL: James, check the phone again—it should be back on.

[James picks up the phone, clamps it to his ear, and taps the tone button several times.]

JAMES: Still dead. *[Places the phone back on its cradle.]* This is not good at all. Maybe we should have taken a chance and run like everyone else. The entire staff felt sure they could outrun that cloud. They might be—

[A low, muffled sound like banging is heard. They all look at each other nervously. Sara rushes to the monitors, looking at the screens while activating the buttons.]

WILL: Are you sure this bunker is as safe as Central Office claims?

ERIC: Relax, Will. We are several dozen feet underground, covered by concrete and steel, with special radiation-proof materials covering everything. A missile couldn't damage this bunker. Not to mention the fact that we have a radiation-filtering ventilation system.

WILL: If sound can seep in, what about radiation? It's obvious this thing isn't soundproofed.

ERIC: That is just the vibration from the pounding overhead. As you can hear, it's muffled considerably.

WILL: *[Sighs and takes a seat.]* Turn on the TV. Let's see if the emergency broadcast is back. Turn on the radio as well.

[James turns on the TV and gets nothing but static. He then turns on the radio and receives the same results. He plays with the dial and then turns the radio off.]

WILL: Keep both of them on, will you? Keep the volume low. That way, if a broadcast pops on, we won't miss it.

JAMES: *[Flops down in a cushioned chair, agitated.]* Why didn't I relocate when Debby begged me to? I don't know what was on my mind. I always knew this was possible, but I never thought it could really happen.

ERIC: The minute the NRC and FEMA refused to close down Indian Point and Bush started bombing everybody who didn't bend to his agenda, this became a catastrophe waiting to happen. Let's just be thankful our families are out of the peak zone.

WILL: I thought you were all for Bush's expansionist endeavors. Having second thoughts, Eric? It's a little late in the game for that.

SARA: *[Points to monitors.]* The surveillance cameras are picking up inmate movement in the corridors of the administrative building.

[Will and James rush over to the monitors and stare down at the screens. Eric peers over their shoulders.]

ERIC: You know what this means, don't you?

WILL: *[Seconds from losing control; stomps back to his seat.]* Damn it! I can only imagine what's going on out there. With a set of keys, they're all over areas they don't belong in. James, are you sure there are no secondary keys to the visitors' processing area?

JAMES: Of course I'm sure. *[Makes eye contact with Sara.]* You know as well as I do that policy requires those keys to be locked in a vault when not in use.

ERIC: If you're worried about the inmates walking out of here with a key, you can relax. The keys are obviously inaccessible, even if they find a way to get to the visitors' area.

SARA: What if they decide to climb the wall? If they're desperate and creative enough, I don't see how they can be stopped when there is no one in the gun towers.

WILL: Thanks, Sara—that's why I hired you. No tongue-holding or sugarcoating antics with you. What you see is what you get.

JAMES: Before we start pulling our hair out, I think we oughta—

[An emergency alarm sounds loudly. All four of them are hurled into a state of terror.]

WILL: *[Screaming over the alarm.]* What is going on, Sara? *[Rushes to monitors.]*

SARA: *[Struggles to find the right words.]* I . . . I . . . Oh, no!

WILL: What is it?

SARA: The . . . the radiation! It's here!

[The lights go down fast as they all stare at Sara with their mouths open.]

Act II

SCENE I

The lights come up on the recreation room. The thirteen prisoners are scattered about, some are sitting while others pace. They all have deeply saddened expressions.

GRIPPER: *[Stands abruptly, looks up.]* What about the vents up in the ceiling? That might work.

SHONDU: The same types of bars are up there as all over this damn prison. All that stuff up there is blocked off.

ZIGGY: How you know all this? It can't hurt to try.

JAKWAN: Be my guest, but you're wasting your time. I used to be a rec porter, and I saw those bars up there with my own eyes.

BONES: *[Desperate.]* Let's do something. Anything.

DONDI: What are we gonna do about food? *[Rubs his stomach.]* I'm starving. The way this is going, we're gonna be here for a while.

BLACKJACK: *[Angrily.]* This shit is foul, what these devils are doing to us.

[The remark causes an avalanche of comments agreeing with Blackjack.]

JAKWAN: Let's stay calm. If we start letting our minds run wild, the fear of starvation alone will accelerate the process.

RUSTY: How can we not worry when we see what the fuck is happening? *[Stands and paces.]* We should try to tear down those gates again and again until those fuckers come down!

SHONDU: We better preserve our energy. The more work we put in, the more our bodies are gonna need food.

ZIGGY: I ain't sitting around waitin' for shit to happen! *[Grabs a weight.]* I'm gon keep tryin'.

[Exits stage left.]

RUSTY: Yeah, I'm down with that. *[Follows Ziggy. Dondi, Mel, and Blackjack follow Rusty offstage.]*

KEV: That's good determination. I wish it could make a difference.

[Intense banging rings out.]

BONES: *[Stands up, heading stage right, but stumbles.]* Damn! Feels like I gotta throw up. *[Rushes offstage. Shondu and Jakwan look at each other nervously. Kev, Gripper, Drama, Da'ud, and Rashien see their expressions and become nervous.]*

DA'UD: *[To Jakwan.]* What's up? You think he's getting sick?

RASHIEN: Nausea is one of the symptoms of radiation sickness, ain't it? *[Sees Jakwan nod.]* Ah, fuck! The broadcast said the radiation shouldn't reach this area for several hours.

SHONDU: Predictions ain't always accurate. Anybody else feel sick?

KEV: *[Nervously.]* My stomach started actin' up about fifteen minutes ago. *[Shakes his head, unwilling to believe what's happening.]* Are ... I ... I usually get a queasy stomach when I get nervous. I haven't taken my insulin, either. It could be that.

JAKWAN: *[Looks at Shondu while Bones is heard offstage throwing up.]* I'm coming down with a headache. Since I don't normally get headaches, I know something is wrong.

DRAMA: I'm feeling sick myself. I got the same symptoms: a headache, stomachache. My appetite is even gone.

[Suddenly, from stage right Mel barrels onto the stage, holding his stomach.]

MEL: I gotta go to the bathroom. *[Continues past the others, exits stage left.]*

SHONDU: Well, I guess it's a wrap. We're exposed. From the response, I would say the radiation's at a high dose. *[Bows his head.]*

RASHIEN: *[Agitated.]* What kind of people would leave other people locked up with radiation all over the damn place and just run off?

JAKWAN: *[Snorts.]* And they call *us* animals and criminals. But who's the real criminals here?

DRAMA: They been planning this shit ever since 9/11, and all the while the Department of Corrections knew damn well they was gonna lock us in here if that nuclear plant was hit.

DA'UD: They've been trying to close down that nuclear plant for years. It's the only one near a densely populated region in the country.

JAKWAN: *[Shakes his head in disgust.]* Even an idiot could see it was a top terrorist target.

[Suddenly a loud cheer rings out from stage right. Ziggy, Rusty, Dondi, and Blackjack reenter the stage with two additional prisoners.]

ZIGGY: *[Elated.]* They got keys! They got keys!

JAKWAN: *[Lights up.]* Rondu! Primo! *[Hugs both men.]*

[Lights fade, scene shifts to bunker.]

SCENE II

SARA: If the electricity cuts off, the negative air pressure vents may stop functioning. That would mean contaminated air could enter this bunker.

JAMES: I don't think we have to worry about the electricity going out. Besides, the electric company has several backup generators, and so does this facility. We have an overkill of safety with regard to the electricity.

SARA: *[A restrained grin.]* It's good to see we're taking this seriously . . . *[Eyes suddenly grow wide, staring at the monitor.]* Oh my God! There's a mob of inmates at the door leading to this bunker!

[Will, James, and Eric bolt to the monitor.]

JAMES: They . . . they have a key! Look at them! Oh my God, they're opening the door!

[All four of them turn and face stage right. Sara slowly steps backward, as if in a trance. Their eyes are wide, and their mouths hang open in shock. Jakwan enters first, followed by the others. They all look very weak and sickly. Bones, Mel, Kev, and Rashien are in bad shape and are being assisted by other prisoners. When they see Will and the others, they stop abruptly, with shocked expressions.]

SHONDU: Superintendent Wilkinson!

JAKWAN: And the executive team.

JAMES: What are you inmates doing in this restricted area? Possession of keys is a felony offense.

WILL: *[Points to the door.]* I'm giving you a direct order to leave this area!

GRIPPER: *[Moves toward them menacingly.]* And who's gonna make us? You and your crew?

DONDI: *[Steps in front of Gripper.]* Chill, Gripper. This ain't the time to start a fight.

GRIPPER: Can't you see we sick because y'all left us up there to die?

SARA: *[Picks up a dosimeter.]* When you all entered, did a machine come on and blow warm air over your bodies?

[Everyone mutters in agreement.]

SARA: *[Walks toward the group, waving the dosimeter.]* Let's see if the decontamination device is working *[Looks at meter, sighs in relief.]* It's good. The radiation is at safe levels.

DA'UD: *[Angrily.]* But what about the damage that's already done?

JAKWAN: Yeah, because once we're exposed, the damage is irreversible.

ERIC: *[Holds up both hands.]* Listen, gentlemen, this unfortunate situation was not our fault.

RASHIEN: *[Tiredly.]* Maybe not the explosion at Indian Point. But what's happening now is.

KEV: There was no evacuation plan for us, and you didn't do a damn thing to make sure it wouldn't go down like this!

ZIGGY: Y'all got some nerve. Y'all down here safe and sound while we up there dying from radiation. You think that's right?

RUSTY: *[Points at Eric.]* Ain't you the one who told them to put me in the box last year?

[Moves menacingly toward Eric.]

ERIC: *[Nervously.]* I . . . I don't know what you're talking about. *[Tries to hide behind Will.]*

BONES: *[Coughs as he grabs Rusty's arm.]* Let it ride, Rusty.

DRAMA: I wanna hear the answer to Ziggy's question. Do you think it's fair that we're up there dying while y'all down here safe?

[There is a tense silence as Will, James, Eric, and Sara look at each other awkwardly.]

DRAMA: Just like I thought.

[Interrupting all conversation, Mel falls to the floor. He curls up into a fetal position, trembling and convulsing in pain. As the prisoners rush to Mel, Bones, Kev, and Dondi double over in pain and collapse to their knees. The prisoners try to assist them by carefully laying them on the floor. Drama stumbles, and Ziggy grabs him. The two stare at each other for a moment. The others look on as if waiting for the fight to begin.]

ZIGGY: *[To Drama.]* I'm sorry about that sucker move back there. *[Sticks hand out for a shake.]* I hope we can do this thing as a team.

[Drama pauses and reluctantly shakes Ziggy's hand.]

JAKWAN: *[To Will and the others.]* We need help over here! I know you got medical supplies down here.

[Will, James, Eric, and Sara do not move a muscle. They make eye contact with each other.]

PRIMO: What's wrong with your ears? They need help!

SHONDU: Please, Superintendent Wilkinson, help us.

[Will, Eric, Sara, and James stare at each other as the lights go down fast.]

SCENE III

The lights come back up on the bunker, but this time the sick prisoners are lying on the floor, covered with blankets. Sara, Primo, and Da'ud are monitoring the prisoners while Will, James, Eric, Blackjack, Shondu, Jakwan, Drama, and Ziggy are downstage at a table talking.

JAKWAN: I want to personally thank you, Mr. Wilkinson. I can understand your apprehension and all, but we ain't trying to make your life miserable. We just wanna make it through this alive.

WILL: You're welcome.

BLACKJACK: *[Picks up a set of keys.]* Are these keys to the prison?

JAMES: Yes, they are, and please put them back.

[Blackjack sets the keys back down on the table and folds his arms.]

SHONDU: *[Shakes his head.]* So all those brothers out there in the blocks are gon die from radiation, huh?

JAMES: Yes, this is terrible. And we are really sorry, even if it doesn't seem like it. This is truly a tragedy.

ERIC: In all fairness, no one expected this would happen. The government had the National Guard protecting all nuclear power plants all across the country around the clock.

JAKWAN: We understand this situation caught everyone off guard. I guess we could point fingers all day long and start the blame game. That's not gonna help all those poor bastards out there.

WILL: I wish there was something we could do. Hopefully the National Guard will be here soon. Before the phone went dead, we spoke to Central Office. They assured us that help is on the way.

DRAMA: How many people can this bunker hold?

WILL: Twenty-five, maybe thirty.

ZIGGY: Get outta here! I think this joint could easily hold at least seventy or eighty people.

JAKWAN: Maybe even a hundred if y'all ain't got a problem with close contact.

SHONDU: *[To Ziggy and Jakwan.]* Are y'all thinking what I think y'all thinking?

JAMES: Hold it—wait a minute here. There is no way we are going to allow that.

ERIC: *[Nodding.]* Not only is it a security breach to put more people in this area than it can legally hold, but it would endanger the lives of us all.

WILL: I agree. Without security staff to monitor this sort of overcrowding, the inmates may pose great danger to my staff and me. I'm sorry, I cannot permit this.

BLACKJACK: You mean to tell me you would sit by and do nothing to help those people?

DRAMA: How you gonna sleep at night with something like that on your conscience?

ERIC: *[Sighs impatiently.]* Let's say we agree to this plan you're talking about. Who's willing to go out there and expose themselves to lethal doses of radiation while you open the cells and bring the inmates back here?

[Jakwan, Shondu, Drama, and Blackjack raise their hands. Ziggy reluctantly raises his hand only after the others give him a disappointed look.]

SARA: But—but why risk your lives?

JAKWAN: *[Disgustedly.]* You gotta ask? I put myself in the shoes of those unlucky guys out there. If Rondu ain't come looking for us, we'd still be in that rec room. It's only right we do the same for somebody else.

SHONDU: *[Bumps fists with Jakwan.]* I'm willing to do this because I know a few dudes out there who'd do the same for me. Plus, I'm a lifer. I'm never going home. I always wanted to know how it felt to do something positive for a change. I can't think of a better way than to help out my brothers who are still locked up back there with no hope.

DRAMA: I know a lot of good dudes out there. A lot of them brothers don't deserve to be left for dead.

BLACKJACK: I won't be able to live with myself if I don't try to help those cats out there. And I know if it ain't my time to die, I'll make it through this, no matter what.

JAMES: *[Adamant.]* I still object to this course of action. If you leave this bunker, you'll be committing suicide. By now the radiation has increased tremendously.

ERIC: In any event, you'll be wasting your time, because at this moment most, if not all, of the inmates are already dead or irreversibly affected by the radiation.

WILL: *[Sympathetically.]* I'm very impressed with your willingness to risk your lives to help others. However, I'm sorry, gentlemen. As the superintendent of this facility, I must refuse your request to leave this bunker.

ZIGGY: *[Mockingly.]* Well, guess what, Mr. Superintendent? This wasn't a request. Look around you. When is it gonna dawn on you that right about now you ain't got no authority to stop us?

SHONDU: *[Rises to his feet.]* No disrespect, Mr. Wilkinson, but this is something we gotta do. *[Picks up a bottle of pills.]* It's time to load up on these potassium iodide pills, my brothers. *[Taps three pills into each of the open palms.]* Take all three in one shot, 'cause we goin' in the jungle. *[Tosses pills in his mouth and pockets the bottle.]*

DRAMA: Yeah, can't go wrong with triple protection. *[Slams pills in his mouth.]*

ERIC: Those pills will only protect the thyroid gland. All the other organs . . .

ZIGGY: Some protection is better than no protection.

JAKWAN: Blackjack, grab those keys. We got some gates that gotta get opened 'round here. *[Jakwan leads the group offstage as the lights go down fast.]*

SCENE IV

The lights come up on the bunker. There are dozens of new prisoners and one civilian lying scattered all over the stage. There is hardly walking room. Will, James, Eric, and Sara sit huddled upstage right, looking on in awe.

WILL: *[Anxiously.]* We have to stop this! They're going to bring the whole damn prison in here!

ERIC: *[Near panic.]* The radiation residue left on each new inmate who enters this bunker will cause the radiation to reach a dangerous level. The decontamination system isn't designed to get rid of every speck of radiation.

SARA: I hate to say this, but I think this is going to be their last trip, whether they want it to be or not. The way they stumbled out of here, I doubt if they even make it back.

ERIC: I tell you, Will, we're committing a crime by letting them go out there. They are killing themselves, and we are just sitting here watching and doing nothing.

WILL: Well, Eric, you have my permission to stop them.

[Just as Eric is about to respond, Jakwan, Ziggy, Shondu, Drama, and Blackjack enter stage right, practically dragging weak and sick-looking prisoners. Two men dressed in civilian clothing stumble in on the heels of the prisoners. Jakwan and the others carefully lay the prisoners down on the floor as Sara rushes to them, waving the dosimeter over the newcomers' bodies. Will and James rush to the two civilians in an excited fashion.]

WILL: My God, Bob, what are you doing here?

JAMES: Why didn't you get out with the others?

BOB: I . . . I didn't think it was going to be this serious. John and I stayed back to help the inmates.

JOHN: *[Looking around the bunker.]* Why didn't anyone inform us about this place? Is it really radiation-proof, like these inmates claim?

[Will nods as Jakwan turns to leave but trips and falls flat on his face. He's breathing very hard. Ziggy, Blackjack, and Drama flop down to the floor. They are beyond exhausted. Bob and John go to the fallen inmates, trying to assist them.]

ZIGGY: I—I'm out. My head is spinning.

JOHN: Just take it easy. You have to give your body some rest.

DRAMA: *[Breathing hard.]* I feel sleepy. I can't go back out again.

SHONDU: *[Staggers to his feet.]* I'm going . . . *[His legs give out, and he falls to the floor. Bob goes to him.]*

JAKWAN: *[Rolls onto his back.]* We did all we can do, Shondu. We made four trips, found three civilians and a whole lot of prisoners. We did major work.

BLACKJACK: Shit! We promised those cats in A Block we'd come back for them. But . . . but I don't think I can do it. That's it for me.

DRAMA: Our bod-bodies won't allow any more. *[Grabs his stomach.]* Oh, shit! I gotta throw up! *[Struggles to hold it back.]*

SARA: Wait! *[Grabs a plastic pan, heading for Drama.]* Do it in this! *[Places pan near Drama's face just as he vomits. Sara walks over to Will, James, and Eric, who watch Drama with pitying expressions. Will approaches the prisoners laid out on the floor. He stops in front of Jakwan and Shondu, peering down at them while nodding. Jakwan starts coughing, which causes the others to cough as well. Will glances around the room at the others. His eyes return to Jakwan as he starts to tremble violently.]*

WILL: *[Kneels and squeezes Jakwan's arm.]* Hang in there, big guy. You men are truly remarkable. I just pray to God you all make it through this. You showed amazing courage and concern for others out there today. You deserve to be recognized for what you have done.

[The lights go down rapidly.]

SCENE V

The lights come up on a room with a hearing in progress. Upstage right is a long table with five men dressed in suits and three women similarly attired. One of them is Superintendent Will Wilkinson, who sits in the last chair to the left. Upstage center, Jakwan sits in a wheelchair, facing the panel.

MALE #1: Mr. Jakwan Robinson, the Board of Pardons would like to thank you for appearing before us. Are you aware of why we summoned you here?

JAKWAN: Not exactly.

FEMALE #2: Superintendent Wilkinson, along with Commissioner Goldwater, made a request that this board consider you for a pardon in the form of a reduction in your sentence for your heroic deeds during the Indian Point nuclear power plant catastrophe.

MALE #4: *[Looks up from the report in front of him.]* You and four other inmates, with no concern for your own safety, saved the lives of three civilian employees and sixty-one inmates. That was a very honorable act that shows you've made great strides in your rehabilitative journey.

MALE #1: We're very sorry the other four inmates aren't with us today. This board intends to honor them for sacrificing their lives to save others.

FEMALE #1: Mr. Robinson, you are currently serving a fifteen-year sentence for armed robbery, of which you have completed two thirds. How would you it like if we knocked off the other third?

JAKWAN: With all due respect, do you really want to reward me for those lives I saved?

[The panel, including Will, look at Jakwan and each other with confused expressions.]

WILL: Why, of course, Mr. Robinson. That is why we are here. What you did deserves—

JAKWAN: Excuse me for interrupting you, Mr. Wilkinson, but if you really want to reward me, please let me say my piece first. And if possible, please allow my words to guide you to do the right thing.

[Jakwan pauses, collecting his thoughts. He draws a deep breath and expels it slowly.]

I'm sure we all can agree the Indian Point nuclear power plant incident was a disaster of epic proportions. I also think we all can agree this was a foreseeable situation. It was so foreseeable that all sorts of evacuation plans were put in place for every citizen in or near the peak zone. National Guard troops were stationed all over the place months, maybe even years, before this disaster occurred. The prison even built an underground radiation-proof bunker. And most of all, because the citizens living near or within Indian Point's peak zone were forewarned, and therefore ready, the casualties were reduced tremendously. All of this is good, but it presents a whole lot of questions that scream for answers.

[Jakwan shakes his head and struggles to hold his tears as the silence reaches uncomfortable levels.]

The most obvious question is, why weren't prisoners included in that evacuation plan, even though we were well within the peak zone? *[After looking into each of the panel members' eyes, he continues.]* Why wasn't a radiation-proof shelter put in place for prisoners? Why did the corrections officers lock us up and flee the prison? Why wasn't one single person penalized for the deaths of the eleven hundred or more prisoners who died as a direct result of the failure of the Department of Corrections to protect them? Why weren't potassium iodide pills given to the prisoners beforehand, like it was done with all the other hundreds of thousands of Westchester County residents? Why did it take three days for the cleanup crew to arrive at the prison? *[Shouts.]* Why? Why? Why? Why?

[Three corrections officers enter from stage right in a very excited fashion. The entire panel waves them away, clearly indicating that everything is under control. The three officers exit apprehensively. Jakwan wipes away tears.]

I know there will never be answers to these questions. I guess that is because it is socially acceptable to believe a prisoner's life is not as valuable as a free person's life. If this is not the case, then fact and reality are in conflict with my lying eyes. You asked me if I would like to have five years knocked off my bid. *[Pauses while nodding.]* Yes, of course I would like that. Even one day knocked off would be an event worthy of praise and appreciation. But . . . If you truly want to honor, commend, and reward me and my friends for the lives we saved, I ask that you please allow me to choose the reward. In other words, I want you to swap this time cut you are offering me for a bigger and better good, and I'll gladly do the five remaining years I was sentenced to do.

[Jakwan stares at the panel as if waiting for a response. The silence holds for a moment.]

MALE #1: We can't make any promises until we hear what it is you would like us to do.

JAKWAN: I want you to go to the state legislators and get a bill passed that not only says that inmates are to be included in all evacuation plans regarding any and all disasters but provides for that to happen.

FEMALE #1: *[Protesting.]* But inmates *are* included in these plans—

JAKWAN: *[Interrupting.]* If that was the case, I don't think I would be sitting before you all . . . The way things are going, terrorist attacks are becoming a fact of life in this country, and we're going to have to learn to live with it. Some even believe that this last disaster is just the tip of the iceberg. Hopefully, such a law will prevent other prisoners from ever experiencing what I went through, and it will save lives. This will be the greatest honor or reward this board can do for me. As a member of the human race, I don't think this is an unreasonable or unattainable request. *[Makes eye contact with Will and holds the stare for a moment.]* And I truly believe you all will do the right thing.

[Before anyone on the panel is able to respond, Jakwan wheels himself off stage right. The members of the panel all look at each other. Will nods with a smile, causing all the others to nod as well.]

[Curtain.]

Gary Hicks

Gary Hicks is a man of principle; he is a poet, a man who reads constantly, and a man who will fight for what he believes in regardless of the cost. He is "an old-school convict." His associates call him Hippy, and it suits him. In keeping with that tradition, he sees it as his duty to battle the establishment, and he looks the part as well. "When I first came to prison in 1983, I went directly into the college program, and I got an A.A. Then, in 1997, all of a sudden my beard and hair became a security risk. They took my job; they took my red card, which allows me to leave the cage on weekends, holidays. If you don't have a job, you are locked down most of the time. When they first took our red cards, we couldn't go to the law library, and we were cell fed; we couldn't even shower. When I won in court, everyone was given back their status except for me. I can't go out to night yard, I can't go out to the yard on weekends or holidays, and on weekends I have to lock in the cell at 2:15 for the night."

Gary told me this as we sat in the Arts in Corrections program at Soledad Prison and talked about the trials and turmoil that are part and parcel of doing time. At fifty-two, he is in the twenty-fourth year of a fifteen-to-life sentence for second-degree murder. "For eight years they took me out of the writing program. They threw me in the hole because I wouldn't shave or cut my hair." Gary has spent the better part of the past twenty years fighting the system about something. Sometimes he wins and sometimes he loses, but he always fights for what he believes are his rights.

"Are you finished having to fight with them about hair?" I asked.

He chuckled. "Well, not exactly. Now they are trying to say the beard has a half-inch restriction, but I have them in court on that too."

Gary told me about a time when he was working as a program clerk and he and a CO were having a difficult time. The CO wanted Gary to correct the disciplinary reports, which were riddled with errors, and Gary refused. He would type them as they were written and send them on their way. The reports would get returned with the statement "retype, re-issue," because they were poorly written. The CO would get upset; it was making him look bad. But Gary always kept a copy, which he would pull out and hold up for the CO to see. "I told him that this is a legal document. I have neither the authority nor the desire to clean up the work, and it will go out as it is." Gary nodded his head as if to say "There it is."

"Did it end well?" I asked.

"No, he sent me to the North Yard as revenge," Gary said.

I knew enough to know that wasn't a good thing, and images of segregation ran through my head. Gary has done enough time to be used to rolling with the punches; he has seen it all. He is pragmatic. He hasn't had a visit since 1986. In many ways he is glad that he doesn't get visits; they can be very stressful. "The attitude of the COs is that anyone who would lower their standards to visit a convict is a piece of crap. They are a low-class citizen." Gary wondered about what that must do to visitors. When I asked him if he missed visits, he said, "I can't miss getting visits. It wouldn't do me any good." There are things you worry about, and then there are things you just let go. Gary has done time his way, on his own terms.

When it comes to writing and reading, there seems to be nothing that can stop Gary Hicks. He reads continuously; he always has a book. In fact, he reads while he is walking, while he is standing waiting to go somewhere, or while he's just waiting, and there is plenty of that in prison. You always have to be prepared to wait. "You can come up from C Wing, just a couple hundred yards from the library, just to see if the library is open, and it can take you two, two and a half hours to get back to the wing," Gary told me. It is just a way of life, and he has adapted by always having something to read with him.

"How did you find writing?" I asked.

"I always wrote when I was a kid," he replied. As a child, he had a little cubby area where he kept all of his work. Even then he felt the need to write. Like many writers, he was critical of his work, but that didn't stop the creative process. "One day I found my stepmother reading my work. I told her it was no good because I couldn't spell and I didn't know where to put the periods. She said, 'I can spell most words in the dictionary, and I know where to put the periods, but I can't write like this. I don't have a creative mind like you do.'" She also told him, "You can hire a flunky like me to fix your spelling."

Gary chuckled at the memory, and then he said, "I have been in writing classes for a lot of years. I have always written. I fell into poetry and it took over. I have written a poem a day since 2000." He went on to add, "To get to this class is not easy. You have to jump through hoops. You have to fight to get something that is supposed to be offered."

Gary pulled out a black-and-white composition book filled with poetry. "I've got probably about two thousand pages of writing like that," he said as he showed me poetry written so small that an entire poem might take up a half an inch of space. When you live in a six-by-nine cell with someone else, conservation becomes imperative, and he has spent years perfecting his space-saving techniques.

For Gary, writing is a calling; he walks around with words in his head looking for a place on the page. When he is working on a poem, he is not satisfied until he has found the exact word, but it is all part of the process. "You can go crazy looking for one word. In poetry, sometimes I can spend hours looking for one word. I'll do other things, but then it will come to me, and I'll run back and fix it. I'll know the poem is done when I realize I've been there before, when the word I find is one I have already tried."

Gary has even been known to interrupt a five-mile jog to get something down on paper. "I will do a five-miler jogging along around the yard, and I will have to stop and run over to my stuff and write something down," he said with a laugh. We chuckled about how long it must take to finish the run with all the writing that he does. Gary Hicks lives with words and ideas; they are there floating just below the surface, waiting to be captured and used by this man whose sharpened wit and intellect have kept him alive and well in a system that doesn't deal well with either.

For all the time Gary has spent behind the walls, in places that are designed to kill you young, he has managed to survive without losing his humanity. The yard at Soledad used to have a number of feral cats that were starving and scared. Gary spent weeks taking food out for the cats, slowly working to gain their trust, and before long they were running out to greet him, twining themselves around his legs, purring like housecats. They depended on him, and soon Gary had COs and inmates alike saving food for him to give to his newfound dependents.

Gary's poetry is a vehicle that allows his voice to soar beyond the walls. In "Cellie" we can clearly hear a prisoner's lament for spending day in and day out with someone who hasn't learned to do time, thus making life more difficult for anyone in close proximity. "Recede" defines time as more brutal with each passing year, each decade moving more slowly than the last. Gary demonstrates that his humor is still intact in "Game," and we breathe a sigh of relief because he can still appreciate the absurdity of it all.

In Margaret Atwood's novel *Amazing Grace,* the narrator describes her battles with the administration of the prison where she has served fifteen years: "If you have a need and they find it out, they will use it against you. The best way is to stop from wanting anything." Gary Hicks is a man who has mastered the fine art of not wanting.
　　　　　　　　　　　　　　　　　　　　　　　—Susan Nagelsen

Poems

GARY HICKS

Garden

The mirror has bent away from kindness.
Though never kind enough to reflect handsome,
It now leans toward cruel.
Life,
Like a garden,
Grows through stages.
They run from seed to fertilizer.
When I look into the mirror today
There's no doubt which stage I've stepped into.

Reason

If age were reason
Allowed as valid excuse
I'd be fat and bald

Love

Grape and yellow night
A full week past black and blue . . .
The swelling's gone down.

Madness

Each spring opens with
A momentary madness
That lasts all year long

Gary Hicks

Sodium

Stars don't exist here.
Nor do the wishes carried upon them.

Blocked not by buildings, trees, or clouds,
They're bleached by lights.

A dirty yellow sodium glow covers all like smog.
Even the full moon must compete.

It moves across the sky in challenge of weakness,
Some weakness beneath the sodium glow.

It won't be found here.
These lights never go out.

Recede

One more yesterday is pasted to life,
To time,
To history.
Neither slow nor fast, only constant.
Constant with static change.
Life in life is short,
Life in prison isn't.

Each year,
Every decade,
Is longer . . .
Crueler than the last.
Hell has no flames,
Only windows that won't open,
Doors sealed shut . . .
Year after year.

Error

Gut with realistic sharpness
Time's scars run deep,
Deep across my brow.
There was a time in life,
In youth,
When I knew it would never happen to me.
I was different.
I was wrong.

Cup

His eyes were filled with wisdom,
They said more than words could ever express.
They showed the difference between difficult and hard . . .
Life is difficult,
It's hard to understand why.
I put a dollar in his cup.

Eleven

Another sleepless night,
Without meditation or comfort.
Eleven, twelve . . .
One, two, three, four.
Moments after five,
As the sun rises,
So do I.

Too Long

Once,
Too long ago,
I flew freely.
Far beyond body, gravity, ground . . .
Imagination soared.

Today . . .
Such separation's stopped.
Reflections are grounded,
Flight's flown away.
I've fallen into an age of anchor.

Too Often

Unspoken.
Once again
Things were left . . .
Unspoken.

Too often,
Too many things
Are politely left . . .
Unspoken.

Now
It's too late to say
What we've left . . .
Unspoken.

Cellie

Whining again.
First words spoken each morning,
Last words every evening
Are complaints.
This is always wrong,
That's never right . . .
Life's a torture chamber.
Not for all;
Only for him.
Every break goes to another.
His plate is always empty.
He searches for sympathy,
Seeks pity from all.
Though it may seem callous
I passed caring months ago.

Again

It's happened again.
I've survived another day,
But night's still to come.

Annoyance

Red card program.
Wing's tables fill,
Games commence . . .
Cards, chess, dominos.
All are slammed with force to the tables,
Territories are marked . . .
Claimed.
Time's 10:30 A.M.
Hours past breakfast,
Almost lunch,
Yet my bunkie's in bed.
Wasting time,
Wasting life.
Suddenly standing, he stomps to the door,
Kicks it, and yells,
"That's what it sounds like in here.
Goddammit, shut the fuck up!"
Noise slows for a moment,
Maybe two.
He lies back down and continues,
Continues to complain.
"Porch monkeys,
Niggers being niggers . . .
Goddamn disrespectful bastards."
I put my headphones on,
Turn the radio up.
Their noise I can tolerate,
His ignorant whining . . .
That's the real annoyance.

Wash

Night,
Like water,
Washes over all.
Swept away,
I surrender to darkness,
Drown in emotion . . .
Silently.

Sunrise

> Transparent morning.
> Cold cereal without milk.
> Then the sun rises.

Place

> Many have loved me.
> Now,
> With the passage of years,
> I've fallen into an existence without.
> What mattered so much once is mere minor to me now.
> Love no longer is.
> Not anymore . . .
> Not for me.
> I've fallen into a place where the only love to be found
> Is found in dreams.

Promise

> Prison is . . .
> Hypnotic boredom.
>
> Prison is . . .
> Draconian dreariness.
>
> Prison is . . .
> Stone cold.
>
> Prison is . . .
> Life without.

Grinch

> It's happened again,
> I awoke in prison.
> Christmas approaches but never arrives.
> There's no such thing here.
> Holidays aren't allowed.

Faith

My inability to believe
Absolutely in God's demands:
For God demands
All sheep be passive.
I bow my head in prayer,
In hope God won't notice
My doubt.
My fear there may be no God.
No afterlife.
That death will be fatal.

Door's Open

I, too, hesitate.
Caught somewhere between apology and anger.

Conundrum

The crippled ant struggles:

Is she in pain,
Or is it some senseless insect need
To complete her mechanical mission?

Others pass:
They stop to touch.

Alligator sympathy,
Then . . .
Abandonment.

An accident on the freeway . . .
Gawkers.

In mercy, should I kill her,
This nameless,
Numberless ant?

My foot hovers.

Shower

Thirty-five swinging dicks shuffle into place,
To wait.
There are but four showers.

Prison suffers each inmate only three pairs of socks,
Two boxers
To last a week.

We're allotted twenty minutes.
This time's not enough,
It's never enough
To get clean.

Once

I did that then,
Then,
Too,
I also did that.

I'm not the same
As the he
Who was me Then.

He had
Different views,
Other plans, concepts,
Ideas and dreams.
I liked him too.

Pause

Twilight parts night and day
Separates the world into maybe.
Shadows stall,
Contemplate moving forward or back.

Follow

With age comes realization.
One realization hit like a truck,
A Mac truck.
A Mac truck at freeway speed . . .
Head-on.

All my friends,
My good old friends,
Have come to term.
The term they've reached is death.

How can it be
That I would live to see
A time where the remainder
Is me?

I hope they all know
Even though
I love and miss them so,
I'm not ready yet
To go.

Reflections

Wishes . . .
Both large and small,
Are made by many.

Gods . . .
Created by myth or man,
Are questioned.

Responses . . .
Imagined or real,
Are interpreted
By choice.

Eclipse

Environment is a cage,
Wake up,
Leave from,
Return to,
Go to sleep in a cage.

How much longer will this last?

I've missed comets,
Planets' alignment,
Eclipses.

Tonight I missed a full moon
Reborn from earth's shadow.

I've missed life in a thousand different ways.

Rehabilitation,
Damnation.
My thesaurus doesn't link them together,
Though here . . .
They are synonymous.

Earthquake

Rubble, broken bricks, splinters, and dust,
Choking dust,
Are all that remains.
She was here when I left,
So safe and secure before the earthquake.

Would it have made any difference,
Any difference at all if I'd been here,
Been home with her when it happened?

When she needed me most,
When the need was really there,
I wasn't.

Game

Dear Jesus,
For me,
Please do this one little thing.
I know you can, Lord,
My faith in you is true.
He seems certain,
So certain,
But I have my doubts as I listen to him pray.
I wonder,
Really wonder,
Does Jesus care what the final results will be?
Personally,
I don't believe Jesus watches football on Sundays.

Cool

His arms are canvas for art,
Tattoos.
Some are color,
Others aren't.
Tattooed shoulders to nails,
Only his palms remain plain.
Twenty-five,
Maybe thirty years ago,
While he was still young and wild,
It may have looked cool,
But he's fallen out of focus.
Unlike Van Gogh's *Starry Night,*
Some art wrinkles.
His body has blurred.

John Yarbrough

My nearly twenty-five years of teaching undergraduate classes and doing research inside prisons should have prepared me for the Texas prison system. It did not. We traveled down the two-lane road toward the Ramsey I Unit, and we passed fields of corn on either side of the road. I knew that in another month prisoners would be out in those fields sweating, under the unforgiving Texas sun, slaving under the watchful eyes of men on horseback with shotguns, who would make sure they did their jobs and stayed put.

We turned right at the end of the road, following the sign directing us to Ramsey I. On the right were houses with beautifully maintained lawns, where prisoners were trimming hedges and weeding flower beds. I was sure these were the houses of the warden and other administrators at the prison, and the trustees were responsible for keeping everything looking just so. They had done their jobs well; everything was pristine and clearly well tended. Welcome to Texas, death penalty capital of the United States, a place where they take the incarceration of inmates very seriously.

In Texas, the men who are held behind the walls are never referred to by name; they are called "the offender." When we were finally granted permission to meet with John Yarbrough, it was clear that we were intruders and would be treated as such. "You will be allowed to meet with the offender for one hour," said the e-mail that granted us permission to visit.

At the front gate, once the paperwork had been located, we proceeded through the man trap, a cage within a cage designed to trap a man in a contained space, and into the courtyard of the unit. The courtyard was lovely. There were flowers and plants everywhere, and they had been tended with great care; there wasn't a dying bloom or a wilted leaf to be seen. We walked up to the double doors that led to the administrative building, our CO escort leading the way. In the lobby, we were told to have a seat. Over the doors leading out to the "world" were the words "Through these doors pass the greatest correctional officers in the world." I wondered what the prisoner thought as he painstakingly hand-lettered those words.

On the wall opposite where we sat were pictures of the prison administration and the parole board, and around the pictures, painted in the crimson and gold color scheme of the prison, was scrollwork. I watched as a trustee walked though the lobby and stooped to pick up a piece of lint from the polished linoleum floor, and I contemplated the conditioning that had made the man feel a sense of pride about a place such as this.

Our escort appeared and told us that it was time for us to meet with "the offender," and we were buzzed into the main part of the prison. After we passed through the door, the first room on the right was a barbershop. The sign over the door indicated that this was the barbershop reserved for officers, and when I glanced inside I saw a black prisoner with his back to me, working steadily at polishing a pair of boots. The next room, once again painted in crimson and gold, was small, and the sign above the door said VISITING ROOM. It was a no-contact visiting area, and there in the last cage sat John Yarbrough.

"Excuse me," I said to the officer, "but I think there has been a mistake. We are here to interview and take photographs of Mr. Yarbrough, and this is going to make our task very difficult."

The officer, a second-generation correctional officer who, at thirty-two, had twelve years on the job, replied, "According to the paperwork, you are allowed to meet with the offender for one hour during a regular visit, and a regular visit is a no-contact visit, so that is what you are going to have, ma'am."

I asked the officer if there was anyone I could talk with to try to make some other arrangements. He shrugged his shoulders and told us to follow him back to the lobby. Once there, I decided that I would try to speak with the warden, to see if he would intervene. I spoke with his administrative assistant, and she told me that he was in a meeting but that she would talk with him. She smiled at me, winked, and said, "Honey, I am sure we can work something out." I walked back to my seat feeling much better.

Fifteen minutes later, a dapper-looking African-American man walked up to me and introduced himself as the warden. He told me that they were working on finding a room that would be more suitable for our purposes. I was thrilled. I felt as though we had won a small victory for John Yarbrough, a man who has spent the last seventeen years in prison, isolated from normal human contact. In Texas, with few exceptions, all visits are no-contact, something that surely can be seen as cruel and unusual, and prisoners in the Lone Star State are allowed only one two-hour visit a week.

Our escort appeared before us again and asked us to follow him. We walked outside and back into the courtyard. We were taken into a small building, and as he was turning on lights and the air conditioner, I looked around. My temporary sense of victory vanished.

"Excuse me, but this is a no-contact visiting area," I said, trying to keep my voice even.

"Yes, ma'am. As I explained to you earlier, you are allowed to meet with the offender for one hour during a regular visit."

"But I just spoke to the warden, and he told me that we could have a contact visit and that he was working on finding a room for us," I said.

"Well, ma'am, the warden is in a meeting, and I can't get in touch with him. If you want the visit, this is the way it is going to be." He said it all with a slight smile on his face.

I turned as I heard the door open, and in walked another CO, and with him was John Yarbrough. It was this or nothing, so we sat down with Plexiglas and a metal louvered area for speaking between us, and we began our visit. Nothing could have prepared me for the look in John's eyes. The look was a confluence of pain and resignation, the same pain and resignation that inform his poetry. We see it in "Colors of Prison"; we wince as we read "Pain," and the man who sat before me had "That Look," the one that comes from fighting to stay alive in a system that seems determined to beat him into submission and keep him until he dies of old age or defeat, whichever comes first.

We talked about writing, and Texas prisons, and his case. John's southern drawl was slow and easy; I leaned in close so I could hear, as the room around me disappeared. "Writing is not that easy for me. I can't just sit down and decide I am going to write something and then write. I have to wait for an idea," John said when I asked him if he was a disciplined writer. I asked him about authors who had influenced his writing, and he spoke fondly of D. H. Lawrence and O. Henry and Elizabeth Bishop.

John told me that he had been writing with a friend for a while now. "I write with another guy. We wrote a book together. We would each write a chapter and go back and forth. Then I would give him my work and he would give me his, and we worked on it for about two years. After a while you couldn't tell our voices apart. It is called *Holy Day,* and it takes place in the 1500s, and it is about daily life in India." As he spoke about this collaborative effort, there was a spark of light in his eyes, but it was fleeting. Texas prisons do not foster happiness and light.

John had just turned sixty; he was forty-three when he was imprisoned. He had been a police officer for twenty-two years when he was convicted of murder and given a life sentence. He had been working in a small, tight-knit department, and he was the outsider. John says it was a corrupt department, with officers on the take, getting kickbacks from bail money. John admits he was a part of the corruption, but he did not have anything to do with murder. "I was in a bad position because I pled guilty, because they were gonna kill me if I didn't. I felt like I would be better off to try and stay alive and try to fight it. 'Cause I know how quick they'll kill you—you're gone in about eight years, so I've been fighting it ever since. I told the newspapers from the moment I was sentenced that I was innocent and I was gonna fight this."

He has been trying to find a way out of this "mess" ever since. But finally, after seventeen years, he has some hope. "My case is back on appeal right now. I have the Innocence Project trying to help me. We are in the Waco court of appeals now, and the State Judicial Commission is investigating the judge in my case." John is one of the lucky ones, because even after all this time, "they still have all the evidence. I was kind of surprised. I'll give 'em credit for that," he said. The DNA evidence would exonerate John, and the ballistics evidence would show that the gun used wasn't his, and yet he remains locked up in the Ramsey I Unit because the system is loath to surrender what it has conquered.

John has been fighting for his life in Texas, and he has given it everything he has. He has gotten a master's degree and written award-winning poetry, and with the exception of one disciplinary report for having an extra blanket, he has a clean record. In the process, John Yarbrough has lost touch with his children, his wife left him after four years, and he has faced the grim possibility of "doing forever" behind bars. "Parole is very difficult to make in Texas," he told me with a look of resignation. "The parole board doesn't put that much emphasis on what you do in here; they only care about the crime."

Our escorts signaled that our hour was over and it was time for us to go. I asked John how he made it through each day. "One day at a time, I guess. I just find things to stay busy." The guard who had brought him in came up behind him and placed a hand on his elbow. As I turned to leave, I reflexively put my hand up to the Plexiglas. John's hand joined mine, and our eyes met as we nodded our good-byes. "Thank you," he said. "I can't imagine that ya'll went through all this just to see me."   —SUSAN NAGELSEN

Poems

JOHN YARBROUGH

Pain

My life is a universe of pain.
I deal with it one planet at a time.
It will not marry me.
It will not bury me.

Grandma

Grandma would chase me
around the house with a butcher knife
she a tortoise me a hare.
In prison I learned
she should have gotten me at night
as I slept in my bed.

Colors of Prison

Lonely blue
Dull gray
Painful red
Scared yellow
Dead white

That Look

I hear that a lot of ex-cons are asked,
"Where did that look in your eyes come from?
It wasn't there before . . ."
We see it, too. We know it's there.
We know where it came from. It came
From sitting on the middle toilet in the row
and pretending you're alone.
From standing ass to ass in the shower
and acting like that's normal.
From not wanting to look too closely
at what's on your food tray.
From waiting in the pill line, the mail line,
the anything line.
From watching the guard hand out visitation slips
without slowing down at your cell.
From staring through razor wire at passing cars.
From looking anywhere but in someone else's eyes,
because you don't want to see
that look.

Freedom

Preachers come here talking about freedom. You can be free
　　　even in here they say.
The word will set you free they say. All you have to do is
　　　believe they say.
When they are through talking about freedom
They leave and all us free people
Return to our cells.

Tracy Atkins

Tracy Atkins is forty-two years old and serving a seven-and-a-half-to-fifteen-year sentence for accomplice to armed robbery. She is a Vermont country girl who is out of her element in the harsh environs of prison. Her hair curls softly around her face, which has a fresh-scrubbed look. She has been in prison a little over five years, and each day has been difficult, stressful, and above all lonely. Tracy has not made the adjustment to prison easily. When I asked her to describe the days when she first arrived at Bedford Hills Correctional Facility in New York, her eyes grew wide, and there was a fleeting look of fear.

"I was so, so afraid. I was on a handful of pills. I was screwed up. I think that was the doctor's way to help me through the transition into prison. I was really unstable." Tracy spent the first six months medicated as a way to ease her fears and anxiety. "I was so afraid that someone was going to jump me in the corridor, and I was going to have to fight, and I didn't want to do that because I know me, and I was afraid that I would seriously hurt someone because I believed I was fighting for my life."

She realized from her first encounters with other prisoners that she had a lot to learn. "I used to say before I came to prison, why are we sending our decent young boys off to fight? We should just send prisoners instead." Then she looked at me. Her face showed softness and understanding, and she said she had met some wonderful women, women accused of terrible crimes, and she couldn't believe how wrong she had been. She was very naive; she believed the things she had heard and seen on television and in the movies.

"When I first got here, they had to put me in a segregated area. In the reception area everyone would go to breakfast early, and that's when the officer would let me take a shower. One morning while I was in the shower, the officer yelled, 'Hey, Atkins, you straight?' Well, every prison movie I had ever seen ran through my head, because I thought she was talking about being straight or gay. But here that means 'Are you okay?'"

It took her four years even to begin to settle in, and she is still not used to it. "I never want to get used to it. It is always a different dilemma. There is always a different scenario that starts the day and another scenario that ends it."

"How have you managed?" I asked.

Tracy looked at me and laughed. "It could be worse. It could be better, but I don't like to dwell on that. I choose to make it better because I choose not to make it worse."

To accomplish this, she has chosen to stay to herself, to smile, to make the best of each day. For Tracy, prison has been isolating beyond normal expectations. She has actively worked to remove herself from her past life.

Tracy's shame is palpable, and her eyes dropped to the table when I asked her about packages from family. "I don't like to ask anybody for anything. This is my own fault. I did this to myself." Tracy feels that she doesn't deserve any kindnesses because she brought this on herself by leaving her daughters behind, by not standing up for herself. But her face lit up when she spoke about her sister. "My sister has been wonderful! She takes good care of me. She sends me pretty paper to write on; she makes sure I have enough good food." Tracy writes to her daughters once a month. She lets them know that she is doing fine, but she doesn't want to burden them with her struggles, so she keeps her letters light.

Tracy will not let people visit; she tried it but found that it was just too difficult. "I don't want any visitors. My friend Missy came to see me. She drove five hours just to see me. That was great." When Tracy was telling me about her visit with Missy, her voice was filled with incredulity; she was amazed that Missy would come all that way just to see her. She went on to say, "My dad visited once. He came all the way from Georgia, and that was just too hard. I just couldn't take it, knowing that I had to go back to my prison cell." I could see the pain, even in the telling of the story; it was as fresh as if it had just happened. Tracy will never be comfortable in prison. It will always be a place of shame, a house of fear and loathing.

Tracy joined the Puppy Behind Bars program, which has probably saved her life. In order to join she had to make it through the first year without a disciplinary report. It gave her focus. She has had four dogs to love and train as service or guide dogs, and when she spoke of her dogs, she was alive; she was Tracy Atkins, dog lover, dog trainer, sharing the joy of being involved in the lives of these animals, not someone locked up in a prison far from the people she loves. "At home I was a provider—I was someone people came to when they needed something. If a neighbor needed a friend, I was there. But in prison, in the beginning, there was nothing, and I felt worthless." Tracy stopped and smiled. "In the puppy program I am able to participate in a giving project. This program has helped give me back my self-worth."

Tracy has always had a difficult time interacting with people, and the puppy program has helped her overcome these difficulties. She attended classes to learn the art of dog training. "I don't like being the center of attention, and in puppy class I had to learn to do that. I mean, five years ago, I would have had a difficult time sitting down talking to you." The program gives her a purpose; it gives her something to do. Tracy takes her dog everywhere she goes; training is a full-time responsibility. "It is time-consuming, but it also consumes your time." Passing the time is all that matters, so she makes each day the best it can be and pushes on toward the next one.

Tracy loves writing and science and reading and everything except math, but school was not for her: "The highest grade I completed in school was the seventh grade." Math was her undoing. She just didn't get it, and she was someone who couldn't tolerate the restrictions of the formal educational system. "My mother died when I was young, and nobody could tell me what to do." Tracy was adamant that she knew best, so she quit going to school. "I just said, I'm not going." She hung out, ran away, got caught, got sent to foster homes, and ran away again; this cycle continued until she got pregnant and married at seventeen. But through it all Tracy never stopped reading. "I was always reading something. I was self-taught."

When Tracy came to prison, she started writing as a way to get all of the anger out of her. Before she knew it, her character, Harvey, had developed into a very bad guy, and she had two hundred pages of his ugliness stacked up in her cell. When her cell got tossed one night and a CO started asking questions, she decided to send the manuscript home for safekeeping, but it is something she will finish one day. Tracy's writing is drawn from the things she hears and her own experiences. "The Funeral" provides a window into an already fragile world being blown apart, leaving only sadness behind. It is the story of many incarcerated women.

In "The Funeral," Tracy offers poignant observations of the bleakest days of her life. Her life was disintegrating as the unimaginable unfolded before her very eyes. "It was a reflection of how I felt. I felt like I had died. At home you have friends, you feel unforgettable. Then when something like this happens, it is like you died. As the years go by, people forget." Tracy has learned that prison swallows people, leaving little trace of them behind. "You want so desperately for someone to write you a letter, or to acknowledge your existence, and it doesn't happen. And you really feel like you died inside." Tracy wrote "The Funeral" at a time when her divorce was being finalized and she was just beginning to understand the full ramifications of all that had happened; the fog was lifting, finally. "I realized how badly I had been used and abused. I knew that I had been such a fool."

Tracy is philosophical about her possibilities for parole when she appears before the parole board for the first time, two years from now. She has remained discipline-free; she will continue to hope. "I'm glad this happened to me. I have learned so much. I have finally learned to stand up for myself, and that is a good thing." Her only priority, if she makes parole, will be getting back in touch with her family and her life. "When this is all over, I am going to write about these years. I am going to call it 'The House on the Hill.' It will be a chronicle of my evolution from the scared basket case to a woman who can stand strong." —SUSAN NAGELSEN

The Funeral

TRACY ATKINS

Some people believe that the day you are born is the day you begin to die. Others may believe it is the day that you are diagnosed with cancer, AIDS, or some other terminal affliction.

My slow and painful death began on a cold and blustery February evening when I came upon a love from the past. That old spark rekindled a new flame, soon to be a raging fire burning out of control.

My peculiar funeral took place in August some years later, although I was unconscious of the fact of my dying.

There was no pain from my inevitable death. Love is such a soothing mask.

As my funeral procession scaled the immense stairs and gathered in a great room, there was a man draped in black. About his head was a halo of "In God We Trust."

At my funeral the man draped in black, the man beside me, the twelve people to my right, and my friends behind me all would soon know my fate.

The word "guilty" still seizes me like an isolated hallucination in a vast wilderness of nothing.

At my funeral the man playing God sentenced me to a far greater punishment than fit the crime. The crime I did not commit. My love did it, not I . . .

I lied and perjured myself throughout the hellish months before. I could have exonerated myself with the truth, yet I listened to and believed in him.

I have been imprinted by a master manipulator. "Just stick to the story—it will all be okay," he told me.

What a perfectly conditioned fool I have been, a dying fool, a jester, a dead puppet on a string, swinging by his interpretation of what would be.

Since the day of my phantom funeral my love has abandoned me, leaving me lost, loveless, and lonely, yearning for a way to turn back time, to right this wrong, to live, not to be in this persistent dead zone. For you see, he had two words to his verdict: "not guilty."

My dear friends and treasured family were bitterly angry with me for protecting this spineless coward: my love. I am bitter and angry with myself for contributing to my own funeral.

My loved ones tried to understand, to be there for me, but as the hypnotic years pass, their contact fades away. I realize that I am dead to them, as dead as though I had faded from their memories, dead because I attended my own funeral.

I live now in a place with no horizons, no importance, no perception of what could be, what should have been.

I was once a kind and gentle soul; now my tears fall like pebbles from my stone-cold heart.

In this hellhole, satanic butterflies whirl in the pit of my stomach as news from home is called out. I close my eyes; I offer a little prayer to my God, who has rejected me, asking him to please let someone think of me.

There is no communication tonight, last night, or any of the nights before. I pray for the morrow to bring some ease in this death with a single word from a loved one from my life long ago.

I was once unforgettable, so vibrant and full of life. Why is it that I've been forgotten?

I am dead, gone from their lives. Their memories no longer have space for me. They have forgotten my smile, misplaced the blue of my eyes, the way I once inspired and touched their lives.

When we lose loved ones, we are saddened in the beginning. Our heartfelt emotions are akin to a salted wound filled with pain.

Alas, the pain diminishes, and our lost ones weakly recede to the furthest recesses of our being.

We may think of them, shaping and reshaping their faces in our minds, which brings a smile. Then we go about our day without them or their memory. They are dead.

I have not passed away! I must convince myself that it was not a funeral but a criminal trial for something I did not do. I am not a figment of my brittle imagination!

My spirit may be dwindling, but it is still here. Can they not hear me calling from what once was?

As I exist through this dead phase in my life, I scream, I beg, and I plead for someone to please lift me from this mortuary of my mind. But no one hears my wails.

I cry each and every night when this cold, evil steel door slams shut, locking me into my six-by-nine-foot coffin. I pray and I die just a little bit more to make my funeral complete.

Afterword

SUSAN NAGELSEN

The only persons swept up in the criminal justice system whom most Americans know are the ones they see on television or read about in the newspapers, usually the famous (Michael Jackson, Robert Blake), the infamous (Scott Peterson, Ted Bundy), or the famous and notorious (O. J. Simpson). Even when the public thinks it knows the person arrested, its judgment is usually distorted by either preconception or the spin put on the story by whatever media happen to be reporting it at the time. Often these images bear little relation to the actual persons behind them, and in the case of the insignificant men and women whose personal tragedies get buried in a two-inch column in the local section of the paper, there are not even images to compensate for their seeming anonymity.

Moreover, once convicted, those same men and women disappear from the public's consciousness just as effectively as if they had dropped off the face of the earth. At best, they are relegated to the dim collective memory as tragically flawed individuals unable to overcome their personal problems. At worst, they become subhuman specimens who preyed on the physically defenseless and morally superior members of society. In either case, they are "untamed, and perhaps untamable, represent[ing] the 'Other,' hostile, threatening, and, above all, different."[1]

Tacitly accepted but rarely admitted, however, is the counterintuitive proposition that society needs its villains—its barbarians, in John Elliot's term, who "stand for savagery, treachery, and violence." This, of course, is incompatible with a society that stands for "civility, trustworthiness, and peace."[2] The result is a meshing of societal and governmental goals that produces a public dynamic in

---

which the accepted beliefs are strengthened, the political power base is increased by get-tough-on-crime rhetoric, and people are incarcerated at an alarming rate.

As long as society can identify its barbarians and justify their confinement and execution without further explanation, it does not need to undertake an examination of either their humanity or the motives for their behavior. The obvious problem with this approach is that 95 percent of the men and women in prison will be released one day. Unless the outside world takes a serious look at who they are and what they have to tell us, the simplistic solutions of imprisonment and execution will always be inadequate. An objective of *Exiled Voices* has been to provide a voice for those men and women, so that we may know them as human beings rather than as monsters who are so frightening that we are willing to banish them and even kill them.

However, the rush to imprison in the last quarter century has left us with institutions that discourage this kind of reflection. Indeed, the opaque nature of prison operations guarantees the perpetuation of this failed social experiment. We must therefore demand both access and accountability, an opening of the doors and windows, to ensure public participation in the discourse about what is taking place in America's prisons and jails. As Margaret Winter, associate director of the National Prison Project of the American Civil Liberties Union, put it, what these facilities need is "light, light, and more light."[3]

There is much to be learned from imprisoned writers, possibly because the deprivation of liberty, the isolation from family, loved ones, and normal society, imposes time for profound reflection. Within one hundred years, Miguel de Cervantes, imprisoned for tax violations, wrote *Don Quixote;* John Bunyan penned at least part of *The Pilgrim's Progress,* while imprisoned as a Dissenter; and Daniel Defoe, social polemicist, was jailed for satirizing the Church of England, before becoming famous as the author of *Robinson Crusoe.*

Today we can be enlightened by the writings of imprisoned men and women who help us step outside our parochial lives to peer inside and correct a system that no enlightened society should tolerate, much less encourage.

In my twenty years of working with men and women inside prisons, I have learned that without both philosophical and operational transparency, prisons will serve neither the public interest nor the needs of the prisoners, which are inextricably related. Left to their own devices, prisons create a *cordon sanitaire* between society's expectations and the methods employed for achieving them, because of a lack of oversight and accountability. The direct result of the secrecy under which the system operates is the numerous examples of unprofessional, even criminal, conduct by prison staff, most of which would remain hidden if not for prisoners' ability to be heard.[4] The alternative is an enforced code of censorship that transforms the prisons into fiefdoms ruled by autocratic wardens who command the loyalty of personnel who operate without constraints. Jack Crowley, who served for more than twenty years as a warden in the Oklahoma system, described the result: "When we're not accountable, the culture inside the prisons becomes a place that is so foreign to the culture of the real world that we develop our own way of doing things."[5]

In such an environment, prison guards adopt attitudes that mirror the operational ethos of Blackwater USA, accountable to no one and openly disdainful of any claims of civil rights or human rights violations. We begin to hear the echo of Henry Clay in 1816, advocating the mass deportation of African slaves: "Can there be a nobler cause than to rid our country of useless and pernicious, if not a dangerous portion of the population?"[6] Without a formal, consistent, and reliable method for evaluating prisons, the failures of prison administrations will continue to go unremarked and uncorrected.

Improving prison conditions, eloquently and poignantly described by the men and women in *Exiled Voices,* therefore requires the proactive cooperation of both the civilian sector and prison personnel, a collaboration that is often prompted by the intercession of prisoners whose writings first illuminated the problems. *Life Sentences,* by Wilbert Rideau, is one example. This collection of articles written for *The Angolite,* an award-winning journal produced by prisoners incarcerated in Angola, revealed the plight of inmates at one of the most dangerous prisons in America. Transgression by either the authority or the inmate dooms the process of incarceration from the outset, a process that currently results in an average recidivism rate of 60 percent.[7]

A proactive cooperative approach is hardly innovative. Our schools and hospitals, for example, require periodic, objective assessments by neutral agencies. Any school that failed approximately 60 percent of its students would be closed immediately. Any hospital that repeatedly failed to meet accreditation standards would see its doors shut indefinitely. Prisons, unlike other public institutions charged with improving the lives of their clients, appear to operate without similar oversights and constraints. It defies logic and common sense to permit prisons to operate in the shadows, requiring no outside assessment, when these institutions record such an abysmal success rate. Yet only 43 percent of prisons and 4 percent of jails in America are accredited by the American Correctional Association.[8] No responsible parent would send a child to a school or hospital that was not accredited.

Yet many politicians and prison administrators continue to insist that prisons are a necessary evil and that society simply does not understand the methods required to contain and control social predators. Such claims justify virtually any mistreatment of prisoners, as illustrated in various essays in this book. The spurious nature of these Potemkin villages can therefore be exposed only by someone on the inside, often at the risk of retaliation, public skepticism, and a hostile judiciary.

But writing in prison is far more than a means to document prison abuses. I have learned what creative pursuits can do for men and women who have spent years behind bars with little or no interaction with the outside world. In the years I spent teaching at the New Hampshire State Prison, men who had spent decades in small cells, believing that they had little to offer the world, came to realize that they were poets and writers, thinkers and scholars, with contributions to make, even with potential futures. They took this new-found sense of purpose back to those cells and used it to become better citizens, thus making doing time easier for everyone.

John "Divine G" Whitfield described similar results at Sing Sing in New York: "When you deal with someone who goes to college or is proactive in some sort of education, you get a whole different energy from him." There is a huge difference, Whitfield says, when people are not creatively engaged: "We walk the yard with people who are just running the yard, doing nothing with themselves, and you can feel the toxic energy resonating from them, but then, if they get into a program, you can see the change."

Finding sustenance for that kind of change is enormously difficult. Certainly the term "struggling writer" has become a cliché, but these men and women create under psychological pressures and physical constraints that would crush many others. They live in isolation, deprived of the ability to share their work with other people in traditional and mutually supporting settings. They face a constant battle against cuts in programs designed to encourage them and promote their work. Spending priorities always target educational programs as the first casualty, even in the face of statistics that prove that such programs are the preeminent rehabilitative tool. As counterproductive as this practice is, Marie Gottschalk's research confirmed that "budget cutters have targeted 'nonessential' prison programs [that] include educational and vocational programs."[9]

The absence of programs is affecting prisons across the country, leaving prisoners with long days spent in their cells and few avenues available for growth and development. The effects of these cuts are felt well beyond the prison walls, as prisoners are released with no viable skills and with no meaningful opportunities to contribute to society. A sergeant at the Oregon State Penitentiary, whose testimony was published in *Confronting Confinement: A Report of the Commission on Safety and Abuse in America's Prisons*, which was submitted to a congressional committee, spoke about the wide range of educational and vocational programs that he had seen available to inmates in his twenty-five years of service. Inmates had been able to earn a GED (General Educational Development) diploma and continue on to a doctorate. But over the years, such programs had been so reduced that teachers were no longer retained. Today Oregon doesn't even offer a GED for inmates; in fact, out of twenty-four programs, only three remain.[10]

Supreme Court justice Anthony M. Kennedy said, "Rehabilitation should be the chief goal of incarceration."[11] With the system bursting at the seams and politicians screaming for cost cuts, the safety of prisoners is questionable, and rehabilitation has taken a back seat to a lock-'em-down attitude. Many correctional officers believe that when prisoners are locked in their cells, they are more easily contained, and they are therefore safer. Mary Livers, deputy secretary for operations for the Maryland Department of Corrections, argued just the opposite: "We're moving away from having that feeling of being safe when offenders are all locked up, to one where we're actually safer because we have inmates out of their cells, involved in something hopeful and productive."[12] In order to change the system, there must be a progressive administrator, someone who believes in education and rehabilitation.

In many ways prisons are like schools; some have money, and some have none. If the correlation ended there it would be bad enough, but it is more insidious, because some prisons or states have money and attract administrators who make informed, humane decisions, while other prisons have little money and therefore attract poor administrators who often make decisions that are not in the interest of prisoners' rehabilitation but favor punishment and confinement. Paul Moran, a prisoner at California's Soledad Prison, confirmed this: "They will lock us in our cells during education time so the COs can do training drills. They are supposed to train on their time, not our education time." Yvette Louisell, imprisoned in Iowa, told me that conditions became so bad under one administration that "it wasn't just the inmates who were impacted; there was a high staff attrition rate too. Everyone suffers when the administration is bad."

The United States is suffering from the effects of legislative zeal. The get-tough-on-crime policies of the eighties resulted in mandatory sentences with lengthy minimum sentences, which necessitated the expansion of the prison system to almost five thousand prisons.[13]

However, what these same legislators failed to consider were the financial resources necessary to sustain these mandates over time. Walter Dickey, former secretary of the Wisconsin Department of Corrections, described the results: "If you don't have programs, whether they're schools, jobs, factories, you're much more likely to be relying on force and handcuffs."[14] Rehabilitative programs are thus the key to helping prisoners become citizens who contribute to society upon their release, because, as Colin McGinn reminds us, "education is necessary in order to correct and transcend our innate cognitive slant on the world."[15]

Writing, as these literary works by the imprisoned writers illustrate, develops prisoners' ability to look beyond the walls, beyond the narrow world of egocentricity. My work has shown me how creative writing sustains a level of appreciation for learning and intellectual discourse that counters the isolation imposed by imprisonment. Men and women who have been set adrift in a world devoid of stimuli, with a constant undercurrent of violence and fear, are transformed when given the opportunity to step out of that world for the briefest of moments.

In the past, the shame that attends a prison experience has engendered silence, but that is changing. People are telling their stories, leaving nothing to the imagination.[16] We are only now recognizing that men and women who have a longitudinal prison memory as a result of decades spent behind bars can provide unique insight into such issues as overcrowding, violence, imposed segregation, rape, other sexual abuse, and medical horrors, which continue to plague the prison system.

In an attempt to address the alarming number of prison rapes, the Prison Rape Elimination Act (PREA) was passed into law in 2003, and while it is a major step forward, it has done little to solve this horrific human rights violation.[17] PREA's intent was "to establish a zero-tolerance standard for the incidence of prison sexual assault in America's lockups, jails, juvenile facilities, and prisons; and to protect the Eighth Amendment rights of Federal, State, and local prisoners." Yet when I asked prisoners if they thought PREA was helping men and women come forward to report rape and sexual assault, the answer I received, without hesitation, was "Absolutely not."

Rape and sexual assault in prisons are common; however, they are inadequately documented because of incredible fear of retaliation. In a comprehensive study, 21 percent of male prisoners in seven midwestern male prisons reported that they had been pressured to have sex against their will, and one in ten had been raped.[18] If a prisoner is raped and it is reported, the victim is immediately sent to solitary confinement. This is done for his or her protection, but "the hole" is still where he or she will spend the next several months, until the officials can arrange a transfer. For many prisoners, rape is not a one-time event. "Two-thirds of the victims [in the midwestern study] had been violated repeatedly, some more than 100 times a year."[19]

I have encountered men and women who talk about what life is like today in prisons that are filled beyond their capacity, where dayrooms serve as extra housing facilities. Rows of men are lined up, as you might see in a hospital ward for the indigent. The common areas are gone, and the showers are too few, filthy, broken, dangerous, and difficult to get to. It is no surprise that tempers are short, patience is rare, violence is common, and life wears thin under these conditions.

When facilities are crowded and the air is vibrating with tension, people can get hurt. When prisoners get out of hand, the officials use segregation, or SHU (segregated housing unit), or ADSEG (administrative segregation), or the hole. It doesn't matter what they call it; solitary confinement is designed to create a significant change in a prisoner's attitude.

Segregation has been used as a management tool by prison

officials since the beginning of incarceration, in spite of the harm it is known to cause. But in recent years the use of segregation for problem prisoners has reached an all-time high, and men and women are being sentenced to increased time in isolation. What was originally meant to be used as a management tool for the most dangerous prisoners is now being used for problem or nuisance prisoners, often causing irreparable damage. Fred Cohen, a witness quoted in *Confronting Confinement,* stated that "segregation is now a regular part of the rhythm of prison life."[20] Prisoners in long-term isolation suffer from depression, psychoses, and other serious medical problems related to their lack of exercise and interaction with others, and this in turn causes more problems, which means more time in the hole because of outbursts of unacceptable behavior. The long-term negative effects of segregation led the commission to urge in its findings that segregation be used as a last resort, and it called for an end to the use of isolation as a punishment tool.[21]

While medical care in some institutions has improved since the 1970s, the gains have not been seen everywhere. Dr. Robert Greifinger, the leading correctional medicine and public-health expert, told the commission, "Some health-care programs are really excellent, and others in this country—too many of them—are shameful, not only in terms of what we do to the individuals but shameful in terms of the risks we expose our staff to and the risks to the public health."[22]

Prisoners are routinely medically mistreated, misdiagnosed, and then sometimes left to die, often alone and sometimes unnecessarily. The lack of diagnosis of infectious diseases such as hepatitis C and HIV is a danger to the individual as well as to society at large. In *Confronting Confinement,* it is reported that "more than 1.5 million people are released from jails and prisons each year carrying a life-threatening infectious disease."[23] Now the impact of medical neglect is reaching out beyond the prison walls into our communities.

Even prisoners with terminal illnesses may face uncaring medical staff with indifferent attitudes. Yvette Louisell was transferred to a prison in Virginia because of overcrowded conditions in Iowa. During her stay in the Virginia system, she had a friend who was dying of AIDS. Her friend was failing, and one afternoon she was so sick that the women in the unit decided she needed to be taken to the infirmary. When they got her to the nurse, she took one look at this gravely ill woman, unable to stand on her own two feet, and said, "I told her she was dying and there is nothing I can do for her. Now take her back to the unit."

The mentally ill prisoner who needs constant care is also frequently left untreated and often without medication. Such disturbed individuals are at risk in the general prison population, but they also put others at risk. On any given day, it is estimated that the number of incarcerated people with serious mental disorders is as high as 54 percent, if you include anxiety disorders, and these people are suffering unnecessarily.[24] Our prisons and jails are attempting to function as mental institutions, and they are failing miserably.

Jamie Fellner, director of U.S. programs at Human Rights Watch and an author of *Ill-Equipped: U.S. Prisons and Offenders with Mental Illness,* in his testimony before the commission said it all: "We should aspire to a zero-tolerance policy for psychological misery and pain that could be alleviated by appropriate mental health treatment, but that standard cannot be met without better funding."[25] It is not enough to build prisons; we must staff them appropriately, with qualified professionals, and offer programs that meet the needs of those individuals whose lives depend on that care. It is morally irresponsible to do otherwise.

Far too many of our citizens are imprisoned in this country for the current practices and philosophy of incarceration to support an institution that thrives on darkness, away from the eyes of those outside the system. On their release from prison, damaged men and women are returning to the communities they left behind without the skills necessary to function in society; too many are reoffending and repeating the cycle, leaving communities devastated.

The issues facing the men and women behind the high walls, razor ribbon, and concertina wire are grave, life threatening, and it is critical that we bring them to the forefront of our discussions. We have the ability to correct the wrongs that are being inflicted; we can create a prison system that operates with dignity and respect, one that works to provide the men and women who are held within the walls the rehabilitative opportunities to ensure a chance at a successful reentry into society, and we can accomplish this while working to eliminate the problems affecting prisoners' health and safety.

Any society that creates and maintains a system that too frequently destroys the human spirit in those entrusted to its care has an obligation to understand how that system works and to be aware of its results. As Justice Kennedy reminds us, "A decent and free society, founded in respect for the individual, ought not to run a system with a sign at the entrance saying, 'Abandon Hope, All Ye Who Enter Here.'"[26] Regardless of the difficulty, the time has come to raise our heads and face our shame.

Notes

Yvette Louisell

1. Juvenile Life Without Parole, 1999–2005, April 2007, http://www.petitiononline.com/lwopj6us/petition.html.

John Corley

1. Louisiana State Penitentiary Museum, http://www .angolamuseum.org.

2. Wilbert Rideau and Ron Wikberg, *Life Sentences: Rage and Survival Behind Bars* (New York: Times Books, 1992).

3. John Corley, "Yesterday's Child," *The Angolite* 31, no. 2 (March–April 2006): 29.

William Van Poyck

1. William Van Poyck, *A Checkered Past* (Bloomington, IN: 1st Books Library, 2003).

Afterword

1. John Elliot, "Barbarians at the Gates," *New York Review of Books* (Feb. 23, 2006): 36.

2. Ibid.

3. John J. Gibbons and Nicholas de B. Katzenbach, co-chairs, *Confronting Confinement: A Report of the Commission on Safety and Abuse in America's Prisons* (New York: Vera Institute of Justice, June 2006) 78, available at http://www .prisoncommission.org.

4. A former guard in New Hampshire was recently indicted for sexually assaulting three female inmates. Another was sentenced to twenty to forty years for raping one prisoner and faces twelve additional counts. See Annmarie Timmons, "Former Guard Charged with Sex Assault," *Concord Monitor,* (Sept. 21, 2007): A1, A6.

5. Gibbons and Katzenbach, *Confronting Confinement:* 79.

6. Anthony Appaih Kwame, "What Was Africa to Them?" *New York Review of Books,* (Sept. 27, 2007): 41–45.

7. U.S. Department of Justice, Bureau of Justice Statistics, "Reentry Trends in the United States," Aug. 20, 2003, available at http://www.ojp.usdoj.gov/bjs/reentry/reentry.htm.

8. Gibbons and Katzenbach, *Confronting Confinement:* 89.

9. Marie Gottschalk, *The Prison and the Gallows* (New York: Cambridge University Press, 2006): 243.

10. Gibbons and Katzenbach, *Confronting Confinement:* 27.

11. Ibid.

12. Ibid.: 67.

13. Ibid.: 20.

14. Ibid.: 28.

15. Colin McGinn, "How You Think," *New York Review of Books* (Sept. 27, 2007): 40.

16. Kerry Max Cook, *Chasing Justice* (New York: William Morrow, 2007).

17. Alan Eisner, *Gates of Injustice: The Crisis in America's Prisons* (New York: Prentice Hall, 2004): 62.

18. Ibid.

19. Ibid.

20. Gibbon and Katzenbach, *Confronting Confinement:* 14

21. Ibid.

22. Ibid.: 38.

23. Ibid.

24. Ibid.: 43.

25. Ibid.: 46.

26. Anthony M. Kennedy, speech at the American Bar Association Annual Meeting, Aug. 9, 2003, available at http://www .supremecourtus.gov/publicinfo/speeches/sp_08-09-03.html.

Recommended Readings

Bogira, Steve. *Courtroom 302: A Year Behind the Scenes in an American Criminal Courthouse*. New York: Vintage, 2006.

Conover, Ted. *Newjack: Guarding Sing Sing*. New York: Random House, 2000.

Eisner, Alan. *Gates of Injustice: The Crisis in America's Prisons*. Upper Saddle River, NJ: Prentice Hall, 2006.

Gibbons, John J., and Nicholas de B. Katzenbach, co-chairs. *Confronting Confinement: A Report of the Commission on Safety and Abuse in America's Prisons*. New York: Vera Institute of Justice, June 2006. Available at http://www.prisoncommission.org.

Gottschalk, Marie. *The Prison and the Gallows: The Politics of Mass Incarceration in America*. New York: Cambridge University Press, 2006.

Johnson, Robert. *Hard Time: Understanding and Reforming the Prison*. 3rd ed. Florence, KY: Wadsworth, 2002.

Johnson, Robert, and Nina Chernoff. "'Opening a Vein': Inmate Poetry and the Prison Experience." *Prison Journal* 88, no. 2 (June 2002): 141–167.

Liebling, Alison, and Shadd Maruna, eds. *The Effects of Imprisonment*. Portland, OR: Willan Publishing, 2006.

Maruna, Shadd. *Making Good: How Ex-Convicts Reform and Rebuild Their Lives*. Washington, DC: American Psychological Association, 2001.

Mauer, Mark, and Meda Chesney-Lind, eds. *Invisible Punishment: The Collateral Consequences of Mass Imprisonment*. New York: New Press, 2003.

Owen, Barbara. *In the Mix: Struggle and Survival in a Women's Prison*. Albany: State University of New York Press, 1998.

Pollock, Jocelyn. *Women, Crime and Prison*. Florence, KY: Wadsworth, 2002.

Prejean, Helen. *Dead Man Walking: An Eyewitness Account of the Death Penalty in the United States*. New York: Random House, 1993.

———. *The Death of Innocents: An Eyewitness Account of Wrongful Executions*. New York: Random House, 2005.

Toch, Hans. *Corrections: A Humanistic Approach*. Albany, NY: Harrow and Heston, 1997.

Tonry, Michael. *Thinking About Crime: Sense and Sensibility in American Penal Culture*. New York: Oxford University Press, 2004.

———, ed. *The Future of Imprisonment*. New York: Oxford University Press, 2004.

Travis, Jeremy, and Christy Visher, eds. *Prisoner Reentry and Crime in America*. New York: Cambridge University Press, 2006.

Warren, Jenifer. *One in 100: Behind Bars in America 2008*. Pew Center on the States, 2008. Available at http://www.pewcenteronthestate. org.

Western, Bruce. *Punishment and Inequality in America*. New York: Russell Sage Foundation, 2006.

Wynn, Jennifer. *Inside Rikers: Stories from the World's Largest Penal Colony*. New York: St. Martin's Press, 2002.

Acknowledgments

In making it possible for us to visit and photograph most of the imprisoned writers whose work we are privileged to publish in this book, certain authorities went out of their way to help make the road a bit smoother, and I offer each of them my heartfelt thanks.

Jack Bowers, *Arts and Corrections Program Director, Soledad Prison, Soledad, California*

Lt. Dan Pherigo, *California Department of Corrections and Rehabilitation*

Lt. Michael Siebert, *California Department of Corrections and Rehabilitation*

Terry Thornton, *California Department of Corrections and Rehabilitation Office of Public and Employee Communications*

Johnie Hammond, *Iowa Board of Corrections*

Patty Wachtendorf , *Deputy Warden, Iowa Correctional Institute for Women*

Linda Foglia, *New York Department of Corrections*

Jeff Lyons, *New Hampshire Department of Corrections*

I would also like to thank Bell Chevigny, for her unwavering support of incarcerated writers, and Margaret Vernon and her family, for opening their home and their hearts to us while we were in Iowa.

The publisher is particularly grateful for the assistance of Bill M. Moushey, *Associate Professor of Journalism and Mass Communications* and *Director of the Innocence Institute at Point Park University, Pittsburgh;* and Colin Starger, *former staff attorney at the Innocence Project, New York;* and Stephen B. Bright, *former director, the Southern Center for Human Rights, Atlanta.*

Book design: Elton Robinson

Production manager: Susan Hayes

Copy editor: Liz Duvall

Proofreader: Barbara Jatkola

Susan Nagelsen is Professor of Special Education and Director of the Writing Program at New England College. She taught writing classes at New Hampshire State Prison for many years, and she is associate editor of *Journal of Prisoners on Prisons.* Her work has been published in *Bleak House Review* and *Entelechy International.*

Lou Jones travels the world from his studio in Boston, with a particular interest in photographing socially significant subjects. His clients are as diverse as *National Geographic* magazine and Major League Baseball. He has taught and lectured at a number of educational institutions, and his photographs have been exhibited in in the Corcoran Gallery, the DeCordova Museum, the Smithsonian Institution, and other museums. His books include *Final Exposure; Portraits from Death Row* and *Travel +PHOTOGRAPHS: Off the Charts.*

Robert Johnson is Professor of Justice, Law and Society at American University and an authority on criminal justice, prisons, and the death penalty. He has testified or provided expert affidavits before the U.S. Congress, federal and state courts, and the European Commission of Human Rights. He has published a number of scholarly articles in his areas of expertise and is the author of *Death Work: A Study of the Modern Execution Process* and *Hard Time: Understanding and Reforming the Prison.* His fiction and poems have been published in many journals, and he is the author of two collections of poetry: *Poetic Justice: Reflections on the Big House, the Death House, and the American Way of Justice* and *Burnt Offerings: Poems on Crime and Punishment.*

The text of this book is set in Bulmer, designed by William Martin c. 1790 for the Shakespeare Press. The contemporary digital revival used in this book is by Monotype Imaging, based on a 1928 revival by Morris Fuller Benton of the American Type Founders.

The display type is Univers, a 1956 design by Adrian Frutiger.

Paper: Sterling, 100 pound Sterling Matte.

Printing and binding: Worzalla: Stevens Point, Wisconsin.